MW00563713

The House of Condulmer

THE MIDDLE AGES SERIES

Roland Betancourt, *Series Editor*
Edward Peters, *Founding Editor*

A complete list of books in the series is available
from the publisher.

The House of Condulmer

The Rise and Decline of a Venetian Family in
the Century of the Black Death

Alan M. Stahl

PENN

UNIVERSITY OF PENNSYLVANIA PRESS

PHILADELPHIA

Published by
University of Pennsylvania Press
Philadelphia, Pennsylvania 19104-4112
www.pennpress.org

Printed in the United States of America on acid-free paper
10 9 8 7 6 5 4 3 2 1

A catalog record for this book is available
from the Library of Congress.

Hardback ISBN 9781512826197
Ebook ISBN 9781512826203

CONTENTS

PREFACE

In the course of four decades of researching and writing about medieval Venetian history, I have come across the names of thousands of people and have wondered how much could be learned about them, either in terms of the course of their lives or their relationships with other individuals. A year of teaching from 2001 to 2002 at Rice University, whose library held little relevant to my research interests, served as the impetus to assemble a FileMaker database of individuals living in Venice in the second half of the fourteenth century. My starting point was the published *Estimo* of 1379, which lists 2,150 Venetian heads of household and the amount each was assessed to fund the war against Genoa.

The receipt in 2008 of a fellowship from the John Simon Guggenheim Foundation gave me the opportunity for an extended stay in Venice to search through the Venetian archives and to initiate a project entitled "The Nexus of Money and Power in Medieval Venice," exploring the extent to which the financial elite of the city correlated with the holders of important policy-making positions in this city-state that has often been termed a "Merchant Republic." Further support from the Gladys K. Delmas Foundation, whose five grants have been the mainstay of my archival work throughout my career, has allowed me to analyze a total of about ten thousand archival documents and to bring the population covered in my database to more than ten thousand individuals involved in about twenty-eight thousand interactions including the holding of office and engaging in trade and family relationships.

An invitation from the Program in Renaissance Studies of Princeton University in 2013 to give a talk on my research in progress gave me the impetus to work through my data and find a topic that could be covered in an evening lecture. The Condulmer family came to my mind because I had taken extensive notes on three individuals from their accounts and personal documents preserved by the Procurators of San Marco acting as the executors of their estates. I also knew them as members of one of only a handful of non-noble families that had joined the ranks of the nobility in the fourteenth century through extraordinary support for the war effort against Genoa. It did not take much more looking to determine that another member of the family had been the leading partner of a commercial bank that had suffered a notorious bankruptcy at the beginning of the fifteenth century. He also had a brother who went on to be only the second Venetian pope and the organizer of the celebrated Council of Ferrara-Florence of 1438, which brought the Byzantine emperor to Italy to seek Italian help in the fight against the Ottoman Turks in exchange for agreeing to the unification of the Latin and Greek churches. I also learned of the important role played by the stepmother of these two brothers in integrating the family into the nobility through the heavily financed marriages of five of her daughters and stepdaughters to noble men.

From this point on, it was a question of going through wills, dowry arrangements, court cases, and other documents in search of any references to members of the Condulmer family. Luckily the name Condulmer is easily recognizable and distinguishable from other family names, even in the shorthand used by notaries. In the course of this research, I believe that I have come to recognize distinctive traits and even personalities of the various members of the family, which reflect the range of motives and actions of other Venetians and of medieval-era people in general.

Most of the contents of this book derive from information in documents in the Archivio di Stato di Venezia. Due to fires and other incidents over the past centuries, many of the records of the medieval Venetian state have not survived, most notably those offices having to do with commerce and finance. Medieval Venetian chronicles are, for the most part, records of the military and diplomatic encounters of the state, with little usable information on the internal workings of the government or the lives of its citizens. Nor do personal diaries, letters, or even account books survive in significant quantities for medieval Venice. The greatest resource for this study has been the collection of documents saved by the Procurators of San Marco for the estates for which they were executors. In addition to personal papers of the deceased, these *commissarie* as they are called, often have the accounts of the procurators as they settled the estate in the years following the testator's death, which allow historians at least a partial reconstruction of the commercial and personal financial activity of the individual. The records of the various Venetian courts are extremely fragmentary and unindexed for the fourteenth and fifteenth centuries, but the Sentenze a Giustizia of the Giudici di Petizion (whose responsibility included commercial activities) often contain a detailed description of the matter under litigation from the viewpoint of both plaintiff and respondent and a final verdict. The records of the hundreds of notaries of medieval Venice, containing collections of testaments and the abbreviated records of such documents as dowry agreements and business contracts, offer a rich source for research, but they are barely indexed (at best only the principal participant in an interaction) and themselves survive in a representation that is at once overwhelming and fragmentary.

I have followed the convention of giving the personal names of Venetians in their Italian equivalents but keeping family names in Venetian; thus, a name that appears in a Latin document as Georgius Georgi would be rendered here as Giorgio Zorzi. Exceptions are made in the case of the common Venetian personal names such as Alvise (for Ludovicus), Menego (for Domenicus), and Cataruza (for Catarina). I have made an exception for names of members of the Condulmer family whose nicknames are repeated in documents and help differentiate members of the family with the same name—hence, Nicoleto, Jacobello, and Vielmo. The Venetian year began on March 1, with documents made in January and February bearing the number of the previous year. I have consistently modernized these, as in 2/24/140[4].

Most monetary sums are given in the text in terms of the Venetian gold ducat (3.53 grams of pure gold), sometimes converted from the money of account in which they are recorded. It is difficult to give an understanding of the value of the ducat in modern terms. Salaries for state offices that appear to have been full time and received no additional fees from users ranged from 35 ducats a year for low-level mint foremen, to 72 ducats a year for galley oarsmen, to 90 ducats a year for supervisors in the arsenal (the shipbuilding complex), to 100 ducats a year for the mint masters and the chamberlain of the commune, to 120 ducats a year for merchant consuls, to 150 ducats per year for provisors of grain. Many wills left provisions for ongoing support for widows, children, and former enslaved persons. For the widow of a merchant of reasonable wealth, a portfolio of 2,000 ducats worth of *prestiti* (state bonds) giving an annual revenue of 100 ducats a year was normal (this in addition to the return of her dowry plus any other capital she might have). An allowance to servants and other people of modest rank of the income from 300 ducats of *prestiti* (an income of 15 ducats per year) seems to have been about standard. For example, Vielmo Condulmer left 300 ducats worth of *prestiti* to one person whose enslavement he terminated and 200 to another. All in all, it seems that an income of about 50 ducats per year would have represented subsistence for a low-income family, 100 ducats a year would mean comfort for a family, and 200 ducats a year relative prosperity. Put in terms of the salaries and costs of living today in such modern merchant centers as New York and Milan, we could, in gross terms, consider one ducat to have the buying power of about 1,000 dollars or euros.

There are many individuals who have helped me through the years of this project. I am especially grateful to Stanley Chojnacki, Georg Christ, and Maarten Halff, who have gone through drafts of the entire manuscript and have offered suggestions that have been vital to getting the book in the form it now appears. As in the case of all archive-based books on Venice, my research has depended greatly on the learned and dedicated work of the staff of the Archivio di Stato di Venezia, especially that of Maria Francesca Tiepolo, its director in decades past, and of Michaela dal Borgo, until recently the director of the Sala di Studio. Especially during the period of inaccessibility of documents during the Covid-19 pandemic, I have relied greatly on the publicly available digitization of the records of the main councils, which went under the rubric of Progetto Divenire and is now called More Veneto. Other scholars who have helped me in the course of researching and writing this book are Hannah Barker, Patricia Fortini Brown, Nicola Carotenuto, Linda Carroll, Lillian Datchev, Consuelo Dutschke, Julian Gardner, the late David Jacoby, Lorenzo Lazzarini, Pamela O. Long, Reinhold C. Mueller, Dennis Romano, Deborah Walberg, and Nicolò Zennaro. I am very grateful to Jenny Tan, Cal Turner, and Noreen O'Connor-Abel of Penn Press and to John Wyatt Greenlee, who drew the maps and figures for this book. I would like to take this opportunity to record my gratitude to my mentor Edward Peters, founding editor of this publication series, for guiding my development as a medieval historian. And, finally, I offer thanks to my husband, William R. Hanauer, for all the support he has given over the past half-century.

CHAPTER 1

The Condulmer Family Before the Plague

"Ille de cha' Condulmario"

In 1408, the noble members of the Venetian Senate were engaged in an arduous debate over whether to continue to support Pope Gregory IX, the first Venetian to ascend to the papal throne, or to switch its allegiance to Alexander V, the compromise candidate chosen by the Council of Pisa in an effort to end the schism that had divided the Western Church for the previous three decades. The Senate proponents of Alexander, who was from Venice's colony of Crete so technically also a Venetian, railed against two papal advisers, both Venetian, on whom they blamed the refusal of Gregory to honor his promise to step down in such a circumstance—the pope's nephew, Antonio Correr, Cardinal Bishop of Porto; and Gabriele Condulmer, who bore the titles Bishop of Siena, Clerk of the Papal Chamber, and Cardinal Bishop of San Clemente. The enraged senators referred to Antonio Correr correctly if blandly as *nepos domini pape* (nephew of the lord pope) but dismissed Gabriele as *ille de cha' Condolmario*, (that one of the Condulmer house, or family), injecting an unparalleled level of scorn and disdain into the usually dry records of the august body charged with Venetian foreign relations.[1]

The house (*casa* in Latin, *cha'* in Venetian) was the basic genealogical unit of Venetian social life, referring to all people, noble and non-noble, male and female, who bore a common family name.[2] All of the members of the *cha'* shared a heraldic emblem, which might later become quartered or embellished with subordinate charges but in the Middle Ages was generally simple.[3] Within the *cha'*, there could develop many lineages, each often associated with the parish in which the palace of the founder of the lineage was located and in which several nuclear families might reside. Even members of families that contained both noble and non-noble lineages—as with the Condulmer after 1381—were all considered to belong to the same "house." In 1413, five years after the Senate's contemptuous dismissal of Gabriele Condulmer, Giacomo Erizzo, the noble husband of Gabriele's sister Ursia, stood before the Great Council to introduce Antonio Condulmer, a young man from the distant ennobled branch of the family, into adult membership in the nobility through the Balla d'Oro process.[4] Antonio's career as a naval captain would become closely linked to that of Gabriele as pope in the succeeding decades.[5]

Clearly, the House of Condulmer was well enough known in Venice to need no clarification and carried a negative connotation for the nobles of the highest political and social levels who made up the Senate. The Condulmer family had clawed its way back from its exile for participation in a conspiracy against the state in the beginning of the fourteenth century, buying and marrying its way into the nobility and the world of banking, with even a non-noble member presenting himself in public with the trappings of the highest nobility. Gabriele himself had been a business partner of his merchant brother while successively (and in some cases simultaneously) being a monk, priest, deacon, canon, and even a prior in half a dozen Venetian ecclesiastical institutions of various affiliations. It was only the year before this Senate debate, in 1407, that Gabriele had broken his financial connections to his bankrupt brother and followed Antonio Correr, his fellow monk and nephew of the newly elected pope, to Rome, where he had risen amazingly quickly through the ecclesiastical ranks to the offices of bishop and cardinal. Though there were many grounds for the proud senators to look down on "that man from the house of Condulmer," the opportunistic striving of members of the family to rise above their non-noble status must have figured prominently in the senatorial disdain.

Efforts, both legal and performative, to rise in social status were not unusual in medieval Venice, nor were bankruptcies or the use of influence for progression through the church hierarchies unknown. Rather, what seems to have rallied the members of the Senate and others at the top of the Venetian power structure against the House of Condulmer was a history of their flouting the demonstration of civic virtue subsumed under the rubric of the "Myth of Venice." This outlook envisaged Venetian government and society as existing in a state of unchanging internal harmony, with a balance of power keeping any family from asserting dominance.[6] This balance of power was, however, exercised among the men of the nobility; the remaining

95 percent of the population, including all women, were expected to accede to the decisions of the Great Council and its subsidiary institutions.

In the central Middle Ages, from the tenth through the thirteenth centuries, Venice was one of hundreds of Italian communes, or city-states, governed by elected officials—a democracy of the wealthy male citizens. In the course of the fourteenth century, most of the other communes came under the rule of individual men or families, such as the Visconti in Milan, the Gonzaga in Mantua, and the Medici in Florence.[7] Venice was one of a handful of Italian city-states that held on to elected government into the modern age. In this respect, the Myth of Venice bore some relationship to reality in that Venice experienced few of the kinds of rebellions against the aristocracy by the citizen class that undermined the political regimes of so many other Italian city-states or attempts of military or financial leaders to seize the reins of power. The maintenance of republican institutions was attributed to a general loyalty of Venetians to their elected councils and the lack of family-based factions acting as political forces. The Myth was promulgated by the refusal of medieval Venetian chroniclers to include information on the inner workings of the republic or factional successes in influencing elections or votes of the assemblies. The kind of inside reporting that permeated medieval Florentine chronicles and would feature subsequently in the gossipy diary of the Venetian Marin Sanudo in the sixteenth century is lacking for fourteenth-century Venice. The image of Venice as a seat of unified harmony was undoubtedly a myth, but it was sustained by the success of the Venetian Republic both in the maintenance of its republican institutions and in military victories in Italy and overseas.

From the start, the Condulmer family can be seen to have scoffed at the myth of Venetian cohesion through civic participation. In the last decades of the thirteenth century, when the members of the Great Council were elected from among the citizenry in general, no member of the Condulmer family was to be found among its participants. Soon after the "closing of the Great Council" at the end of the thirteenth century, when this failure to participate in the communal government led to its exclusion from the nobility, two members of the Condulmer family joined in a notorious conspiracy to overthrow the government and put it in the hands of the Tiepolo and Querini families. They were from one of only two non-noble families in this rebellion. Two later members of the family, Minello and Nicoleto, both of whom appear to have died in the Black Death of 1348, are known to us to a great extent from multiple records of infringements of regulations and grants of clemency from punishments. However, as such *grazia* documents are one of the most complete sources for information on individuals in this period, it is not clear whether their violations of commercial regulations were actually greater than that of the average Venetian.

It is in the period after the Black Death that the individual careers of members of the Condulmer family can be plotted more fully and their bending of the social norms of Venice can be put into context. Jacobello Condulmer must have flown high in the eyes of his contemporaries, especially those like him outside the nobility, for his founding of a confraternity of merchants and the provision of it with a miracle-working statue, for his service on the board of a hostel, and ultimately for his generous contributions to the war effort against Genoa, which earned him and his descendants the rank of nobility. It was not long after his entry to the Great Council, however, that he died, leaving evidence of having raided the funds he managed as trustee of his orphaned nephew and leaving his widow with debts that would take the rest of her life to settle. Vielmo Condulmer, from the same branch of the family as Jacobello but not his descendant so denied noble rank, used the proceeds from his lucrative business as a money changer to outfit himself in clothing that would be appropriate only for a man of the highest social status or even for a cardinal.

The Santa Lucia branch of the Condulmer family across the Grand Canal from Jacobello's palace in San Tomà, was no truer to the myth of the Venetian as a virtuous citizen working for the communal good. In the course of fulfilling the mandate of her late husband to get his many daughters married into the nobility and thus indirectly raise the social status of the family, Franceschina Condulmer resorted in at least one case to requiring a prospective groom to put up his own family's funds to procure the astronomical dowry attached to his fiancée. One of her stepsons, Simoneto, flew high as the lead partner of one of the few deposit banks of Venice, but led it to a disastrous bankruptcy that left his descendants in debt for generations. Simoneto's efforts to recoup his lost fortune by a series of lawsuits against his former business associates, some of them his relatives, could hardly have raised his profile in the small world of Venetian finance. His brother Gabriele, as we have seen, was to rise to the highest level of the church hierarchy as cardinal (and finally as Pope Eugene IV), but only after jumping from local monastery to monastery and then attaching himself to the coattails of his former business partner whose uncle was Pope Gregory IX. During his pontificate, Eugene never once visited Venice and consistently went against the express wishes of its political leaders.

It is little wonder that the reputation of the House of Condulmer sank in the fifteenth century within the closed world of Venetian society as quickly as it had risen in the decades following the Black Death of 1348.

Social Class in Medieval Venice

The common conception of the social history of medieval Europe is of a division into three classes: those who ruled, those who prayed, and those who labored.[8] Nobles or aristocrats were at the top of society, their power deriving usually through inheritance of land and occasionally from military prowess; governmental authority was restricted to this group, which was also responsible for providing military service. A second social group comprised churchmen. Below these two was a vast number of people engaged in agriculture, tied to the nobles with various kinds of legal and financial obligations. Italy, where ancient cities survived into the Middle Ages with some physical and social structures intact, is considered a special case in this paradigm. In most of medieval Italy, the line between aristocrats and city dwellers tended to be less clear than elsewhere in Europe, with local lords participating in the urban social and political structure and collaborating with merchants to form autonomous communes that exerted political power over the surrounding countryside.[9]

Venice, born in the early Middle Ages as an island settlement with few ties to the adjacent mainland, differed from other medieval Italian communes in having a government made up mainly of merchants, with no landed aristocracy to contest their power. In the course of the thirteenth and fourteenth centuries, the division between these wealthy merchants and the classes below them became increasingly clear, and opportunities for rise in status were limited. By the end of the thirteenth century, a process of governmental reorganization, which included the formal definitions and regulations of the various councils and magistracies of the Republic, came to equate noble status with membership in the Maggior Consiglio (Great Council), and, in a process known as the *Serrata* (closing), limited the future membership in the council to the families of men who had served in it in the preceding decades.[10]

Within the noble class of Venice, however, there was a vast range of wealth and of political power, with some nobles dominating the commercial and financial networks of the city while others followed a career path of holding various salaried positions, both abroad and within the domestic branches of government, that were reserved for nobles.[11] About 150 families who were

declared noble as a result of the *Serrata* remained active through the fourteenth century, constituting what has been estimated as about 5 percent of
the population.[12] The nobility itself was divided in the minds of contemporaries into those from families considered the oldest in Venice and those
whose presence was considered more recent. Within the old families, there
was moreover a division between the 24 oldest families (the *longhi*, or long
families), who dominated the highest offices of the republic, including that of
doge, until late in the fourteenth century, and 16 additional ones (the *curti*,
or short families) who came to monopolize the office of doge after the last
decades of the fourteenth century.[13] Even within the most prestigious families
of the nobility, such as the Contarini and Morosini, there was an enormous
discrepancy between the wealth and political status of the various members,
who might number as many as 60 adult male heads of households at a time.[14]
Although the line between nobles and non-nobles was, in theory, specified
and fixed during the fourteenth century, it was not until the systematization
in 1414 of the Balla d'Oro (golden ball) procedure that there was a straightforward mechanism for determining if an individual was indeed a member
of the nobility; this was especially significant in the cases of the many houses
that had some lineages recognized as noble but others who were not.[15]

There were many concrete advantages that came with noble status. In
addition to the Great Council, there was a proliferation of lesser councils (the
Senate, the Forty, the Ten) that were in essence subcommittees of the Great
Council and thus restricted to nobles.[16] The highest of offices (for example,
the six procurators of San Marco and six ducal councilors), judgeships, and
heads of the departments of revenue and regulation were likewise limited to
members of the nobility, as were the salaried positions of governor or rector
of the various colonies and outposts of what was increasingly becoming a
maritime and continental empire.[17] Captains of the commercial and military
fleets had to be noble, as did those who bid on control of the precious cargo
space on the annual merchant convoys that were the backbone of Venice's
commercial economy. Below this level, there were hundreds of positions,
both domestic and abroad, that were reserved to nobles and paid salaries that
sustained the less wealthy of the rank. Besides these official perquisites, noble
status (as well as regular participation in government bodies) gave individuals informal access to information and to alliances, both commercial and
by marriage, that could greatly increase their wealth and standing.

Those excluded from the nobility were defined as being part of the
popolo (general population), of which about 5 percent made up the *cittadino*

(citizen) class.[18] This group of *cittadini* was further divided between those who claimed citizen status as members of a family that boasted generations of Venetian presence and those who originated outside the city but had been granted the status after a residence and the payment of taxes for many years. There was a subset of the *cittadini* known as the *popolo grande* who had wealth equivalent to many members of the nobility and were most visible in the religious confraternities and certain branches of government, including the ducal chancellor.[19]

The Origins of the Condulmer Family and Their Social Standing Before the Black Death

In the sense that, as Sandro Carocci has argued, social mobility can be viewed as a "any shift that not only brings individuals and groups, but also objects and values, to a new position within the hierarchy of wealth and professions," the different modes of social mobility within medieval Venice can be seen as exemplified by the lives of various members of the Condulmer family in the fourteenth and early fifteenth centuries.[20] There are Venetian families widely known to scholars for their contributions in many fields of history and culture and to tourists for the magnificent palaces that bear their names; such families as the Barbarigo, the Morosini, the Contarini, and the Corner come to mind. The Condulmer family, however, was almost as obscure for most of the centuries of Venetian history as it is today, entering the historical record with the participation of two of its members in a failed conspiracy, buying its way into the nobility only to have its noble member die within two months of his election, and finally becoming known to the European world as the family of Eugene IV, one of the most consequential—and reviled—of Renaissance popes. After the death of Eugene, known to us as Gabriele Condulmer, the family slipped back into obscurity, remaining one of the dozens of such families that carried on the business of the Western world's center of commerce in the fifteenth through eighteenth century.

The Condulmer family appears first in Venetian sources before the year 1200 as residents of the outlying parish surrounding the monastery of Santa Lucia, a newly drained frontier region at the furthest reaches of the Grand Canal (Map 1).[21] In early documents, the name was spelled Gondolmario, Gondolmero, and Glomdomero and was possibly of Lombard origin as suggested in the much-later tradition that the family came from Pavia.[22] The

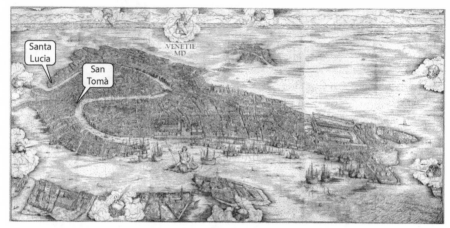

Map 1. Parishes of the pre-plague members of the Condulmer family, super-imposed on a bird's-eye view of Venice engraved by Jacopo de'Barbari, 1500. Barbari engraving: Wikimedia Commons, public domain.

earliest members of the Condulmer family are known only from occasional mentions in documents, and it is difficult to draw a continuous narrative of their lives or to place them within larger family groupings.

Conspiracy and Exile: Meneghello Condulmer and His Son Marco

The first member of the family whose life we can follow at all is Meneghello, whose name is a Venetian diminutive of the Latin name Domenicus. He appears first in a list dated 1289 of the lay brothers of the confraternity of Santa Maria della Misericordia, in Cannaregio but closer to the center of Venice than his home parish of Santa Lucia.[23] He is identified as Menegel-lus Gondolmero *stazonero*, that is, owner of a shop. Neither he nor anyone of his family name appears in the lists of those participating in the Great Council of Venice in the second half of the thirteenth century; for this rea-son, the family was excluded from membership in the council following the *Serrata* of 1297.[24] Meneghello Condulmer next appears in 1302 in an inquest by the State Advocates into the contested will of his neighbor and in-law Pietro Sabatino.[25]

Meneghello's son Marco Condulmer became notorious in Venice for his involvement in the Querini-Tiepolo conspiracy of 1310 (see Figure 1 for

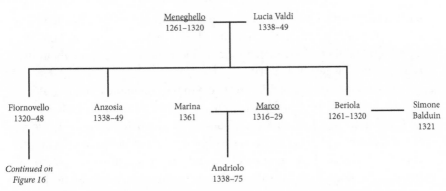

Figure 1. The family of Meneghello Condulmer, parish of Santa Lucia. Underlined names are for people featured in Chapter 1. No last name is given for Condulmer. Years are of documents in which each is mentioned, while † denotes
the year of death.

the family tree). This was one of the infrequent uprisings that challenged
the myth of Venice as an efficiently run commune, immune from the kind
of internal factions and strife that threatened and eventually overthrew the
elected governments of such rivals as Padua, Verona, Florence, Milan, and
Genoa.[26] As is evident from the name by which it became known, the 1310
revolt against the constituted government of Venice was led by members of
two of its prominent noble families, Querini and Tiepolo; a total of about
three dozen nobles fled to neighboring cities following the discovery and
defeat of the conspiracy, though some returned and were imprisoned.[27]

The sixteenth-century historian and diarist Marin Sanudo lists Marco
Condulmer, along with his unnamed sons, among the non-noble conspirators (along with thirty nobles) identifying him as a *stazzonarius de pannos de
lana* (shopkeeper of woolen cloths); the same identification is contained in
the sixteenth-century chronicle of Giovanni Giacomo Caroldo.[28] Also implicated in the plot was Simone Balduin, the non-noble husband of Meneghello's daughter Beriola and their neighbor in the parish of Santa Lucia.[29] By
the end of 1310, Marco Condulmer's father Meneghello, not listed among the
conspirators, had been removed from his position as procurator, chief lay
administrator, of the monastery of Santa Lucia.[30] The Condulmer conspirators were among those who suffered a milder form of exile than the leaders
of the plot; their ban from Venice was not considered permanent, and their
property there was not forfeited to the state.[31] Though they suffered a great
loss in terms of social standing within Venice in their exile, the Condulmer

participants in the Querini-Tiepolo conspiracy were among only a handful of non-nobles in an enterprise dominated by nobles of prestigious families, a position that men of the family were to find themselves in throughout the course of the fourteenth century.

In 1316, Doge Giovanni Soranzo wrote to the commune of Fermo, along the Adriatic coast south of Venice, on the subject of the exiled Meneghello Condulmer and his son Marco, both said to be living there.[32] The doge accused Marco of having fled there with the goods of Venetian merchants, and he threatened the commune of Fermo if it refused to return Marco to Venice. The doge then turned to the case of Marco's father, Meneghello, whom he characterized as the author of evil deeds and reported to have received the stolen merchandise that Marco brought to Fermo. In the end, the doge demanded that Fermo seize and return father and son and their possessions with a threat of Venetian reprisals. The last we hear of Meneghello is in a directive of the Council of Ten in 1320 to transfer the bonds held in his name to his creditors.[33]

In 1321, the Council of Ten granted Marco Condulmer the right to administer the capital goods of his imprisoned brother-in-law Simone Balduin.[34] In the next year, the council passed a series of resolutions concerning the strictures that had been applied to the Condulmer and Balduin families in 1312, denying them the right to lease their lands without specific permission from the government.[35] In February 1322 both families were instructed to give three weeks' notice to the current tenants to vacate the premises and thereafter not to rent at all to foreigners and to rent to Venetians only by express permission of the doge and the Council of Ten.[36] A year later, the Ten passed a measure restoring to Marco Condulmer the right to occupy his own house in the parish of Santa Lucia for the following two years, after which it could be renewed by the council's permission.[37]

By this time, Marco Condulmer appears to have reestablished himself in commerce and in the eyes of Venetian society. In 1323, a private galley that he co-owned with two other non-noble Venetians was captured off the coast of Barletta by a Genoese vessel; three years later, the Venetian state negotiated a compensation to him of 1,450 ducats for his losses.[38] The last we hear of him is in 1329, when he sought reprieve for an import fee on twenty-two bales of gray cloth worth 800 ducats that he had tried to export to Apulia but brought back unsold.[39]

In September 1336, Lucia Valdi made out her will in Trani in Apulia, in which she identified herself as widow of the late Meneghello Condulmer and mother of the late Marco.[40] She declared herself near death and asked to be buried in the Franciscan church of Trani. She left a modest legacy to her daughter Beriola, wife of Simone Balduin, and a smaller amount to her other daughter Anzosia, whom she designated as her executrix. The remainder of her estate was left to Marco's son Andriolo. Lucia apparently survived and returned to Venice; two years later, in 1338, she entrusted Anzosia with about 77 ducats to look after her grandson Andriolo until he turned sixteen.[41]

Meneghello and Marco were by no means the only members of the Condulmer family active in Venice in the first decades of the fourteenth century; no fewer than seven other male heads of household are attested for the period. Fiornovello Condulmer of Santa Lucia first appears in a document accounting reparations made in 1330 for the attack on a Venetian vessel in Apulia; it notes that he had carried out an exchange of Neapolitan coinage for Venetians on behalf of the Bardi and Acciaioli banks of Florence.[42] Nicolo Condulmer of Santa Lucia was fined in 1334 for having exported cloth to Apulia and then reimporting the unsold cloth without paying customs duty.[43]

Minello Condulmer, Far-Ranging Merchant Venturer

Minello Condulmer appears in the historical record in 1336 with an appeal to extend his property in Santa Lucia into the swampy land contingent with it (see Figure 2 for his family tree).[44] In this period, he owned and commanded a commercial ship that plied the Mediterranean, one of the sail-driven private vessels that carried on trade between Venice and its eastern trading colonies and were supplemental to the state-owned, rowed galleys that participated in coordinated annual commercial convoys (the *mude*). In May 1340, a Venetian merchant in Tana on the Black Sea wrote to his agent in Venice to ask Minello to supply him with pelts of small animals to sell there.[45] Later that year, Minello was forgiven a fine for not declaring three pieces of camlet, camel-colored woolens of northern European origin, which were found by the customs masters undeclared in his ship.[46] The following year, he was forgiven another fine for lacking the requisite number of sailors on his ship when it stopped in Constantinople on the way to Tana.[47] In July 1346 a merchant in Venetian Crete was waiting for the imminent arrival of the Condulmer ship to carry to Venice a shipment of saffron that had been sent there from Alexandria via Rhodes.[48]

Later in 1346, Minello was charged by the State Advocates with secretly removing four bundles of silk from his own ship, presumably to avoid paying

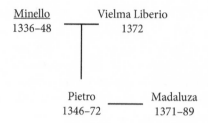

Figure 2. The family of Minello Condulmer, parish of Santa Lucia. Underlined names are for people featured in
Chapter 1. No last name is given for
Condulmer. Years are of documents in
which each is mentioned.

duty on them.[49] According to testimony, the nobleman Marco Barbarigo
came by boat to the house of Minello in Santa Lucia and rowed him out to
the ship, which presumably was lying in anchor in the lagoon. The two broke
into the ship's cabin and retrieved the silk. Minello was convicted and fined
5 ducats, which he paid, and Barbarigo was fined 100 ducats. Another nobleman, Benedetto Emo, was fined 5 ducats for his role in the escapade, while
Nicoleto Contarini, also identified as noble, was acquitted; one other man
implicated in the case was given a lesser fine and another was acquitted. This
association, albeit illicit, with members of three prominent noble families
shows Minello participating in activities that would establish him as being in
the social world of the nobility, if not legally sharing their noble status.

Despite his ownership of a sailing ship and active participation in the trade
of spices, cloth, and fur, Minello Condulmer does not seem to have been an
extremely wealthy man. In 1346, both Minello and his wife, Vielma, daughter
of the non-noble Cristoforo Liberio, wrote out their wills. Minello, dictating
his will in March, specifically noted a fear of shipwreck as was common in the
wills of sailors and named as his executors his wife, their son Pietro, his sister Nicoleta, and Andrea, bishop of the neighboring coastal town of Caorle.[50]
The list of pious benefactions that began the specification of legacies is extensive, but the sums were not extravagant. Nicoleta was given lifelong room and
board in his main house if she could get along with his widow; if not, she
could lodge in one of his small houses. Vielma was given the choice of remaining in his home as a widow with her dowry and proceeds from his estate to
subsidize her expenses, or, if she remarried, she was to get only the return of
her dowry and her personal clothing. In the latter case, she would also lose
her status as executor and any claim to his goods. The residue of Minello's
estate (of unknown value) was to go to his son Pietro. Any male child born
between the making out of the will and his death would share in the residual

estate, while any female child would be cared for until marriage and then get the reasonably substantial but not extravagant sum of 200 ducats as a dowry.

Vielma made her will with the same notary in July 1346.[51] She named Minello and Pietro as her only executors. Her pious distributions were smaller than those of her husband; her confessor (*patrino*) at the church of San Lucia was to get 1.5 ducats, and sums to other Venetian institutions were even smaller. Somewhat more significant were the 2 ducats she offered to a poor man or woman to make a pilgrimage to Assisi for an indulgence for her and 3 ducats to someone to go to Rome for her soul. Her mother was to get 5 ducats, and the residue of the estate was to go to Pietro.

Minello lived at least until June 1348, when he was named executor in the will of his nephew, the noble Nicolo Avonal; marriage between members of the Condulmer family and of the nobility clearly went back at least into the early decades of the fourteenth century.[52] Vielma lived at least until 1372, when she made out a new will, identifying herself as widow of Minello and naming her son Pietro as one of her executors along with her sister Francesca.[53] Her new will was considerably more generous with pious bequests than her earlier one had been, the intent of which was made clear by the final provisions: all of her personal effects were to be sold and added to the estate, which was to be distributed as her executors saw fit for the benefit of her soul, that is, to religious institutions or to the needy.

Pietro, the son of Minello and Vielma, apparently inherited his father's wealth in accordance with the 1346 will and in 1363 received a dowry of 450 ducats from the family of his wife, Madaluza, which she reclaimed in 1377 after his death.[54] He made out his will in 1371, leaving her his estate if she remained a widow and only her clothing if she remarried, in which case 100 ducats would go to his mother with the rest to be sold for the sake of his soul.[55] In 1380, Madaluza inherited 250 ducats from the estate of her sister's daughter Cristina, also married to a member of the Condulmer family named Pietro.[56]

Thus, the early history of the Santa Lucia branch of the Condulmer family, fragmentary though it may be, shows several examples of the members engaging in criminal, commercial, and marital activities with members of the nobility, their non-noble status notwithstanding. The themes of the ownership of relatively small sailing ships, as opposed to the large, oared galleys whose activities were monopolized by the nobility, and commercial dealings with Apulia were also characteristic of the Condulmer family in this

era. Their grants of the bulk of their estates to churches and other pious institutions were typical of wills written during or after the Black Death of 1348,
contributing greatly to the wealth of such institutions.

Nicoleto Condulmer of San Tomà, Early Victim of the Black Death

Like his distant relative Minello, Nicoleto Condulmer appears to have died
of the plague, or Black Death, of 1348. Nicoleto was one of four sons of Giacomo, after whose death in 1339 his lands in the nearby parish of Sant'Agostin
were divided among his own three sons and the three sons of his deceased
son Pietro.[57] Nicoleto probably remained in his father's palace in the parish
of San Tomà (location of the Frari, the leading Franciscan church and monastery of Venice) and provided a home there for his three orphaned nephews
until they reached maturity. Most of the land holdings of this branch of the
family were in the half of Venice known as *de Ultra*, that is, on the far side of
the Grand Canal from San Marco. Both of Nicoleto's surviving brothers are
documented as long-distance merchants in the second quarter of the fourteenth century.[58]

In 1329, Nicoleto Condulmer and his business partner the nobleman
Giovanni Dandolo (a member of one of the most prestigious noble families)
went to the Turkish coast of Asia Minor in search of grain to bring back to
Venice but, finding none, brought back alum (a fixant for dyes that was found
only in that region), which they were not authorized to carry; they paid their
fine and were forgiven further penalties in a document in which both are
identified as noble.[59] In 1339, Nicoleto exported vair pelts, leaving a pledge
of 5 ducats with the customs agents; his ship foundered off of Apulia, and
when he brought the soaked pelts back to Venice, he was forgiven the import
duty for them and received his pledge back.[60] He had similarly poor luck the
next year when with two partners he sent a shipment of horsemeat, chickens,
and lambskins to Apulia worth 900 ducats and had to bring them back to
Venice, for which the duty was forgiven.[61] In 1342, he was fined for not paying customs duty on 170 pounds of cheese within the requisite six weeks; he
was forgiven half the fine.[62] Such infractions were common and part of doing
business for successful merchants, noble and non-noble alike.[63]

In May 1348, a few months after the Black Death had arrived in Venice,
Nicoleto made out his will; at that point, he was living in the parish of San
Cassian, not far from San Tomà.[64] He named his wife, Fiorenza Miorato; her

non-noble father, Pietro; and his son Zanino as his executors; the instructions that these executors give the customary tithe to the poor if they should survive him testifies to the uncertainty of the times. He also named the Procurators of San Marco among his executors; it is thanks to this latter fallback provision that the elements and disposition of his estate survive in unusual detail.

According to Nicoleto's will, Fiorenza was to receive a bequest of about 115 ducats, the return of her dowry (*repromessa*) of about 240 ducats, plus the valuables she had brought in her wedding chest (*cofano*) valued at about 100 ducats, that is, her trousseau (*corredo*) as well as all of her clothing and cloth.[65] If she continued to live with her son as a widow, she would get 5 ducats a year; if she remained a widow but did not live with Zanino, she would get 40 ducats a year for food and expenses and keep her upstairs bedroom and a chamber in the San Cassian palace as well as a downstairs room facing the street for the rest of her life. If she remarried, she would get back only her dowry and chest. Nicoleto and Fiorenza had a daughter, Agnesina, who had received her dowry in 1346; her name appears nowhere in his will, as was typical for daughters already dowered. However, as we shall see below, Nicoleto's estate would have to deal with the fact that he had given her groom only half of the 580-ducat dowry in cash, with a complicated scheme of payment of the balance. Nicoleto's son Zanino was to receive the residue of the estate when he turned eighteen; until then, the executors were to invest half the value of the movables of the estate in commercial ventures (*colleganze*) within Venice and half in maritime trade; no more than 500 ducats was to be put into any single investment. If Zanino should die without heirs, the estate was to be used to build a hospital.

Nicoleto Condulmer died on June 20, 1348, three weeks after making out his will; as this was soon after the beginning of the devastation wrought by the Black Death in Venice, it is likely that he died of the plague.[66] A week later, the Procurators of San Marco began to settle the estate with the purchase for 1.5 ducats of a notebook for the estate records and a sack for coins; on June 30, Pietro Miorato, Nicoleto's father-in-law, entered into his status as executor.[67] In February of the following year, the executors made the payment of 115 ducats to Nicoleto's widow, Fiorenza, in accordance with a decree of the Court of Procurators.[68] By March, however, the two individual executors, Nicoleto's son Zanino and his father-in-law, Pietro Miorato, had died, and Fiorenza had remarried.[69] Zanino had made a will leaving his mother as his sole heir and executor, and she sought sole executor status for herself for Nicoleto's estate as well, but the court left it in the hands of the Procurators of

San Marco, giving her jurisdiction only for aspects of the estate for which the will had granted discretionary choice to her and Zanino. Wrangling over the administration of the estate continued for several months, but the Court of Procurators removed Fiorenza's rights to control it in June 1349.[70]

An examination of the numerous business ventures that Nicoleto was involved in at the time the Black Death struck Venice gives a view of his diversified and dynamic investment strategy, typical of that of hundreds of middle-level Venetian merchants. Because the estate of Nicoleto Condulmer was administered by the Procurators of San Marco, there survives a complete record of its settlement, including receipts for about two years after his death that allow a reconstruction of his mercantile activities, income from his *prestiti* (bonds of the Venetian state), payments for the transactions needed to settle the estate, and finally payments to beneficiaries of his will. These details of his finances, which survive for few merchants of his generation, show him to have been a mid-range, non-noble merchant, with much of his activity in foodstuffs from the Adriatic coast of Italy and from the eastern Mediterranean brought to Venice by small sailing ships, in some of which he held part ownership.

At the time of his death, Nicoleto owned shares in five ships, for which the estate received profits and freight charges at the end of each voyage, as well as the sale price of goods brought in, almost all within two years of his death.[71] In November 1348, the estate received 109 ducats for the profits from Nicoleto's one-eighth share in a ship owned by the non-noble Tomadi family, followed by another payment of 155 ducats the following April and 50 ducats in December. Nicoleto's merchandise from the voyages of this ship, including pepper, ginger, soap, and lard, was sold off in January and December 1349, bringing the estate an additional 911 ducats. Nicoleto's partial ownership of various small sailing vessels brought his estate freight charges and heavy commodities, such as grain, oil, and cheese, as well as metals including lead, tin, copper, worked silver, and forty-one Persian gold tanka coins. All told, Nicoleto's outstanding merchant ventures at the time of his death brought the estate 824 ducats from investments in ships and boats and 2,008 ducats from the sale of imported commodities.

There were also proceeds from investments within Venice. At the time of his death, Nicoleto was receiving rent of 21 ducats a year for land in the parish of San Cassian (probably a few rooms within his palace) and less than 2 ducats a year from land in Santa Lucia.[72] He got 19.5 ducats a year for the rent of his house in San Tomà to Giacomo Moioli of Cremona, which was split evenly with his nephew Matteo.[73] In October 1353, the Procurators sold off his house in San Tomà to Nicoleto's nephew Jacobello Condulmer for 250 ducats, and in 1357 the main house in San Cassian was sold for 1,000 ducats.[74] The estate of Nicoleto Condulmer received regular distributions on the basis of the 1,300 ducats' worth of *prestiti* he held at the time of his death.[75]

In June 1349, one year after Nicoleto's death, the Procurators of San Marco paid the tithe officials 39.6 ducats based on a 3 percent levy on 1,320 ducats.[76] The 39.6 ducats paid in tithe amounted to about 0.5 percent of his total wealth, far less than the *decima* (tenth) name of the payment would imply.[77] Regular distributions from the estate to religious institutions and members of the extended San Tomà branch of the Condulmer house began in September 1349, over a year after the death of Nicoleto, but due to the ravages of the Black Death, this delay may not have been typical.[78] The executors also had to deal with the dowry that Nicoleto had bestowed on his daughter, Agnesina, when she married the nobleman Moise di Jesolo, a merchant who would eventually become a lawyer and judge.[79] In 1349, Moise produced in the Court of Procurators a promissory note written in 1346 in which Nicoleto recognized a debt to him of 290 ducats as the balance of the dowry of about 580 ducats.[80] Nicoleto had promised to invest the 290 ducats in the state galleys every year and transmit to Moise the profits reckoned as about 84.5 ducats a year (almost 30 percent). The court ordered the estate to pay that year's profit as well as the capital of 290 ducats; the executors paid the capital in March and the profits in June of that year.[81]

The investment of Nicoleto's wealth was continued by the Procurators after his death. As executors, they had to follow the prescription in the will that the value of the movables of the estate be invested in *colleganza* ventures at land and sea at the rate of not more than 500 ducats per venture. Though initially a form of partnership in commercial expeditions (equivalent to the *commenda* investment contracts of other Italian cities), by the mid-fourteenth century the Venetian *colleganza* was basically a loan given to one or more individuals for a given time period whose repayment rate would be based on the success of the venture. These investments did not start until October 1355, when the Procurators gave 50 ducats to Nicoleto's brother Almoro and to Jacobello, the son of his late brother Pietro, for investing within Venice. Almost two-and-a-half years later, they received back the 50 ducats plus a profit of 6 5/6 ducats, a return of almost 6 percent per year on the investment; the Procurators reinvested the capital with Almoro and Jacobello on the same terms. When they closed the first register of estate records in 1360, the Procurators noted that they had a total of about 292 ducats outstanding in *colleganza* ventures.

From these postmortem accounts, we can deduce that at the time of his death, Nicoleto Condulmer owned three pieces of land in Venice worth a total of about 1,300 ducats. His movable goods, as derived from the value of the *colleganze*, seem to have been worth about 300 ducats. He held about 1,300 ducats worth of state bonds, which produced about 65 to 100 ducats of interest per year. At the time of his death, he owned shares in five ships, ranging from a small *marano* for local coastal trade to large sailing ships capable of voyages to the Black Sea; the total value of these investments was about 650 ducats, and the profit in freight fees was 166 ducats from the four smaller ships. The total value of the merchandise brought back to Venice after his death was over 2,000 ducats. In general, with a total wealth of about 7,500 ducats, Nicoleto Condulmer can be placed in the upper range of wealthy non-noble merchants.

A provision in Nicoleto's will to give regular payments for masses to the hospital church of Santa Maria della Misericordia from the proceeds of Nicoleto's state bonds was of indefinite duration, and this may have been the aspect that impelled him to include the Procurators of San Marco among his executors and the courts to give them exclusive status after his death; these payments to the church carried on until 1596.[82] The provision that the residue of his estate in the absence of a male descendant go to build a hospice had an even longer afterlife in the Ospizio de' Santi Pietro e Paolo on Murano. In 1357, the Procurators disbursed from Nicoleto's estate about 841 ducats for two-fifths of the expenses of buying and restoring a hospice on the island of Murano and began an annual dispersal of 75 ducats a year for its expenses.[83] The remaining three-fifths of the hospice's costs were paid from another estate administered by the Procurators, that of the nobleman Paolo Signolo, who in his will of September 1347 left 100,000 ducats to build and endow a hospice in Murano.[84] The two endowments were managed separately until 1684, when they were merged, and were continued until 1734; the hospice was still active in the nineteenth century.[85]

When he made out his will in May 1348, Nicoleto Condulmer must have been aware of the death rate from the plague that was increasing exponentially within the city. Nevertheless, with a young and presumably healthy son, wife, and father-in-law he made little in the way of contingency provisions for his widely ranging investments or sizable estate. The death of his son before his own estate could be settled put a quick end to his particular branch of the Condulmer house and ended up channeling his significant wealth to a hospice on Murano, which outlasted him by more than five centuries.

The Black Death and the Condulmer Family

While the case of Nicoleto offers an example of the benefit that the plague brought to religious and charitable institutions in Venice, in other cases the sudden disappearance of a sizable proportion of the Venetian population in 1348 and immediately thereafter ended up concentrating the wealth of widespread families in the hands of a few survivors. In our case, it was the San Tomà and Santa Lucia lineages of the House of Condulmer who came out of the plague years in a stronger economic and eventually social position.

The Black Death ravaged Venice in 1348 and 1349 as much as any place in Europe.[86] It is difficult to quantify the effect of the plague on the House of Condulmer. Of seventy-seven members of the family (including women married into it) recorded in the period from 1330 to 1369, thirteen appear in documents of 1330 to 1339, forty-four in documents of 1340 to 1349, twenty-one in documents of 1350 to 1359, and twenty-nine in documents of 1360 to 1369. Of these, nine women and six men are known only from wills of the years 1348 and 1349, as testators, executors, and heirs. In all, thirty-seven of the forty-nine members of the Condulmer family who appear in documents of the two decades leading up to the Black Death—that is, about three-quarters of them—do not appear after 1350; a good proportion of them may have died between 1348 and 1349.

There has long been an ongoing debate between those who see the Black Death as an end point to the dynamic growth of medieval Europe's population and economy and others who see it as a stimulus for a new Renaissance society with capital concentrated in the hands of fewer families.[87] When we look at the specifics of the Condulmer family, we can see a concentration of wealth in two main branches in the second half of the fourteenth century as compared with the decades leading up to 1348 (Figure 3; see Figures 12 and 13). It is almost certain that Nicoleto Condulmer died of the Black Death, which hit Venice in the winter of 1347–48 and raged for the next year and a half. It appears that his son and only heir also died, bringing Nicoleto's line of the San Tomà branch of the house to an end. The lines of his three brothers survived the plague. Almoro lived in the parish of Sant' Agostin into the 1350s, and his three sons succeeded him. Nicoleto's second brother, Pietro, had three sons: Rafaele, who appears to have died of the plague; Alvise, who wrote out a will in 1348 but survived at least until 1355; and Jacobello, who served as caretaker for Alvise's young son Zanino.[88] As we shall see in Chapter 2, Jacobello not only carried on Pietro's line but brought glory to the whole

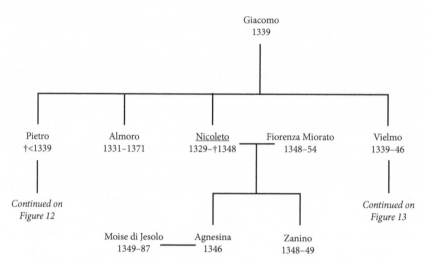

Figure 3. The family of Nicoleto Condulmer, parish of San Tomà. Underlined names are for people featured in Chapter 1. No last name is given for Condulmer. Years are of documents in which each is mentioned, while † denotes the year of death.

Condulmer family with his entry into the nobility. Nicoleto's third brother, Vielmo, who had appeared as a cloth merchant in a document of 1346, was dead by 1350, also presumably a victim of the plague, but was the grandfather of his namesake, the money changer, who will be the subject of Chapter 3.[89]

The other main branch of the house of Condulmer to survive into the second half of the fourteenth century was centered on the parish of Santa Lucia in Cannaregio, home of the earliest well-documented members of the family, Meneghello and Minello. The main lineage of this branch in the decades after the plague was that of Fiornovello, identified as deceased in a land survey of Condulmer holdings in Santa Lucia just after the Black Death.[90] His branch of the family, however, seems to have come through the plague strongly, as he was survived by at least two sons and two daughters and several nephews. The descendants of Fiornovello on the Santa Lucia side of the family would bring it to financial heights and depths with the rise and collapse of the bank of Simoneto Condulmer and to international stature with the papacy of Gabriele Condulmer, Pope Eugene IV, as will be traced in Chapters 4, 5, and 6.

CHAPTER 2

Jacobello Condulmer,
Merchant and New Noble

Jacobello Condulmer of the parish of San Tomà must have appeared to contemporary Venetians as the most visible member of his house in the decades
after the Black Death. Through a series of pious, fraternal, and public benefactions he established himself and his family as one of the leading non-noble
lineages of post-plague Venice and, through an extraordinary commitment
of resources to the military effort at the time of the War of Chioggia, brought
his branch of the Condulmer house into the nobility. He was the embodi-
ment of the literal definition of social mobility in medieval Venice—the rise
from the ranks of the non-noble populace to admission to membership in
the Great Council for himself and his direct descendants, with all of the
rights and privileges that this carried.

Jacobello's Personal and Professional Life

The Black Death had winnowed the ranks of the Condulmer house as it did
for Venetian society as a whole and concentrated its growing wealth in a few
hands. Jacobello was the son of Pietro, a brother of the plague victim Nicoleto, who was already dead when Nicoleto made his will in 1348.[1] One of
Pietro's sons, Rafaele, was also dead by the time Nicoleto made out his will.
Alvise, Jacobello's other brother, made out a will in 1348, leaving a dowry for
his daughter of 50 ducats but making his brother Jacobello and their mother
his principal heirs.[2] Alvise survived the plague, and by the time of his death,
at some point after 1354, entrusted to his young son Zanino to the guardian-
ship of his own brother Jacobello.[3]

Jacobello appears in documentation in 1332 as a married man, so he was probably born between 1300 and 1310; in 1339 he was named an heir of his grandfather Giacomo.[4] After the Black Death, his resources grew through inheritance and the management of estates. As executor of the estates of his uncle Vielmo and his brother Rafaele, he made investments in a company of three merchants among whom was his brother Alvise.[5] Jacobello got barely 4 ducats in 1353 directly from the will of his uncle Nicoleto, plus an additional amount as executor of Rafaele's estate; however, he was one of the merchants entrusted by Nicoleto's executors with 50-ducat investments for commerce (in partnership with his uncle Almoro) within Venice in 1355 and again in 1358; the first of these *colleganza* (joint investment) contracts brought the estate a profit of about 6 percent per year.[6]

As guardian for the underage son of his brother Alvise, he used that estate (for which he was coexecutor with the Procurators of San Marco) as the source of investment in his own merchant activities. He received two one-year *colleganza* investments in 1366—one of 1,000 and the other of 1,230 ducats; one of 2,280 ducats in 1367; one of 2,400 ducats in 1369; one of 2,480 ducats in 1370; and one of 2,600 ducats in 1371.[7] In all these cases, his share of profits is not specified. In view of the incremental increase in the *colleganze*, it appears that each year's profits to the estate may have been added to the next investment, in which case the estate's return would have been about 2.25 percent for the first year of 1366, 5.25 percent for the two-year period following, 3.33 percent for the following year, and 4.75 percent for the 1371 contract. If the division of profits was equal between investor and merchant, as was common in this period, Jacobello's profits would have been the same as the sums added to the investments, amounting to 370 ducats over five years.

Jacobello also used funds from the estate of his nephew for investment of about 300 ducats in state bonds, for which he claimed half of the value as his own as compensation for expenses he had made for the estate.[8] Over the objection of his coexecutors, the Procurators of San Marco, who said that Jacobello had no permission to buy such bonds, the Court of Procurators, which exercised jurisdiction over estates, awarded him half the value of the bonds. Later that year, he bought another 151.5 ducats' worth of bonds, of which the court awarded him half the value.[9]

Starting in his early adulthood, Jacobello used the profits from his mercantile investments to buy real estate, often plots of land that his wife, Agnesina, had purchased and sometimes in partnership with her. From 1332 on, he and Agnesina acquired land around Venice; in that year she (identified as his wife) bought land in the Cannaregio parish of San Marcuola, which she sold to Jacobello in 1361.[10] In 1351 she bought land in the Santa Maria del Giglio parish for 350 ducats from a Giovanna Condulmer of the parish of San Felice, probably a relative of Jacobello's uncle Vielmo.[11] In 1355, Jacobello together with his brother Alvise, bought from Agnesina a property in the family's home parish of San Tomà directly on the Grand Canal for 1,350 ducats.[12] In 1366, Jacobello bought a property in Treviso, on the Italian mainland.[13]

The extent of the couple's landholding is documented in a detailed inventory made shortly after Jacobello's death. In 1383, his widow received a court confirmation of ownership of five pieces of land that he had transferred to her in 1380 (Map 2).[14] The first was the site of the family's main palace, the Cà Grande, in the parish of San Tomà. It included the holdings of the estate of Alvise Condulmer's son Giovanni, to whom Jacobello was guardian, which comprised a dwelling and four shops or storage units. The court found that Jacobello had built an extension containing an iron-framed window in the form of a pergola beyond his property limits and ordered it removed and that piece of land restored to its proper owners. This property appears to have been located between the apse of the Church of San Tomà and the Grand Canal and bordered on the Rio San Tomà. This site was later occupied by the Palazzo Dolfin.[15]

The second and third pieces of land the couple owned were in the parish of Santa Lucia and included a main dwelling (*hospicium*) and rental dwellings (*domus a serzentibus*).[16] The fourth property was in San Marcuola, which included a soap-making shop.[17] The fifth property was a piece of vacant land in the parish of San Geremia in Cannaregio.[18]

In his mature adult life as an independent merchant, Jacobello appears to have been involved in a wide variety of commercial ventures in Venice and abroad. In early 1350, he sought a reversal of the fine of about 115 ducats for refusing to testify to the gold estimators about whether the gold being sold by another merchant was acquired or traded illegally; later that year both the Council of Forty and the Great Council reduced his fine to less than 10 ducats.[19] He was also active in the slave trade, as witnessed by a 1360 receipt for funds for an enslaved person bought in Tana, in the Black Sea region, on his behalf.[20] He was singled out in a Senate decree of 1362 as due for compensation for losses in Apulia, along with Pietro Gradenigo, son of the late doge; Nicolo Contarini; and Nicolo Falier, all of prestigious noble families.[21] In 1364, Jacobello received 1,200 ducats in *colleganze* from the wealthiest non-noble in Venice, Bandino di Garzoni, for investment within Venice for

Map 2. Important sites in the life of Jacobello Condulmer.

one year, after which time he would return the capital and an unspecified
percentage of the profit.[22] In 1376 he was awarded damages by the Court of
Petitions against the nobleman Nicolo Michiel for losses in connection to
shipments of paper he had imported to Venice and cumin he had imported
and then reexported to Bruges.[23]

Jacobello Condulmer in the Public Life of Venice

Jacobello played a surprisingly large role for a non-noble in the diplomatic
relations of Venice, an activity usually reserved for the most experienced
noble members of government councils. He was one of four Venetians who
participated in 1357 in negotiations led by Doge Giovanni Dolfin for reparations for damages done to an Amalfitan merchant in recent fighting between
Venice and Genoa.[24] Five years later, the king and queen of Naples negotiated
with the Venetian government for compensation to Jacobello for losses he
suffered when a ship he owned, captained by another Venetian, was seized
by Manfred of Claramonte.[25] In 1377, Jacobello was involved in proceedings
concerning the loss of Florentine cloth in Constantinople.[26]

In the 1370s, at an age of probably between sixty and seventy years, Jacobello entered into the public life of Venice. Though most of the major offices
of the Republic were reserved for members of the nobility, charitable institutions and confraternities gave non-nobles opportunities for public service

and recognition. The Hospital of Saints Peter and Paul, in the far eastern reaches of the city, near the cathedral of San Pietro di Castello, was the largest such institution in Venice, serving about a hundred patients and prisoners.[27] At the time of the plague, it was put under direct control of the doge, who selected a layman to act as prior and five procurators to govern it, specified as comprising two members of the nobility and three *providi viri*, that is, non-nobles of the highest status, all to be chosen for life with a review every two years by the doge and his counselors.[28] In January 1376, Jacobello Condulmer was elected to this office, with the designation *providus vir*; he presumably held the position until his death five years later.[29]

The following year, 1377, Jacobello rose to a position of prominence throughout Venice with his founding of the Confraternity of Merchants in the church of San Cristoforo in the marshy lands at the northern reaches of Cannaregio, and notably with the provision of a statue of the Virgin that would make the church a center of pilgrimage.

The Church of San Cristoforo of Venice was founded by the Order of the Humiliati, whose origin was in twelfth-century Lombardy and whose participants and supporters were often associated with the cloth trade (Figure 4).[30] As was the case with the Franciscans, the zeal of the Humiliati, their emphasis on preaching to the general populace, and their independence from the authority of local bishops and of popes brought them frequently under suspicion for heresy and unclerical behaviors. They differed from the Franciscans and Dominicans in seeking to earn their subsistence from the labor of the brothers rather than from begging. Like other monastic orders dedicated to poverty and the lives of the working poor, the Order of the Humiliati lavished resources on the splendid decoration of their churches, most notably the Ognissanti Church in Florence, for which they had commissioned in 1310 a panel painting from the great artist Giotto, who had recently completed the Arena chapel in Padua for the Scrovegni family. By the end of the thirteenth century, there were almost four hundred houses of Humiliati, mainly in northern Italy, but for the first century and a half of the order's existence, they had no church in Venice. In 1365, the order's Grand Master, Fra Tibero of Parma, acquired a vast area in the northern reaches of Cannaregio for a new church for the Humiliati dedicated to Saint Cristopher.

In April 1377, Jacobello Condulmer became the founding governor of the Confraternity of Merchants, located at the church of San Cristoforo—"la scuola de messer sen Cristofor di mercadanti" (Figure 5).[31] The *mariegola*, or rule book, of the confraternity begins with fourteen folios of rules and

Figure 4. Venice, the Church of San Cristoforo (Madonna dell'Orto), Order of
the Humiliati, founded in 1365. Photo taken by the author.

procedures of the *scuola*, followed by later additions up to 1524. It ends with
lists of officers and members of various classes. Jacobello appears as the first
governor, in addition to 1 vicar, 12 deacons or rectors, 9 physicians, and 1
scribe. There were 40 noble members and 297 non-noble brothers, all lay-
men, among whom in addition to Jacobello there appears Angelo Condulmer, of the Santa Lucia branch of the family.[32] Though its name indicates
that it was connected to the merchant population of Venice, the Scuola dei
Mercanti was not a guild; such organizations, called *arti* in Venice, were
distinct from confraternities and were closely controlled by the state. The
new merchant confraternity founded by Jacobello Condulmer was one of

Figure 5. Venice, the Scuola of San Cristoforo dei Mercanti, founded in 1377.
Photo taken by the author.

hundreds of so-called *scuole piccole*, in contrast to the four *scuole grandi*
that dominated the social life and identity of the higher levels of non-noble
Venetians, the *cittadini*.[33]

The *mariegola* of the confraternity of San Cristoforo prescribed that the
governor, as the head and protector of the confraternity, be elected annually
by the brothers, as were the other officers, including two who were designated
to wash the bodies of dead members. Members, non-noble and noble alike,
were to pay annual dues of one ducat on the feast day of Saint Christopher,
July 25. Mandatory chapter meetings were to be held twice a year, on the
second Sunday of January and July; in addition, members were expected to
participate in processions to the Piazza San Marco on major occasions and
those leading to mass in the church of the Humiliati on the second Sunday
of each month (Figure 6). Any brother who fell ill or into poverty was to be
visited by the other members. The funeral and burial of each brother was a
primary function of the confraternity; the governor and officers were charged
with accompanying the body of each defunct member to the church for burial
and having twelve masses be said for his soul, and each brother was to say

Figure 6. Gentile Bellini, *Processione in Piazza San Marco*, c. 1496, tempera and oil on canvas, 378 × 745 cm, Venice, Gallerie dell'Accademia. Wikimedia Commons, public domain by Didier Descouens.

twenty-five Our Fathers and twenty-five Hail Marys as soon as they heard of the death.

A contrast with the newly founded merchant confraternity at San Cristoforo can be seen in the documentation for the brothers of the Scuola Grande di San Giovanni Evangelista, whose membership comprised the leading non-noble shopkeepers and manufacturers. As presented in its *mariegola* of 1387, the Scuola of San Giovanni Evangelista, founded in 1261, included 91 noble members in addition to the 1,447 non-noble members, of whom many were identified as owning small manufacturing establishments or stores.[34] The merchant confraternity of San Cristoforo founded by Jacobello Condulmer contained among its membership almost none of the local artisans and shopkeepers typical of San Giovanni Evangelista. The number of brothers of San Cristoforo known to have been active in the international cloth trade is five times higher than for the *cittadino* lists of San Giovanni Evangelista.[35] A relatively large number were newly admitted to Venetian citizenship and identified as coming from other cities, with Como, Verona, and Siena appearing most commonly. Rather than being spread throughout the city, the members of San Cristoforo were concentrated in the sestier of Cannaregio, where the *scuola* was located. It might be that this smaller *scuola* attracted a more local membership, or more likely the distribution can be associated with the identity of Cannaregio as home to a growing number of up-and-coming merchants.

Jacobello Condulmer and the Virgin in the Garden

Four months after the formation of the new confraternity, its governor Jacobello Condulmer met with the sculptor Giovanni di Santi to document the sale of a "figure of the Holy Virgin Mary with son in her arms" (Figures 7 and 8).[36] Di Santi gave a quittance (receipt for payment) for 150 ducats to Jacobello and thirteen other officials of the confraternity and promised to continue to work on the statue to bring it to a state of completion that would be suitable to them.

A month later there was a convocation in the monastery of San Cristoforo to celebrate the transfer of the statue to the church and at the same time formalize the relationship between the merchant confraternity and the Humiliati. An enormous parchment was witnessed by eight nobles (not members

Figure 7. Giovanni di Santi, *Madonna and Child*, 1377, limestone, Venice, Madonna dell'Orto. Photo taken by author.

Figure 8. Giovanni di Santi, *Madonna and Child*, detail, 1377, limestone, Venice, Madonna dell'Orto. Photo taken by author.

of the confraternity), the master general of the Order of the Humiliati, the *praepositus* and nine brothers of the monastery, and Jacobello Condulmer and thirteen brothers of the confraternity. They all confirmed their agreement to a pact (described as written on paper in Venetian), which began with an account of the statue:

> Many miracles have appeared in connection to the stone statue sculpted by Giovanni di Santi, stone sculptor of the parish of Santa Margarita, of the Virgin with son in arms, not yet completed on land next to the home of Giovanni, with many people coming day and night to venerate it. Consequently, the Bishop of Castello [i.e., of Venice] commanded Giovanni to take it into his house so people would not go there or to put it in some church or sacred space. Giovanni then came to brother Antonio, the provost of S. Cristoforo, saying he would give it to the church at his own expense if the church would put an altar immediately in front of the Virgin Mary and after his death have a mass said there daily for his soul. The provost agreed, but Giovanni then demanded

money, which the provost considered dishonest and declared that he could not in good conscience give in to such a demand. Giovanni then reneged on his offer. Hearing this, Jacobello Condulmer, the first governor of the confraternity, in order to help the church, agreed to make the payment, along with his associates, and got the provost to agree to build the altar and say the masses for Giovanni. So, on this past June 18, the statue was erected in the church of San Cristoforo.[37]

It is evident from this account that the statue had become the object of a spontaneous public act of veneration, something that could potentially threaten the ecclesiastical establishment of Venice and that its purchase by Jacobello Condulmer on behalf of the church of San Cristoforo put it into a context in which public devotion to it could be regulated and used to the benefit of the church and the confraternity. The document of donation noted that there had been so many miracles attributed to the statue that the confraternity and the monastery reached an agreement that all the gifts to the statue or because of the statue be put in front of it in a box opened by two keys, one held by the provost and monks and the other held by Condulmer and his successors in the confraternity. All of the jewels, clothing, and ornaments placed on the statue were to be sold and the proceeds added to the box. All the money taken from the box would be spent first for the fabric of the church, second for the chapel and altar of the Virgin in the church, and third and last for the monastery.

Another large document drawn up the same day with the same witnesses enumerated the obligations of the monastery to the confraternity in exchange for the statue and the gifts it attracted.[38] The confraternity was given permission to build its own new building of about fourteen paces on each side adjacent to the church, with an open space of about ten paces; two vaulted arches were to lead into the cloister. When members of the confraternity died, they were to receive burial in the cloister of the monastery for a fee of 4 ducats, with the monks committed to singing monthly masses for their souls (Figure 9). If any members were buried in another church of Venice, two of the monks were to go there to pray; if they were buried outside of Venice, the governor of the order was charged with making arrangements for masses. Burial space within Venice was becoming increasingly sought after in this period, and the assurance of a suitable plot and continuous prayers was one of the chief attractions of such confraternities.[39]

Not only did the purchase of the statue benefit both the confraternity and the monastery; it also seems to have rescued its sculptor from financial

Figure 9. Venice, San Cristoforo (Madonna dell'Orto), cloisters. Wikimedia Commons, public domain by Abxbay.

straits. Giovanni was the son of the sculptor Andriolo di Santi, whose most accomplished work was the portal of the church of San Lorenzo of Vicenza.[40] It appears that in the summer of 1377, Giovanni di Santi was in debt to the Procurators of San Marco for 60 ducats for a loan guaranteed by his recently deceased father, so he must have been desperate for the quick turnaround of the statue he was in the process of carving in his studio.[41] Other than this statue of the Madonna, the sculptor Giovanni di Santi is known to have produced only one other work: in his will of 1384, seven years after the sale of the Madonna, he reminded the brothers of the church of their agreement to bury him there and bequeathed to the church a sculpture of red porphyry so that they might remember to pray for his soul in eternity.[42] The sculpture in question is undoubtedly the burial slab that resides in the church to this day, with an inscription identifying its subject as the stone sculptor Giovanni di Santi who made the statue of the Virgin (Figure 10).

The church of San Cristoforo continued to prosper from the pilgrimage to the statue of the Virgin and child, and in 1414, the Council of Ten officially changed the dedication of the church from Saint Christopher to the

Figure 10. Giovanni di Santi,
self-portrait on tombstone,
c. 1384, bas-relief, porphyry,
Venice, Madonna dell'Orto.
Photo taken by author.

Madonna dell'Orto (the Virgin of the Garden).[43] The Order of the Humiliati, which had founded the church in the mid-fourteenth century, was eventually ousted and replaced by the Order of San Giorgio in Alga, closely identified with another member of the Condulmer family, Gabriele, in his role as Pope Eugene IV.[44] In 1420, the Confraternity of Merchants of San Cristoforo got permission from the Council of Ten to add the name of the Madonna dell'Orto to its original dedication.[45] It would continue to purchase works of art to adorn the adjoining church, including a portal by Bartolomeo Bon in 1460 (expenses shared fifty-fifty with the congregation) and large paintings by Tintoretto for the apse.[46] In 1570, it was merged with the merchant confraternity associated with the basilica of Santa Maria Gloriosa dei Frari, the large Franciscan church, and lost much of its identity and connection to the church of Madonna dell'Orto.[47]

In his guide to the sites of Venice composed in 1493, the diarist Marin Sanudo compiled various lists of must-see attractions, including the ten most beautiful large churches, the ten most beautiful monasteries, the twelve churches most valued for their daily miracles, and the ten churches most visited for personal devotion; the church of Madonna dell'Orto appeared on

all of these lists.[48] Most of the other churches on the lists were large establishments of long standing; the Madonna dell'Orto was a relatively recent
foundation, of modest size, and located in the distant sestier of Cannaregio.
Sanudo explained that the church was originally dedicated to Saint Christopher but got its name because an image of the Virgin, a matchless statue of
white marble, performed miracles in a garden nearby.[49]

Modern academic assessment of the sculpture has not been so generous.
In his corpus of Venetian Gothic sculpture, Wolfgang Wolters dismissed
the statue, saying that it is so damaged that a stylistic comparison of it (with
the work of the sculptor's father Andriolo di Santi in Padua) could give no
secure result.[50] He acknowledged that the tombstone of Giovanni di Santi in
Madonna dell'Orto was also heavily damaged but says that it was worthy of
being protected.

One aspect of the statue that probably has accounted for its popularity
among pilgrims and tourists, if not necessarily art historians, is its colossal
size; few sculptures of fourteenth-century Italy are so much larger than life.
The statue of the Virgin is itself certainly in a terrible state, at first appearing to have suffered erosion from its time spent in a garden. According to a
recent examination of the statue by Lorenzo Lazzarini, a professor of petrog-
raphy at the University of Venice and one of the participants in the 1968
restoration of the Madonna dell'Orto, "The statue is made of soft Vicenza
(Oligocenic) white limestone, a bad choice for Venice but cheap. Although
badly deteriorated and restored, it is clear that it was not finished by the
artist (namely on her right side and on the back). It is also clear that it has
suffered greatly during exposure to rainwater, which has produced diffused
dissolution pits."[51] It would appear that the statue had stood in the yard of
the sculptor for a significant period and that di Santi never performed the
final work on it specified in the purchase document, perhaps in the haste
to get it in place to satisfy the eager pilgrims seeking miracles from it. The
various cloaks donated by such worshipers, including that given by a doge
according to one account, would have covered up the more egregious areas
of roughness.

The church then went on to be the home of the works and tomb of another
Venetian artist, Jacopo Tintoretto. The sculpture of the Virgin by Giovanni
di Santi and the tomb slab with his image were moved to a side chapel. By
1581, when Francesco Sansovino wrote his guide to the sights of Venice, less
than a century after that of Marin Sanudo, he praised the church of Madonna

dell'Orto for the canvases of Bellini and Tintoretto and the exterior sculpture of Bartolomeo Bon but made no mention of the miraculous statue that had given the church its name and its importance as a site of popular devotion.[52]

The War of Chioggia and Its Financing

Two years after Jacobello Condulmer came to public notice as the governor of the new confraternity that brought the miracle-working statue to the church of San Cristoforo, a military crisis brought fresh opportunities to him for social advancement in Venice. The long-simmering conflict with Genoa over influence in the eastern Mediterranean had escalated into the fourth full-scale war between the two powers.[53] The war reached a climax in August 1378 with the capture by Genoa of the town of Chioggia within the Venetian lagoon, an existential threat to Venice itself. In May 1379, the most important part of the Venetian fleet, under the command of the popular captain general Vettore Pisani, engaged the enemy off the coast of Pola in Istria, and Pisani withdrew in defeat with only a few of his vessels intact. The Senate welcomed Pisani home with a charge of treason and desertion. Despite an indictment from the State Advocates that he be beheaded, Pisani was sentenced by a vote of 77 of 138 total votes to six months in prison and a five-year prohibition from office-holding.[54]

At this point, an incident arose that broke through Venice's carefully tended façade of internal unity, or at least the unquestioned ability of the nobility to control all political decisions. In September, members of the classes below the nobility, the *popolo*, rose up and demanded that Pisani be released from prison and be put back in charge of the defense of the city. In releasing Pisani in August 1379, the Senate must have been mindful of the precedent set the previous year in Florence when the Ciompi rebellion had resulted in a government of the *popolo* taking over the commune, a regime that would last until 1382.[55] More crucial, perhaps, was the need to enlist the Venetian populace of all ranks into the defense of the homeland both in terms of participation in the fleets and mainland armies for the retaking of the lagoon town of Chioggia and in providing the wherewithal to fund this campaign.

The main source of state revenue was the traditional recourse of Venice and other Italian communes: the obligatory purchase of state bonds with relatively regular interest payments but carefully controlled opportunities for redemption or sale.[56] In Venice, each individual was required to buy such bonds, termed *prestiti*, in a quantity based on his or her assessed patrimony, that is, the declared value of their immovable (real estate) and movable (goods and cash) possessions. Such assessments were recorded in a document called the *Estimo* that was revised periodically as needed. As the financial needs of the state were felt, levies were ordered in which individuals were required to buy bonds equivalent to a certain percentage of their *Estimo* assessment. In the course of the War of Chioggia, Venetian citizens were subject to a total of twenty-five levies that required them to buy bonds at a cost equivalent to 41 percent of their assessed wealth.[57]

The *Estimo* carried out in 1379 to raise money for the war against Genoa is the earliest to have come down to us in a complete form, but the text is neither contemporary nor totally accurate.[58] The names listed on the 1379 *Estimo*, noble and non-noble, and thus those forced to buy *prestiti*, represent only the wealthiest members of the population; in all, the register lists more than 1,150 nobles and 1,000 non-nobles, estimated to represent about 12 percent of the total population.[59] There were also classes of wealth that were excluded from the assessment on which the *Estimo* was based, including those already held in *prestiti*; estates administered by the Procurators of San Marco were also excluded.

Six members of the house of Condulmer appear on the *Estimo*. Jacobello's assessment of 4,000 ducats is the highest of the San Tomà branch of the family; his son Pietro also appears with an assessment of 1,000 ducats in the parish of Santa Lucia.[60] Nicolo Condulmer of San Felice, also of the San Tomà branch, appears with an assessment of 1,000 ducats. The highest assessment for a member of the Condulmer house is 4,300 ducats for Angelo, son of Fiornovello, of the Santa Lucia branch of the family, listed for the parish of Sant' Aponal.[61] Another member of the Santa Lucia branch is Fiornovello's daughter Cristina, widow of the nobleman Nicolo Alberto, who had died in 1374; she is listed in the parish of San Marcuola at an assessment of 1,000 ducats.[62] She is one of 197 women who appear on the *Estimo*, of whom 139 have names that are usually noble and 58 non-noble; most were probably widows. Andriolo Condulmer, son of the conspirator Marco and grandson of Meneghello, appears with an assessment of 800 ducats.

The bottom level of assessment was for the most part a patrimony of 300 ducats; it appears that a good number of members of the nobility, to say nothing of the non-nobles, fell below that threshold.[63] For example, of the thirteen noble masters of the silver mint active in the years around 1379, only eight appear on the *Estimo*, and only two of the eight noble holders of the lower-paying office of mint weigher in the period appear on the *Estimo*.[64] There are, moreover, many cases of individuals whose names are missing from the *Estimo* that cannot easily be attributed to low personal worth, including important military leaders in the War of Chioggia, more than 10 percent of the men who made up the doge's executive council, the Collegio, and more than one-third of the noble individuals who won the bidding to be captains of the state merchant galleys in this period. It is likely that members of non-noble families like the House of Condulmer and others without power in the decision-making organs of the state fared worse in this system of assessments and forced loans than did the power elite of the city.

The assessments on the 1379 *Estimo* can be divided into deciles for nobles and non-nobles (Figure 11). From this vantage point, the assessment of Jacobello Condulmer of San Tomà of 4,000 ducats would put him in either the top or second decile among non-nobles; the 4,300-ducat assessment of Angelo Condulmer of the Santa Lucia branch would put him solidly in the top decile. The 1,000-ducat assessment of Jacobello's son Pietro would put him in the middle of all non-noble assessments, the fourth to sixth deciles, as would those of Cristina and Nicolo of the Santa Lucia branch. Andriolo's assessment of 800 would put him at the bottom of the sixth percentile of non-nobles assessed.

Figure 11. The distribution by decile of assessments in ducats in the *Estimo* of 1379.

Decile of Those Assessed	Nobles	Non-Nobles
1	7,333–60,000	4,000–50,000
2	5,000–7,333	3,000–4,000
3	3,000–5,000	2,000–3,000
4	2,500–3,000	1,000–2,000
5	2,000–2,500	1,000
6	1,133–2,000	800–1,000
7	1,000–1,133	500–750
8	600–1,000	500
9	500–600	300–500
10	200–500	100–300

The Reopening of the Great Council and
Jacobello's Entrance into the Nobility

With the defeat of the fleet under Pisani in May 1379, the Venetian authorities realized that replenishing the treasury via the *Estimo* was not sufficient
to ensure the survival of the city, and so they decided to take extraordinary
measures. They must also have been wary of a full-scale revolt by members of
the *popolano* class. As in other periods of crisis, the Venetian state suspended
the decision-making responsibilities of its normal councils and put all power
in an executive committee, called in this case, the War Council. The records of
this body were deliberately destroyed at the end of the war, but the decision of
the War Council of December 1, 1379, was copied into the registers of the Senate.[65] As passed by forty-five members of the War Council, with four opposed
and four abstaining, it noted that the fate of the Republic rested in being able
to arm the galleys and that if there ever was a time for proceeding judiciously,
it was the present. The act provided that once the war was over and peace was
made, the Senate be convened with the War Council and that each member
of these bodies be allowed to nominate an individual for admission to the
Great Council and hence to hereditary noble status. Any member of the bodies could speak to the efforts of the individual under consideration, and each
candidate was then to be voted on one by one, with the thirty individuals getting the highest number of positive votes to be admitted to the Great Council
and their heirs to retain noble status in perpetuity. A provision was also made
to distribute 5,000 ducats annually to additional non-nobles and their families
who had contributed substantially to the war effort.

While this authorization was entered into the Senate's registers, other
information concerning the process of the selection of these thirty individuals is preserved mainly in a series of unofficial documents and chronicle
reports, which have led to ambiguity and uncertainty concerning the identity
of those who applied for and were admitted to the Venetian nobility on this
occasion.

An entry in the chronicle of Daniele Chinazzo, composed within a few
years of the end of the war, notes that an announcement was made in the
Rialto market and Piazza San Marco conveying the offer by the War Council of nobility for thirty families and the distribution of 5,000 ducats annually among others, as well as a provision granting citizenship to foreigners
who aided in the war effort.[66] This notice is followed in the chronicle by a
list of ninety-one individuals from fifty-three families who made promises

for wartime assistance and what they offered. Jacobello Condulmer appears on this list offering his two sons to go on the war galleys with servants at his expense and promising to import a thousand bushels of grain that the state could sell.[67] A chronicle written down in 1414, two decades later, conveys the same offer of Jacobello, adding the names of his sons Giovanni and Pietro.[68]

Later sources, however, add the name Angelo Condulmer to the listing of Jacobello and his sons.[69] The only Angelo Condulmer in archival documents of the period is Angelo, son of Fiornovello, of the parish of San Marcuola; he was of the Santa Lucia branch of the house and so only distantly related to Jacobello. The inclusion in late sources of an offer by Angelo, and indeed his election to the nobility, is probably to be connected with wishes to tie his son Gabriele, Pope Eugene IV, to the noble branch of the family.[70]

None of the men listed with Jacobello as elected to the nobility in 1381 appear in any earlier document in an office reserved for the nobility or with a designation as a noble. Six, however, do share family names with men who were already in the nobility. While Longo, Polo, and Trevisan were common names within and outside of Venice, the new nobles with the names of de Mezzo, Nani, and Vendramin probably did share some ancestry with their noble namesakes and their election may well have been fostered by family connections. On the other hand, two men with the distinctive family name of Mocenigo, a noble house that had one member elected doge in 1414, were denied admission in 1381.

The results of the elections cannot be explained totally by the promises made at the beginning of the war. Some of the men who were passed over had offered, and presumably given, as generously as those who succeeded. Giovanni Pavon offered the free services of his son who fought on the Lido and a nephew and two companions on the galleys and forfeited the interest on 10,000 ducats' worth of state bonds until a year after the war, but he received only forty-eight out of ninety votes, so fell below the cut-off. Donato Polo offered the support of his son fighting on the Lido, the pay of five archers, and a gift to the state of 1,000 ducats, but he got far fewer votes than the successful Nicolo Polo, not identified as a relative of his, whose offering was similar but lacked the gift of 1,000 ducats.

Nor does wealth appear to have been an overriding factor in the election of Jacobello. In the *Estimo* of 1379, ninety individuals (about 4 percent of those assessed) had wealth assessed at over 10,000 ducats; twenty-six of these (about 30 percent) were non-nobles. Six of the presumably wealthiest twenty-six of the non-nobles were among those admitted to the nobility, but an equal number were turned down; the remaining fourteen apparently did not attempt to gain noble status. With his assessment of 4,000 ducats, Jacobello was below that of ninety-four other non-nobles in the *Estimo*, in the upper reaches but by no means among the top thirty in assessed wealth. Of those who are recorded as having applied for admission to the Great Council, Jacobello was assessed the same as two other men, below fifteen men and above twenty-three others; of the final thirty elected, he was assessed the same as two, below five and above eight others.

The competition for admission to the nobility during the War of Chioggia was evidently a product of self-selection; only those who had special motivation seem to have made the effort to promote themselves. The final choice was also not based totally on the amount offered or on the wealth of the applicants. As in many aspects of Venetian life, personal ties and quid pro quo deals must have played a major role.[71] In the case of Jacobello Condulmer, his participation in public life in the years leading up to this selection, first as a procurator of the Hospital of Saints Peter and Paul and then as founding governor of the Confraternity of Merchants at San Cristoforo and agent for the purchase of the sculpture of the Madonna dell'Orto, demonstrated a desire to function in the mainstream of Venetian life and also probably played a role in making him more visible than other members of the crowd of upwardly mobile *cittadini*.

Jacobello's Death and Its Aftermath

The only documents in which Jacobello Condulmer appears after his election to the Great Council are two disputes in the Court of Procurators over investments of the trust fund of his nephew Zanino, of which he was coguardian with the Procurators of San Marco.[72] Though the court records are dated to May and July 1381, before the September 4, 1381, date of the list of new nobles, his name appears with the noble honorific *Ser*, probably an indication that the court records were written down after the Senate decree.[73] A suit in the same court on October 30, 1381, appealing the May 31 decision, was filed by the estate of the widow and sons of the late Jacobello Condulmer.[74] Jacobello can be seen to have died less than two months after his elevation to the nobility, probably at an age between seventy and eighty years.

In the records of the court case of October 30, 1381, Jacobello's sons Giovanni Nicolo (*Zancolo*) and Pietro Condulmer are identified with the honorific *nobilis vir*. The original call for pledges of war support in exchange for an opportunity for nobility made it clear that the new status would apply only to the selected individuals and their direct descendants. Noble status thus accrued in 1381 only to Jacobello and his sons, not to his brother's sons or those of his cousins of the San Tomà branch of the house, let alone the much more distant relatives of the Santa Lucia branch.

It was not long after his death that it became apparent that some of the wealth that Jacobello had used to rise in the social world of the non-nobles and then buy his way into the nobility was ill-gotten. In November 1381, one of the Procurators of San Marco, who shared oversight over the estate of Jacobello's nephew Zanino, brought suit in the Court of Procurators, charging that in August 1366, Jacobello had borrowed 1,000 ducats from the estate, which was valued in all at 2,530 ducats, and in November of that year had borrowed an additional 1,200 ducats; neither loan had been repaid to the estate.[75] The Procurators were granted the right to remove the unpaid sums from the estate of Jacobello before it went to his own heirs. It also became evident in 1382 that Jacobello, sole executor of the estate of his father Pietro, had failed to provide the full annual bequest of 6 ducats to his sister Zanina, a nun.[76] In his ongoing quest to raise his own social status, Jacobello had appropriated 88 percent of the inheritance of his underage nephew for whom he was the principal trustee and had withheld a payment of 6 ducats a year that his father had instructed him to pay to his own sister, a nun. It is clear from these court cases that Jacobello's efforts to improve his own standing were done so without regard for and in detriment to the fortunes of his closest relatives.

It was Jacobello's widow, Agnesina, who appears to have suffered the most immediate harm, filing appeals in several courts soon after Jacobello's death to protect her landholdings from his creditors. Her family name is unknown; documents from as early as 1332 identify her as "wife of Jacobello Condulmer," and those after 1381 identify her as his widow. On November 19, 1381, she received back her dowry of about 306 ducats plus the value of her trousseau of about 4 ducats.[77] As we have seen, she had engaged in real estate dealings for half a century by the time of Jacobello's death, in two cases selling parcels to her husband. She clearly played an active role in building the family's landholdings, but it is not apparent whether she did so on her own initiative or with her own funds. On October 3, 1380, Jacobello had gotten a ruling in the Court of Movables transferring his five main properties in Venice to Agnesina's name; Agnesina had this transaction confirmed in the Court of the Palace on October 2, 1383.[78] However, these properties had already been claimed by the Procurators of San Marco as repayment for Jacobello's debts to the estate of his nephew Zanino; they were granted these five properties in a ruling in February 1382, but this would be rescinded in a series of rulings over the next two years.[79] A later document characterizes property in Agnesina's estate as having been given to her by Jacobello ahead of all creditors, that is, as a device for shielding at least his real estate holdings from creditors.[80] Three years later, she got a confirmation from the Court of Procurators for exchanges of parts of these holdings carried out in 1381 with the trust of Zanino Condulmer, Jacobello's nephew and ward.[81]

In 1388, seven years after Jacobello's death, his creditors reached an agreement worked out in the court of Sopra Consoli and confirmed by the Judges of Petition.[82] The following year, on March 10, 1389, Agnesina made out her will.[83] She named the Procurators of San Marco as coexecutors with another widow named Agnesina and the parish priest of San Geremia. She left to her son Pietro her bed and the rights to a judgment that Jacobello had secured in the Court of Movables of 1380. She left 8 ducats to an unmarried daughter and 25 ducats to an "adoptive daughter" in Treviso. She freed an enslaved person, Anna. Her monetary assets, held by Angelo Condulmer of the Santa Lucia branch of the family, and the value of the rest of her goods were to be used for perpetual endowments to the church of San Tomà and other pious purposes.

In May of that year, Agnesina transferred her rights to the five properties to her son Pietro.[84] She had used her returned dowry to purchase part of the family's principal palazzo of San Tomà from the heirs of Antonio Bevilaqua of Verona.[85] Agnesina died in September 1389; the total receipts of her estate collected in the next five years were less than 10 ducats. In 1392, the Procurators handling her estate transferred to Ramberto Querini, presumably one of the creditors of Jacobello, the property in San Geremia with the exception of the access to the canal and the campo.[86]

It is evident that Jacobello had spent all of his movable wealth and indebted his landholdings in his rise through the offices of procurator of the Hospital of Saints Peter and Paul and founding governor of the Confraternity of Merchants, and especially his bid for entry into the nobility through support of the Venetian effort in the War of Chioggia. Some of this wealth had been taken illicitly from the funds he was administering on behalf of his nephew. The chief recompense for this depletion of his resources was the ability of Jacobello's three surviving sons, Antonio, Pietro, and Zancolo, and his eventual grandsons to be elected to the many offices of the state that were reserved for men of noble status and receive the salaries that they offered.

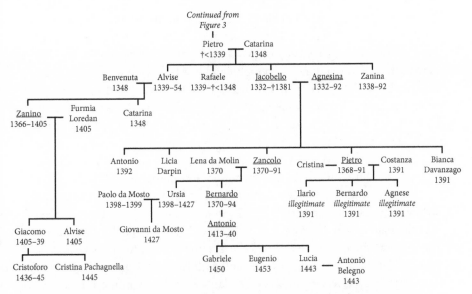

Figure 12. The family of Jacobello Condulmer: the noble branch of the Condulmer house. Underlined names are for people featured in this chapter. No last name is given for Condulmer. Years are of documents in which each is mentioned; † for year of death.

For the most part, these offices lasted for a single year or less and brought salaries that provided a comfortable but not extravagant subsistence. One of Jacobello's sons, Antonio, is known only as a witness to a land sale in 1392 in which he is identified as a "nobilis vir."[87] Both of Jacobello's daughters married into noble families; the Darpin family into which Licia married had one member assessed at the sizable sum of 8,000 ducats in the *Estimo*; none of the members of the Davanzago family into which Bianca married appear in the *Estimo*, so they must have been among the least wealthy of noble families (Figure 12).

Not all of the families that entered the nobility with Jacobello received such modest rewards for their contributions. With his assessment in the *Estimo* of 50,000 ducats, the *cittadino* Bandino di Garzoni stood out as one of the four wealthiest men in Venice.[88] His offer of 200 ducats, the service of his three sons, the use of his ship, the pay of twenty-five archers, and the interest on all of his *prestiti* for the duration of the war was considerably above that of Jacobello Condulmer and among the most generous of all of the non-nobles seeking entry to the Maggior Consiglio. Like Jacobello, Bandino di Garzoni died before he could enjoy the fruits of his sacrifice; he seems to have died even before the end of the war and his election to the nobility. His brother Giovanni received eighty-two votes for his entrance into the nobility, among the highest rankings, and took Bandino's place on the Great Council. Bandino's son Francesco, married successively to women of the prestigious Malipiero and Foscarini noble families, went on to hold high offices in the Venetian government, including ducal counselor in 1431 and patron of the Arsenale in 1443.[89] Francesco's son Marino rose even higher, serving as Duke of Crete from 1484 to 1487 and finally reaching the second highest office of the Republic, Procurator of San Marco in 1501, at the age of eighty-three.[90]

The main difference between the success of the Garzoni house in its rise to noble status compared with the Condulmer house seems to have been wealth. Bandino di Garzoni was rich enough that he could offer generous support for the war effort without severely diminishing his resources, whereas Jacobello Condulmer bankrupted himself in his bid for election to the Great Council, leaving to his descendants formal recognition as noble but placing them among the ranks of poor nobles in constant search of support from the state, an identity that did not greatly enhance their social status.

CHAPTER 3

Vielmo Condulmer, a Money Changer as Would-Be Noble

The Life and Death of Vielmo Condulmer

The noble status offered as a reward for extraordinary donations to the Venetian efforts in the War of Chioggia was limited to the applicant and his direct descendants; collateral relatives and their heirs remained in the *cittadino* class.[1] The money changer Vielmo Condulmer, first cousin once removed of the newly ennobled Jacobello and second cousin to Jacobello's noble sons Pietro and Zancolo, was thus excluded from their accession to the nobility (see Figures 3, 12, and 13). However, before the widespread use in the fifteenth century of the Balla d'Oro process of confirming the nobility of males at the age of eighteen, there was no accessible formal way to determine who was and was not a noble. This ambiguity was all the stronger in the case of people such as Vielmo Condulmer, who came from the same branch of the house as that which had entered the nobility but was not a direct descendant of an ennobled individual; thus, he was in legal terms non-noble.[2] With his frequent business dealings with the wealthiest members of the nobility, Vielmo appears to have adopted a performative aura of nobility in his public and private life through dress, manner, and the furnishing of his residence and workplace, as revealed by the inquisition postmortem of his possessions.[3]

Vielmo was not yet emancipated by his father at the time of the *Estimo* and the entry of Jacobello into the Maggior Consiglio.[4] In 1383 he received a dowry of 175 ducats from the *cittadino* Andriolo Novello for marriage to his daughter Clara with his own father's permission, suggesting that Vielmo was then in his late twenties and thus born between 1348 and 1353.[5] Vielmo appears in the 1387 membership list of the Scuola Grande of San Giovanni

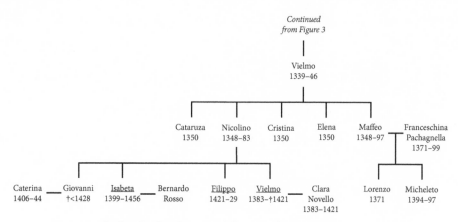

Figure 13. The family of Vielmo Condulmer. Underlined names are for people featured in this chapter. No last name is given for Condulmer. Years are of documents in which each is mentioned; † for year of death.

Evangelista among eighty-five non-noble men listed as *nobili de puovolo,* or nobles of the people, a seemingly contradictory classification that is not encountered elsewhere in Venetian social life.[6] In his will of 1421, he also claimed membership in the confraternity of the church of Santa Maria della Celestia in the Castello sestier.[7] Vielmo seems to have changed his residence in the sestier of Cannaregio frequently: his father was assessed in the parish of San Felice of Cannaregio, and he is identified as living in Santa Fosca when he received his dowry in 1383, in San Marziale in the 1387 register of San Giovanni Evangelista, in the parish of Santi Apostoli in 1402 at the time of a sale of land within the Castello parish of Santa Maria Formosa, and again in San Marziale when he wrote his will in 1421.[8]

Other than the receipt for his wife's dowry, appearance in the registers of confraternities, and a few land sales, Vielmo left little trace in documentation other than his own estate papers. He appears to have had little in the way of active social connections, even within his own family. An exception is his designation as the sole executor of the gold worker (*batioro*) Bartolomeo Bordon, who in his will of 1396 left 1,000 ducats to each of his illegitimate sons, Nicolo and Bartolomeo (an exception to the common naming practice, probably because of the illegitimacy of the son), when they turned twenty-four along with the right to continue living in his house.[9] Nicolo received his inheritance in 1401.[10] In 1403, after the death of Nicolo, Vielmo appeared in court on the question of whether Nicolo's brother or his widow should receive the balance of the *prestiti* left to him.[11] In the 1396 will, Bartolomeo had instructed that if there were no remaining heirs, the house should be sold; this must have happened by 1412, when Vielmo sold the house in question and distributed the proceeds.[12] His involvement with this estate had an echo in Vielmo's will written in 1421; one of the few personal bequests was to Antonia, mother of Nicolo and Bartolomeo Bordon, for the income on 500 ducats of state bonds until her death.[13]

It is because of one provision of Vielmo's will that he is one of the best-documented members of the house of Condulmer and indeed of most contemporary Venetian *cittadini*: in his will he named the Procurators of San Marco his sole executors. While it was not uncommon to include the Procurators among executors, especially where provisions could involve ongoing payments of interest from state bonds for years and even centuries, they usually appeared as a unit within a group of executors that might also include the spouse, relatives, and friends of the testator. Vielmo's choice to make the procurators his sole executors, while it may reveal a lack of close personal ties or a distrust of his relatives, had the results that all of his personal accounts were preserved in a public repository and that a detailed postmortem inventory of the contents of his palace was recorded.

Vielmo's wife, Clara, whose dowry he had received thirty-eight years earlier, was the principal immediate beneficiary of the will. She was to receive all of her own clothes and personal effects and the interest on 2,500 ducats of bonds until her death. She could also keep her bed and an icon of her choice—with the exception of the large icon in the upstairs bedroom, which Vielmo for some reason instructed to have sold. His properties in the parish of San Marziale and in the mainland districts of Mestre and Treviso were also to be sold and to be added to the movables in his possession and used to buy state bonds, *prestiti*, with the returns to be distributed at the rate of one-third to Clara as long as she did not remarry, one-third to his sister Isabeta, and one-third to his brother Filippo. The will is remarkable in that all of the bequests were in terms of state bonds, including those to two enslaved women who were to be freed and to be given 300 and 200 ducats of *prestiti*, respectively. Among charitable bequests, the confraternity of San Giovanni Evangelista received 100 ducats of bonds, while the confraternity of the Celestia got 40 ducats of bonds, as did five churches and monasteries.

In the settling of the estate after Vielmo's death in 1421, the Procurators gathered together Vielmo's account books and stored them with the two notebooks they filled with the accounts they generated for settling his estate, along with the postmortem inventory of the possessions in his Venetian palace.[14] His accounts comprise nine paper account books running from 1389 to 1413, with a gap from 1394 to 1396, probably a single lost account book. There are also twenty-two loose sheets of accounts, covering more or less the same period but containing a few entries starting in October 1388, a year before the earliest entries in the books and to some extent filling in the missing three years. There is no indication in these accounts that he ever worked in partnership with anyone, nor that he took his business over from anyone nor passed it along to anyone. Nor is there any indication that he conducted business before or after the years of his accounts. When he received his dowry in 1383, he was still a dependent of his father, so it may be that 1388 was the year in which he went into business for himself, probably at about the age of thirty. The end of his accounts twenty-five years later and eight years before his death may well represent the end of his business career as well.

Money Changer and Bullion Agent

Vielmo Condulmer was primarily a money changer and silver broker, but he appears as a banker in some sources. He is characterized as "dal ban-cho" (banker) and "cambiador" (money changer) in an account book of rent receipts in the period from 1406 to 1411.[15] In a court case of 1404, covering actions that occurred in 1402, Vielmo Condulmer testified that a document made for a groom's gift had been forged in the name of his bank, and he identified the handwriting as that of one of his depositors but denied any involvement of his bank in the transaction.[16] He does not, however, appear often in documents as a banker of script, those bankers of Rialto who used ledgers and receipts to record deposits, disbursements, and credit. In the period of Vielmo's career—1389 to 1413—the principal such bankers were Gabriele Soranzo (active from 1375 to 1395), Pietro Benedetto (active from 1376 to 1395), and Marco and Simoneto Condulmer, distant relatives of Vielmo of the Santa Lucia branch of the house.[17]

One of the chief duties of a money changer in Venice and elsewhere in medieval Europe was manual exchange, the process of examining and evaluating foreign coins brought into the city and giving back Venetian coins of a similar value minus a fee. There are scant records of this process in Vielmo's accounts, limited to entries on a loose sheet from 1388, but that does not mean that such manual exchange was a minor, or only early, aspect of his

career. Account books were mainly kept for the purpose of recording transactions for which there might be a later need for review, either by the parties
involved or by governmental agencies. Manual exchange of coins had little
need for such documentation, and account books of money changers per se
are very rare in medieval Europe as a whole. In the 1388 entrees, the only
foreign coins Vielmo specified as having taken in and brought to the Venetian mint for refining into silver of the fineness of Venetian coins are *carra-
rini*, minor coins of Padua, and genuine and counterfeit Hungarian coins he
received mainly from someone called Vielmo of Pordenone; in addition, he
recorded acquisitions of foreign ingots and scrap silver.[18] The accounts in the
bound books from after 1388 list the source of the silver he took to the mint
but not the form in terms of specific foreign coins or ingots or scrap silver;
only occasionally does he even note whether the silver in question had been
bought as ingots or as coins or scrap.

Vielmo's Account Books

In addition to documenting bullion taken in and brought to the mint, Vielmo's accounts also record purchases and sales of olive oil from April 1393
through March 1394 and payments to the Ternario, the office in Venice controlling oil sales. This may represent a year-long venture into the oil market,
or it may be that, like the manual exchange of coins, oil transactions were not
something that needed to be accounted fully, so Vielmo stopped recording
them early in his career.

A similar situation arises in the consideration of the recording of gold
in these accounts. Though silver is recorded completely and consistently,
transactions of gold appear regularly only from March 1406 through 1411.
Vielmo did indeed buy and sell gold at other points in his career; there are
occasional mentions of transactions in the accounts of 1391, 1398, and 1413.
However, the inconsistent appearance of gold seems to relate to the much
less rigorous control that the Venetian state put on the trade in gold vis-à-
vis silver in this period.[19] Part of this might be attributed to the importance
of silver in the basic monetary systems of Venice or to the much greater
difficulty of determining the fineness of silver bullion and coins than that of
gold. The chief mechanism of the Venetian state in controlling the market
for silver in the city was the *quinto*, the special imposition put on all silver
that passed through Venice, which brought about the requirement of careful recording of all such transactions. Gold, on the other hand, was eagerly

sought by the state and the mint, and its importation was not taxed and only lightly controlled.

It is evident that the overriding impetus for the careful compilation by Vielmo of accounts of all of the silver he handled, along with the preservation of these records, was to meet the demands of the silver officials at Rialto and the mint officials. This is confirmed by a passage from February 1406 in which he reports having come to agreement with the mint officials about the amount that he owed for the *quinto* and a similar one in December 1411. Most telling is an entry at the very end of his last account book, dated January 12, 1412, in which he writes "I Vielmo Condulmer have been with the mint officials Fantino Morosini, Daniele da Canal and Tomaso da la Fontana and having shown them the accounts of the *quinto* of the state and in the evening of that date I remained in agreement with these officials that I have a credit of 20 marks and 4 ounces [about 5 kilograms]."[20]

By comparison with the scattered and imprecise figures that exist for the total amount of bullion refined and minted by the Venetian mint in the period, it can be estimated that Vielmo Condulmer handled about one-sixth of the silver that passed through the city in the years covered by his account books. The quantities he handled seem to have mirrored the decline in the amount of silver production in Europe in the last years of the fourteenth century known as the Great Bullion Famine.[21]

Most of the silver that Vielmo received back from the refineries was sold as ingots weighing a bit over 5 kilograms each rather than as coins. Such ingots, stamped with the same die as the grosso coins, the standard silver denomination, could be used for trade abroad.[22] In all, he grossed 5,533.2 ducats from the sale of ingots. Together with the 946 ducats' worth of coins, his gross receipts were 6,479.2 ducats on 1,110 marks of silver. The net profit that Vielmo derived from these transactions is difficult to establish with any confidence, as he seldom recorded the price he paid for the silver he purchased or its purity. One entry, however, allows us to estimate the profit that he gained from these transactions; in the year 1402, his profit of 1,210 ducats was about 23 percent over the cost of his purchases in that year.[23]

Vielmo's sales of silver in 1402 were significantly lower than those of the 1390s or the years between 1404 and 1409 leading up to his retirement; his profit in this year may have been significantly below that before and after the bullion famine.[24] The percentage of silver that he brought to the mint on behalf of other merchants was typical of the earlier period, but in later years, the percentage that was on his own behalf declined significantly. The amount that he sold as ingots also varied; in 1402, virtually all of the silver other than that put in the mint for the *quinto* was sold as ingots; in later years, ingot sales represented a smaller percentage of the silver he had refined. While his activity in the years before and after 1402 can be seen to have reflected larger European trends in the minting of silver, it appears that in 1412 and 1413 he was closing down his business and handling only minor quantities of bullion. We cannot estimate the profit he would have made on transactions of gold and olive oil or on those of manual money changing that did not involve the mint. His profit of 1,210 ducats a year on silver transactions in 1402 probably represented about half of his annual income from his dealings as an intermediary between traders of bullion and the mint; in any case, it is evident that he received a substantial but not exorbitant income from what seems to have been the main source of his wealth.

Vielmo's Professional Networks: Sellers of Silver Coins and Scrap

Nothing in Vielmo Condulmer's will or in the general archival record suggests a wide-ranging or close network of social contacts, even within the Condulmer house. From his account books, however, it is evident that he had extensive professional interactions with individuals of a great variety of social and even national origins, many of which continued over an extended range of years.

In the two decades covered in the account books, Vielmo recorded the names of 491 individuals from whom he bought silver or coins. About 70 of these can be identified as Venetian, of which half have family names that identify them as probably noble. As Vielmo gives no patronymics or parishes in his account books, it is seldom possible to identify these names with individuals known from other sources, especially in the cases of large families and popular first names. One exception is probably Silvestro Morosini, a member of one of the largest and wealthiest houses, whose Christian name was quite rare in Venice. Silvestro appears in Vielmo's list in 1400, the same year in which he is documented as a merchant of spices and two years before witnessing the shipment of goods from Famagusta in Cyprus to Venice; in later years, he would appear as the patron of state galleys to Beirut and as the private owner of a ship of the cog type.[25] Other noble suppliers of silver to Vielmo Condulmer with connections to shipping are Fantino Zen, patron of a galley in 1404; Benedetto Marcello, patron of a galley in 1419; Antonio Belegno, patron in 1390 and again in 1416; and Bernardo Querini, who made three sales of silver in 1402.[26] Of particular interest is the appearance of Bernardo Sesto, a non-noble goldsmith and engraver at the Venetian mint, who appears with silver sales to Vielmo from 1401 through 1411.[27]

Perhaps more personally meaningful to Vielmo were the purchases from individuals whose families had sought to enter the nobility in 1379. Girardo Francesco was an early and regular customer of Vielmo's, selling him silver in 1390 and twice in 1391, and making four purchases of ingots from 1391 to 1393. His *Estimo* assessment of 5,000 ducats put him in the top decile of non-nobles assessed. He offered his own service with two servants in the defense of the Lido during the War of Chioggia as well as the pay of fifty archers for two months at 8 ducats per man; he was elected to the Maggior Consiglio by a comfortable margin.[28] Perhaps Vielmo could sympathize more with Lorenzo di Garzoni, son of Marco, who sold him silver in 1400.[29] Lorenzo was of a house of which one branch had been voted entrance into the nobility in 1381: the sons of Bandino di Garzoni became noble, while Vielmo's client Lorenzo and his father, Marco, were left out.[30] Also on the list of suppliers of silver to Vielmo is Tomaso de Buora, of a family of money changers who applied to enter the nobility at the time of the War of Chioggia but was not admitted.

Most of the sellers of silver to Vielmo, however, were not from recognizable Venetian families. His largest single supplier was Marin di Gradi, who sold him 165 marks of silver from 1406 through 1412; his name can be identified with a merchant family in Ragusa (Dubrovnik), a city on the eastern Adriatic coast, which served as a major exporter of Serbian silver.[31] Marin seems to have continued a supply carried out by Matteo di Gradi in the period 1397 to 1404 (28 marks). Other suppliers of silver to Vielmo who have been identified as Ragusan are Luca di Bon (136 marks from 1409 to 1411), the partnership of Ratichio di Menzo and Elia di Tripo (124 marks from 1402 to 1411 individually or as a partnership), Nicola da Poza (78 marks in 1406), Polo di Radin (70 marks from 1402 to 1404), and Bono di Nadal (70 marks from 1408 to 1411). These Ragusans constituted eight of his top eighteen suppliers of silver and accounted for 12 percent of the silver he presented to the mint. A number of his other suppliers of silver were also from cities on the east coast of the Adriatic: four from Zara (7 marks), two from Modruza (10 marks), two from Sibenico (2 marks), and one from Spalato (1 mark).

Padua appears most frequently in the identification of suppliers of silver from Italian cities other than Venice, with eight Paduan individuals selling Vielmo a total of 28 marks; of note is Dona Agnola of Padua, the only non-Venetian woman whose name appears as a seller of silver. Eight merchants from Lucca sold Vielmo a total of 31 marks of silver. Two merchants appear from Treviso selling a total of 9 marks, and single merchants appear from Ancona (22 marks), Pordenone (9 marks), Faenza (91 mark), Monopoli (1 mark), Parma (1 mark), Portogruaro (1 mark), Vicenza (1 mark), and Spilimbergo (1 mark). Of note are two members of the Medici family of Florence, Giovanni (probably Giovanni di Bicci, 8 marks) and Buoso (1 mark). Major suppliers with ambiguous but Italian-sounding names were Simone de Lapazin (176 marks in 1391), Giacomo and Nicolo Granata (199 marks from 1398 to 1410), and Martore di Zan Magno and his sons Tomaso and Lorenzo (206 marks from 1398 to 1410).

A large number of Vielmo's suppliers of silver were from north of the Alps, merchants who had either imported ingots from silver-producing regions or had brought in foreign coins to have them exchanged for Venetian ones for trade with Mediterranean lands where they would be more easily recognized and accepted.[32] Eight merchants identified as coming from Vienna sold Vielmo a total of 162 marks (39 kilograms) of silver. The largest number of individual sellers from transalpine mining regions came from Salzburg, ten men supplying a total of 98 marks. Five merchants from Nuremberg sold him 30 marks; three were from Augsburg (11 marks), one from Cologne (4 marks), one from Frankfurt (2 marks), two from Bratislava (40 marks), one from Prague (1 mark), one from Bohemia (1 mark), one identified simply as German (1 mark), and one identified as a Hungarian (12 marks).

Eight individuals appear on the list identified as Jews: Salamon (21 marks), Michael (17 marks), Manoelo (13 marks), Bonaventura (11 marks), Moise (8 marks), Angolo (6 marks), Bon (4 marks), and Piero (2 marks). Jews had been allowed greater access than previously to Venice following the War of Chioggia, but their status, especially as money changers, was coming under review and greater control in the years around 1400.[33]

Vielmo's Professional Networks: Buyers of Silver Ingots

In contrast to the people from whom Vielmo bought silver, who were chiefly Venetians of relatively low status or foreigners, those to whom he sold refined ingots for trade abroad represented the elite of Venetian merchant society, noble and *cittadino* alike. In all, he sold 5,525 marks of silver ingots (1,218 kilograms) for use in export trade in the course of the twenty-five years covered by his account books. The largest single buyer was the office of grain supply (*proveditori sopra biave*), which from 1404 to 1406 bought 218 marks of silver ingots from Vielmo (4 percent of his total sales). Another leading customer was the office of state provisors (*proveditori di comun*), which was charged with a wide variety of state purchases and purchased 173 marks of silver ingots from the beginning of his career in 1389 through 1405.

The rest of Vielmo Condulmer's customers for trade ingots were 246 individuals (including a few estate trusts), all of whom were Venetian with one exception: the Florentine Giovanni di Bicci de' Medici, whose family established a Venetian branch in 1402 after his visit a couple of years earlier.[34] Vielmo's largest private customer was the partnership of Nicolo Mudazo and Francesco Amadi, which purchased almost 150 marks of silver ingots in two transactions in 1404 and 1405, followed by a purchase of 24 marks by Mudazo alone in 1406. Nicolo Mudazo was a member of a relatively small noble house that had five members listed in the *Estimo* of 1379, two in the second highest decile, one in the third, one in the seventh, and one in the ninth. He began his governmental career as a member of the Council of Forty in 1386, rising to be one of the six ducal counselors in 1400; he was a witness to the 1400 will of the leading banker of the day, Pietro Benedetto.[35] Mudazo's partner, Francesco Amadi, was not a noble; like Vielmo he was listed as a "popolano nobile" in the 1387 membership list of the confraternity of San Giovanni Evangelista; two members of his family had appeared in the *Estimo* in the second and fourth deciles of *cittadini*. In 1395, he had paid 278 ducats for silk imported from Tana by Pietro Stornello, which he paid for through his account at the Benedetto bank.[36]

Members of the nobility, especially of the most prestigious families of the nobility, appear prominently among Vielmo's customers for silver ingots. In the years after the War of Chioggia, election to the office of the doge moved from the control of the families regarded as the oldest, known as "long" families, to another elite group known as the "short" families.[37] Members of fourteen of the twenty-four long families bought silver ingots from Vielmo Condulmer, accounting for 1,151 marks of the 5,524 marks (21 percent) he sold. Among these, the Contarini house was one of the largest, richest, and most respected noble clans in Venice; Andrea Contarini had been doge from 1368 to 1382, the years leading up to Vielmo's marriage in 1383. Sixty-eight Contarini appeared on the *Estimo*, with fourteen in the top decile of nobles. No fewer than twelve members of the Contarini house appear among the buyers of silver from Vielmo Condulmer, accounting for 366 marks of ingots, or 6.7 percent of the total. Maffeo Memmo, a member of a prestigious noble family and assessed in the top decile of the *Estimo*, was one of the silver officials at Rialto in 1387, shortly before buying 42 marks of ingots from Vielmo in 1390 in partnership with Giovanni Contarini.[38] Gabriele Soranzo, one of seven members of his family buying a total of 117 marks of silver, was one of the leading bankers of script in Venice but appears on the list of buyers of ingots only once, in 1398, with a purchase of only 5 marks; the other major script bankers do not appear at all. It may be that these bankers dealt directly with the mint rather than through an intermediary like Vielmo, or they may have been chastened by the continual efforts of the state to limit their presence in the silver market.[39]

Ten of the sixteen "short" houses are represented among Vielmo's buyers, accounting for 475 marks of ingots. Customers from seven of the twenty-six families with members admitted to the nobility in 1381 appear among Vielmo's clientele. The only entry that appears to be for a member of his own Condulmer house, however, is for the "Commissaria of Ser Jachomel": in 1389, for 10 marks, probably the estate of his first cousin once removed, the ennobled Jacobello. Francesco Girardo, whose 5,000-ducat assessment put him in the top decile of *cittadini* in the *Estimo*, took an active role in the government soon after joining the nobility, serving as adviser for wood in 1385 and becoming a member of the Forty in 1387; he sold seven marks of silver to Vielmo in 1390 and 1391 and bought 60 marks of ingots from him between 1391 and 1393.[40] As with the Condulmer house, the di Garzoni had some members who entered the nobility in 1381, and others who were left out. Of the three customers of Vielmo from the family, Alvise di Garzoni was, like Vielmo, a *popolano nobile* member of the confraternity of San Giovanni Evangelista, hence, a *cittadino*; Giovanni di Garzoni might have been the Giovanni, son of Bandino, who was admitted to the nobility or the Giovanni, son of Marco, who was not; Filippo's status is not known.

Vielmo was probably sympathetic to the draper Biagio Mocenigo, a fellow *popolano nobile* in his confraternity, who was one of the few non-noble members of the house of Doge Tomaso Mocenigo, who reigned from 1414 to 1423, during the last decade of Vielmo's life. Biagio Mocenigo sought to join the nobility at the time of the War of Chioggia with a fairly low *Estimo* assessment of 1,500 ducats, which put him in the fourth decile, and a weak service offer for the war (only two archers rather than the twenty-five or fifty of competitors), but he was not admitted; with his brother Pietro (the only other non-noble Mocenigo of seven in the *Estimo*), he bought 26 marks of silver ingots from Vielmo in 1390 and 1391.

There were dozens of houses in the nobility among Vielmo's customers beyond those known as long or short and those who were admitted in 1381.

The second-highest-spending customer of Vielmo, for 128 marks of ingots, was the nobleman Andrea Zulian, whose house had four members in the *Estimo*, one in the second decile of nobles, one in the third, one in the sixth, and one (a woman) in the tenth. Filippo Signolo was silver official at Rialto in 1385 and bought 5 marks of silver from Vielmo, also in 1390.[41]

The great mass of *cittadini*, Venetians like Vielmo in the highest ranks among non-nobles, also appear prominently among his customers. The largest individual purchaser, with 135 marks, was the *cittadino* Nicolo Panciera, identified in the *Estimo* as a varoter (furrier specializing in vair) where his assessment of 1,300 ducats put him in the fourth decile of non-nobles. He appears as a *cittadino* rather than a "noble of the *popolo*" on the membership list of San Giovanni Evangelista. Marco Cavalo, whose 3,000-ducat assessment in the *Estimo* put him in the second decile of non-nobles, purchased 99 marks of ingots from 1391 to 1405; Lucia Cavalo, probably his widow, continued the purchases in 1406 to 1407 with 67 more marks of ingots. The only other women who appear regularly in Vielmo's account books are Fioruccia di Stella, who appears from 1398 to 1400 twice as a seller of small amounts of silver and seven times as a buyer of 40 marks of ingots; and Gerita di Alemano, who appears twice in 1389 with total purchases of 10 marks. The *cittadino* Nicolo dalle Colze bought 72 marks of ingots from 1390 to 1400; he is remarkable for having received 100 ducats in the will of the Doge Antonio Venier of 1400, the only such bequest to an individual outside of the doge's family and household.[42]

Vielmo's Personal Possessions and Simulated Noble Identity

Vielmo Condulmer stood in a position between the *cittadino* class of Venice and the nobility. Though his cousins held noble status as descendants of Jacobello, who was coopted into the nobility in 1381 when Vielmo was in his twenties, Vielmo remained a *cittadino*. In a similar way, his business consisted of acquiring silver and coins from people mainly outside the nobility, often foreigners, and then selling refined silver ingots for trade to the richest Venetians, many of them members of the highest-status houses. The descriptions of his palace and of his personal belongings, his movables in medieval terms, give us a feeling of how this ambiguity of status played out in his personal life.

Vielmo Condulmer made out his will on July 26, 1421, probably while in his late sixties or early seventies.[43] On September 21 of that year, probably soon after his death, an inventory was made of the goods in his palace in the

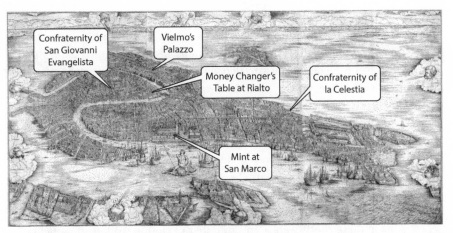

Map 3. Important sites in the life of Vielmo Condulmer.

parish of San Marziale, prior to their being distributed and sold in accordance with the provisions of his will.[44] The cover of this paper collation is blank; then two pages enumerate the contents of five chests, followed by five pages listing objects in upstairs rooms and then one with three items in the wood storage shed. Thirteen pages were left blank, and the book ends with two pages listing the things left to Vielmo's widow, Clara.

The location of the five chests that lead off the inventory is not specified, but as the remaining rooms are identified as upstairs, it is likely that these were found in the main downstairs room of the building, which was normally used as a place of business.[45] Vielmo no doubt had a stand, or *banco*, in the Rialto market where he dealt with the general public under the watchful eye of the silver officials, but the tight control of silver sale was loosened after the War of Chioggia and in the face of the bullion famine of the end of the fourteenth century.[46] He must also have had a space in his home where he stored his coins, bullion, and ingots away from the public eye and probably also met with the wealthy purchasers of ingots (Map 3).

The first two chests inventoried contained Vielmo's clothing; as described by those recording the inventory, these items are similar to clothing worn by the highest members of the nobility in paintings of the end of the fifteenth century (Figure 14).[47] There were eight long coats (*pelande*), of which five were colored with scarlet, a dye derived from the cochineal insect imported from the Aegean, a coloring characteristic of clothes used by ambassadors and princes.[48] Two were colored with *grana*, a local imitation of scarlet, probably died with the kermes insect. The other was of "cardinal" color, achieved with grana, madder, and soluble redwood. As its name applies, this too was a color associated with individuals of the highest status; perhaps Vielmo's acquisition of clothing of this color was associated with the naming of his distant relative Gabriele Condulmer to the cardinalate in 1408.[49] Four of these coats were lined or trimmed with fur; one is specified as vair (a Scandinavian squirrel) and another as marten (a small animal from the Dalmatian coast). One is described as being of scarlet lined with braided strings of kermes glass beads (*conderi*); another was lined with braided lace (*rendado*). Most of these coats are described as having open cuffs, a style that had originally been restricted to the doge (*maniche dogali*) and later allowed to the highest ranks in the state.[50] The coats were stored in the chest between linen sheets.

Also in these chests were a great number of clothing accessories, including three vermeil collarless tunics (*zuparelli*): one of velvet, one of damascene, and one described simply as cloth (*panno*). There were six metal belts, one of vermeil. There were four overgarments: two capes, one scarlet and one black lined with vermeil, and two mantels, both of scarlet, one specifically for horseback riding (*da cavalcar*). Two corsets were of old braid. There is no question that when Vielmo appeared at the Rialto market and in the streets and plazas of Venice he gave the impression of a man of high status and exceptionally flamboyant personal style, emulating the young nobles depicted in paintings of the fifteenth century (Figure 14).

The downstairs room also contained one large walnut chest and two small ones with household objects and those related to Vielmo's business. Included among the items in the large chest were implements that seem to be specific to a money changer's work. There were three small boxes containing balances, presumably two-pan scales; one is characterized as large, two are small. There is no separate listing for the weights for these balances; they must have been in the same box as the pans and included in the description. A particularly intriguing entry in the inventory is "1 orologio da ore 12," a timepiece of twelve hours. Such a timepiece would have been necessary in such processes as the refining of gold via cementation, which required twenty-four hours of slow heating.[51] The storage of a sundial in such a box is unlikely, so this is probably a reference to some form of a water clock, a technology continued from antiquity.[52] Mechanical clocks with escapements came into use as early as 1330. Such machines were large and rare; if Vielmo Condulmer owned such a mechanical clock in 1421, it would have been an object of extraordinary rarity and prestige when displayed on his table with other tools of his trade.Among

Figure 14. Vettore Carpaccio, *Arrival of the Ambassadors*, Saint Ursula Polyptych, detail, end of the fifteenth century, oil on canvas, 278 × 589 cm, Venice, Galleria dell'Accademia. Wikimedia Commons, public domain by Didier Descouens.

other implements listed as being in the chest were ten large and eighteen small engraving tools, which may have been used to mark acquired silver or finished ingots with weights or the identity of the customers.

Within the chest with the silver implements, the balances, and the time-keeping device were also "all of the writings of the testator" (*tute scriture del comeso*). There was separately a "sack with old writings." The first listing probably refers to Vielmo's account books, while the second may be his will, his dowry receipt, and possibly the loose sheets of accounts, all of which are contained in the *commissaria* that the Procurators of San Marco preserved. Also listed separately were five Flemish candlesticks and five large wooden plates. The only item of furniture listed for the downstairs area is a Serbian dark blue bench.

The next section of the inventory is headed "in the upstairs bedroom" (*la camera di sovra*), confirming that all that came before must have been in the downstairs area. In Venetian palaces of the period, the main living space was the *piano nobile*, one flight up from the street and canal level. In this period, staircases were usually exterior, rising from a closed courtyard to the *piano nobile*.[53] This main upper floor usually had a long central room, the *pòrtego*, running from the courtyard in the back of the house to the canal, which was

Figure 15. Venice, Palazzo Mastelli, a typical fourteenth-century palazzo. Artstor, permission of Sarah Quill.

its principal façade, usually with windows at either end (Figure 15).[54] This was the main space for shared family functions and for receiving social visitors. Smaller chambers usually opened onto the *pòrtego* and were frequently disposed symmetrically to either side; these were for sleeping or other private purposes.

The upstairs inventory starts with one of these small rooms. The first item listed is a large, beautiful icon with a silk cover. In this room were two beds, a large one with two covers and one described as *a cariola*, apparently wheeled, both characterized as *pignolata*, covered with a linen cloth that gave the appearance of pine nuts. The beds in the inventory are measured according to the number of bedspreads (*telli*) they would accommodate; one of these was 2 *telli* large and one was 1.5 *telli*. There was a damascene lamp and bolsters, pillows, cushions, and a pair of French-style andirons.

The next room listed in the inventory is identified as the chamber near the well. As there is a later room identified as the one near the small well, we can imagine that this large bedroom looked out over the larger of two wells in the courtyard. This room had two beds covered in *pignolata* (3 *telli* and 2.5

telli, respectively) and one with wheels (*da cariola*) 2 *telli* long and various cushions and other furnishings. The most noteworthy items in the inventory for this room were three sets of curtains, one in front of the largest bed and one set hanging from special curtain racks (*resteli da coltu*), that were embroidered with golden vinework "with the arms of the deceased" (*cum le armi del comesso*).[55] Though Vielmo Condulmer was not of the noble line of his house, in Venice, heraldry was not rigidly limited to the nobility, so technically Vielmo could have displayed the Condulmer family arms, a diagonal white band on a blue background (see Figs. 20, 21, 28).[56] Their repeated display in this bedroom, however, embroidered in gold on three sets of curtains, reveals a personal identification with noble trappings on the part of Vielmo. In this room there was a small icon with an "armory" (*armaruol*), perhaps another iteration of the Condulmer arms, with a gilt damascene lamp. There were more knives and various stone, bronze, and tin implements for cooking, suggesting that this room may have served as a kitchen as well as a bedroom. Another room on the other side of the floor (near the smaller well), held an ironclad casket with sheets and tablecloths, an icon with a hanger, and thirteen large and small shields (*pavesi*) and twelve lances of various sizes.

The inventory next moves to the *camera di mezo,* the *pòrtego* or large central hall that served for public functions. This room contained such impressive pieces of furniture as an armory chest with an icon, a rack (*restello*) with an array of knives, two black chairs decorated with birds, and two sets of horse trappings (without saddles).[57] The most eye-catching item of furniture in the room was no doubt the green accounting bench "cum le armi da cha Quirini" (with the arms of the Querini house). The Querini house was one of the largest and wealthiest of the long noble families. Three members of the family, Fantino, Marco, and Stefano, had been customers for silver ingots sold by Vielmo. Other than the participation of a distant ancestor in the 1310 conspiracy led by Marco Querini, there was no connection between Vielmo and this august family, no intermarriage of even his noble relatives with the house.[58] His display of a desk with the Querini arms in the area of his home reserved for distinguished guests must be taken as a sign of his wish to be identified with the nobility, complementing the festooning of his bed with gilt vinework displaying the Condulmer arms.

The inventory continues with more items in the upstairs storeroom (*salvaroba*), in the small room facing the canal, and in the woodshed. It ends with the objects left to Vielmo's widow, Clara Novello. There are no clothes listed here; these were considered to have belonged to her by right rather than having to be inherited, as was the case with her original dowry of 175 ducats. In accordance with Vielmo's will, she would have gotten the interest on 2,500 ducats' worth of bonds for her lifetime, about 125 ducats a year. As also prescribed in the will, she got one icon, specified in the inventory as having a crucifix. Along with a long list of household furnishings, the inventory enumerates a large bed (2.5 *telli*) and a small "family" one (*da fameia*). The larger bed was accompanied by a green cotton curtain decorated in gold with the Condulmer arms; it would appear that like Vielmo, Clara had slept accompanied by his house's arms, despite the fact that Venetian women generally kept their paternal family name and their own family identity.

There is evidence that away from the city in which his identity was well known, Vielmo Condulmer identified himself as a nobleman. In 1409, toward the end of his career as a money changer, Vielmo purchased land on the mainland in the region of Treviso; the document in which he charged an agent with carrying out this purchase lists him as "nobilis vir Ser Guglielmus Condulmario."[59] In 1416, shortly after he seems to have retired from business, he sold various holdings in Treviso; this time he is identified as "Prudens and circumspectus vir Ser Guglielmus Condulmario," terms appropriate for a non-noble man of wealth.[60]

From the description of his clothing in the postmortem inventory, it is clear that Vielmo Condulmer dressed the part of a nobleman in public, while buying and selling bullion at his station in Rialto and in the processions with other *nobili de puovolo* of the confraternity of San Giovanni Evangelista. At his palace, he greeted important visitors from behind his desk embellished with the arms of the Querini family, and he and his wife slept in beds adorned with fabrics with the arms of his ennobled cousins embroidered with golden threads. It is possible that the noble identity given him in the first document by the notary in Treviso was a simple mistake, but in any event, it is clear that Vielmo Condulmer presented himself (at least outside of the circle of people who knew his true legal status) as a nobleman. His social mobility was subjective and performative but none the less genuine in his own eyes and probably in the eyes of most people who encountered him. Vielmo's palace sold for 1,100 ducats and its contents realized 690 ducats.[61] It must have been the high-value furs, fabric, and trim of his garments that allowed his personal effects to fetch almost two-thirds of the price of his palace.

CHAPTER 4

Franceschina Condulmer, Matriarch of the Santa Lucia Clan

The Santa Lucia Branch of the House of Condulmer

The Condulmer men who were featured in the previous two chapters—Jacobello, who bought himself and his heirs into the nobility, and the money changer Vielmo, who presented himself as a member of the nobility—were from the branch of the family descended from Giacomo of the parish of San Tomà. Their homes and affiliations were in the central part of Venice across the Grand Canal from San Marco (*de Ultra*) and near the Rialto bridge. We now turn to the other main lineage of the house of Condulmer, the one descended from Meneghello, the participant in the Querini-Tiepolo conspiracy at the beginning of the fourteenth century. Their landholdings and palaces centered on a region at the farthest reaches of the Grand Canal, the parish of Santa Lucia (site of Venice's current main train station), which was just being drained and settled in the fourteenth century, and the parish of San Simeone Grande (or Profeta); though these parishes were on opposite sides of the Grand Canal from each other, they were both administratively within the sestier of Santa Croce, that is, *de Ultra*.[1]

Of Meneghello's two sons, Marco and Fiornovello, it was the latter whose descendants had the greatest impact on Venice and the European world in general, thanks in great part to the efforts of Franceschina, wife of Fiornovello's son Angelo. We have seen Fiornovello, who had not been implicated in the conspiracy, as an agent for the powerful Bardi and Acciaioli banking families of Florence in 1330. He apparently died before the *Estimo* of 1379; his married daughter Cristina appears there with a patrimony of 1,000 ducats, situating her among the wealthiest of non-noble women.[2]

Though women in medieval Venice were barred from serving in the governmental councils or holding state office, they could own property, make contracts, execute wills, and bring lawsuits. From the surviving documentation, it appears that a woman's sphere of influence was often within the family and parish setting.[3] At a very early age, usually around fourteen, she played a major role in the social and economic life of Venice through the bestowal of a dowry from her birth family to her husband. The dowry was considered the daughter's share of her family's patrimony, analogous to the sum that was given to a young man at the time of his emancipation from his father's finances.[4] A bride's husband had control over the management of the dowry during the marriage, effectively adding to the capital available to him for commercial and other ventures, but the principal had to be returned to the wife or her heirs upon his death. Throughout her marriage, a woman had control of any assets given or bequeathed directly to her; upon becoming a widow, she often gained access to her dowry as well. It was in their wills, especially, that we can see the mechanisms by which Venetian women exercised their agency over and beyond their families.

Unlike many married Venetian women, Franceschina Condulmer identified herself in documents by the family name of her husband, Angelo, rather than that of her father, Lorenzo Lombardo. The noble Lombardo family appears to have been of moderate size and wealth; it had six members listed in the *Estimo* of 1379, two with assessments of 3,000 ducats (deciles 3 to 4); one with an assessment of 1,200 ducats (decile 6); and three with assessments of 500 ducats (deciles 9 to 10); Franceschina's father was not included in the *Estimo* (Figure 16).[5]

Franceschina made out her first will in 1388; it was an extremely modest affair, written in what was presumably her own hand in Venetian, with a validating note from the notary in Latin at the bottom.[6] She identified herself first as Franceschina Condulmer, wife of Angelo, and then daughter of Lorenzo Lombardo. She designated her mother, Lucia, as her executor, with her brother Antonio to take the role if her mother predeceased her. Her dowry (whose amount is not recorded) would normally be returned to her mother upon her death, but she allowed her husband to continue to use the profit from it on the condition that he make 25 ducats' worth of donations for thirty thousand masses for her soul from the profit of the first year following her death.[7] The capital of the dowry itself was left to her mother along with all of her other possessions; after her mother's death, it would go to her own sons and daughters if there were any and then, in their absence, to her

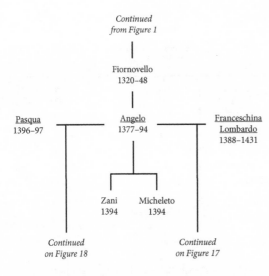

Figure 16. The family of Angelo Condulmer. Under-lined names are for people featured in this chapter. No last name is given for Condulmer. Years are of documents in which each is mentioned; † for year of death.

brother and sister with the ultimate contingent bequest being as charity for sailors to Syria. In view of the hypothetical treatment of children, it seems likely that this will was made soon after her marriage, perhaps during her first pregnancy, as was becoming common practice in this period.[8]

Franceschina's husband, Angelo Condulmer, with an assessment of 4,300 ducats, was in the top decile of non-nobles in the *Estimo* and had a higher assessment than any other member of the house (Jacobello was assessed at 4,000 ducats and Vielmo's father, Nicolo, at 1,000). Like his distant relative Jacobello, Angelo applied for admission to the nobility at the time of the War of Chioggia, probably before his marriage to Franceschina. His offer was the interest on his *prestiti* for the duration of the war, which he estimated at 3,000 ducats' worth, and the imposition on them of about 76 ducats, plus the pay of ten archers until the end of the war. Angelo's bid was rejected, but some-how his name became conflated with that of Jacobello in later sources, which assumed that Jacobello and Angelo were from the same branch of the house of Condulmer and explained the appearance of both names in the listings by reporting that Angelo was selected but died immediately and his place was taken by his son Jacobello.[9]

By the time Franceschina's husband had made out his will in 1394, six years after her own first one, the family situation was much changed.[10] In the first place, Angelo mentioned four daughters of the couple: Fiornovella, Elena, Cataruza, and Polisena (Figure 18). Angelo named two of his sons from

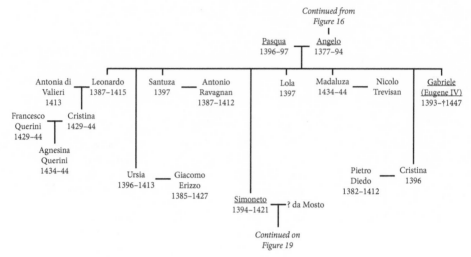

Figure 17. The descendants of Angelo Condulmer and Pasqua. Underlined names are for people featured in this chapter. No last name is given for Condulmer. Years are of documents in which each is mentioned; † for year of death.

before his marriage to Franceschina, Leonardo and Simoneto, as his executors, along with the Procurators of San Marco; his youngest son, Gabriele, was probably too young for such a responsibility (Figure 17). His pious bequests were generous; to the church of Santa Maria dei Servi, he gave 200 ducats' worth of *prestiti* to provide a fund to keep the monks warm and 100 ducats for a fund for candles for the altar. His bequest to his wife, Franceschina, was also generous: the income on 1,000 ducats of *prestiti* (without the common condition that she remain a widow), as well as one of his houses in the parish of San Simeone Grande, all of her household goods, all of her clothing with the exception of silk clothes and rings and pearls, plus an enslaved servant of her choice who would receive a modest sum on her death.

Angelo made provision in his will for dowries of 2,500 ducats for each of his and Franceschina's four daughters. This was in excess of the largest dowry bequests made by the twenty-two men of the extremely wealthy and powerful noble Morosini family in the period from 1371 to 1410.[11] These enormous dowries came with conditions. All the daughters were to wed between the ages of thirteen and fourteen; if they were not married by that age, their share of the estate was to go to any of their sisters who should be already married. This age was just above the legal minimum in Venice at the time

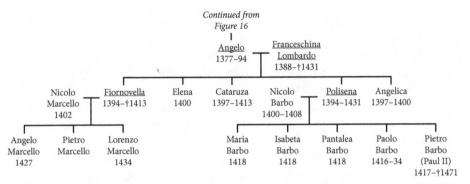

Figure 18. The descendants of Angelo Condulmer and Franceschina Lombardo.
Underlined names are for people featured in this chapter. No last name is given for
Condulmer. Years are of documents in which each is mentioned; † for year of death.

and somewhat below the predominant age of fourteen to seventeen specified in noble wills of the period.[12] The most notable condition of the dowries, however, was that all his daughters were to be married to young men
of the Great Council, that is, to men over the age of eighteen from noble
families. He added that these betrothals would require the consent of his
sons and especially of his wife, Franceschina. A provision in Angelo's will
allowed any daughter who wished to become a nun to have 1,250 ducats as a
novitiate gift as long as she entered the convents of Sant'Andrea della Zirada
(at the extreme west end of Santa Croce), Santa Chiara (on Murano), or the
recently established Corpus Domini near Santa Lucia. In an unusual provision, Angelo allowed that a daughter who did not marry and lived honestly
could, in her will, dispose of half of the 2,500 ducats with the other half to be
divided among his heirs.

The requirement that in order to receive their dowries, the daughters
marry into the nobility represented an attempt to achieve noble status for
Angelo's branch of the house of Condulmer, denied to him at the time that his
distant cousin Jacobello and his heirs gained such status. The daughters would
not themselves enter the nobility, but their offspring with noble fathers would
be considered noble and, most important, the sons of those unions would be
eligible to seek entrance into the Great Council by being proposed in the Balla
d'Oro process at about age eighteen. Thus, Angelo and Franceschina would
have noble grandchildren, though not bearing the Condulmer family name.
In the case of sons, marriage to a noblewoman would not have brought noble
status to their children, and so, in a sense, Angelo and Franceschina were

fortunate to have had only daughters in terms of gaining noble descendants through marriage.[13] As we shall see, Angelo Condulmer had a total of at least ten daughters and five sons by two, and probably three, women. Five of the seven daughters known to have married did so with members of the nobility; of the two sons known to have married, the eldest married a woman from the non-noble di Vialeri family and the second one from the da Mosto family, which had members of both noble and non-noble status.

Angelo's will also made provisions for five sons, apparently born before his marriage to Franceschina. Three were treated very generously: an elder emancipated son, Leonardo, and younger sons, Simoneto and Gabriele, still under twenty and within the financial control of their father. Leonardo had been given 2,000 ducats at the time of his emancipation, and the will gave him title to the palace in Santa Lucia where he was living. Angelo had deposited 3,000 ducats on Simoneto's behalf in the bank of Pietro Benedetto but instructed that the sum not be held against him (that is, be deducted from his eventual inheritance), and, if necessary, an equal amount be given to Gabriele. Simoneto and Gabriele were to inherit the residue of Angelo's estate. At the end of the will are bequests of 200 ducats' worth of *prestiti* each to Micheleto and Zani Condulmer with the provision that they not "touch him or be *signore*"; they were probably illegitimate sons that Angelo refused to recognize, possibly fathered with an enslaved woman.[14]

In 1397, Franceschina made out a new will, nine years after her first, simple one.[15] On the verso of the will, the notary identified her as *Nobilis Domina*, though nowhere did it name her father or identify her by his family name. She identified herself in the body of the will as the widow of Angelo, who must have died within the three years since he had made out his own will. Rather than naming relatives as executors as she had done earlier, Franceschina asked the Procurators of San Marco *de Citra* by name—Alvise Loredan and Giovanni Barbo—to serve as her executors either in an official capacity or as her special friends; if they could not do so, then the executors should be the Procurators of San Marco *de Ultra*, as appropriate for her home parish of San Simeone Profeta.[16] She ordered that her tithe of 80 ducats be paid, if possible, from funds in her house but in any case be her first legacy. The tithe as specified in this will was an exaction unique to Venice whereby a portion of a person's lifetime accumulation of wealth was to be paid to the bishop upon death.[17] We have seen in Chapter 1 that the tithe paid by the Procurators of San Marco on the estate of Nicoleto Condulmer amounted to about one-half of a percent of his total wealth; if the same basis was used by Franceschina in writing her will, it would appear that she estimated her total wealth at 15,000 ducats.

In this will, Franceschina enumerated five daughters, the four included in Angelo's will of three years earlier and a fifth named Angelica. She left 80 ducats to each, to be invested in *prestiti* with the interest accruing until they married. She gave 10 ducats to the church of Sant'Andrea, where she wished to be buried in the tomb in which her mother lay. She left to her sister Andreola Lombardo 80 ducats' worth of possessions and money to go eventually to Andreola's daughter Margarita. To another Margarita, identified as the illegitimate child of her nephew Antonio Lombardo, she also left a dowry of 40 ducats and a bed and bedclothes worth another 40 ducats. She left 30 ducats each to her two stepsons who were still unemancipated, Simoneto and Gabriele, a seemingly superfluous legacy given their huge inheritance from their father and an act that demonstrates the degree to which she had identified with her Condulmer family. She left the residue of her estate to her brother Nicolo, with the instructions that he try to recover the goods of their mother, Lucia, currently in warehouses in Capo d'Istria, with the proceeds to be distributed to charity.

Franceschina's Stepchildren

With the death of her husband, Franceschina had found herself a very wealthy widow with five young daughters for whom she needed to find noble husbands. In addition, there were also three stepsons, Leonardo, Simoneto, and Gabriele, all of whom were mentioned in Angelo's will and Simoneto and Gabriele in hers. No wills are known for any of the three sons; in general, wills of men are encountered much less commonly than those of women in this period, perhaps because of concerns over the disposition of women's dowries in the case of intestate death.[18] Moreover, there were five stepdaughters who do not appear in the wills of either Angelo or Franceschina, probably because they were already dowered and married or had become nuns: Cristina, Santuza, Ursia, Madaluza, and Lola are documented through their own wills.

The identity of the mother of Franceschina's stepchildren has been an ongoing mystery due to the circumstance that later sources for the life of Gabriele Condulmer identify his mother as Beriola Correr, sister of Pope Gregory XII. But there is no archival record of the existence of a Beriola Correr or of any marriage alliance between the Correr and Condulmer families.

Modern studies generally consider the relationship to be the result of later legend.[19] The wills of two of the stepdaughters of Franceschina, however, provide information on their mother's identity, if not a clear picture of the situation. Moreover, they identify her as still alive during the years after the 1388 will that Franceschina wrote as the wife of Angelo. The will of Cristina of 1396, in which she identified herself as a daughter of the late Angelo and sister of Ursia, Gabriele, and Simoneto, names as the first of her executors "mi madona," to be joined by "madona Lucia Diedo mare del marido" (my lady Lucia Diedo, mother of my husband); she included her mother as a potential legatee.[20] The 1397 will of Santuza (who identified herself as a daughter of the late Angelo Condulmer) names as executor, and leaves a bequest of 50 ducats to, "mia mare madona Pasqua" (my mother, my lady Pasqua), who was thus clearly alive after Angelo's marriage to Franceschina and after his death.[21]

As divorce would not have been permitted, especially in the case of a marriage that had produced eight children, it would appear that Angelo and Pasqua had not been married. Given the fact that she was identified only by her first name, Pasqua may well have been of low social status, though as she was named as the executor of a will, she could not have been enslaved. Moreover, there were Angelo's two unrecognized sons, Micheleto and Zani, whose mother was probably of even lower status. The illegitimate nature of his birth and low status of his mother would have given to Gabriele Condulmer, as Pope Eugene IV, or to his early biographers, strong reason for inventing a mythical noble mother. It is a tribute to Franceschina's character that after the death of her husband, she looked after and gave bequests to two of her illegitimate stepsons, Simoneto and Gabriele, as well as her own daughters. Her lack of mention of her stepdaughters in her 1397 will probably derives from the fact that they had been married or otherwise settled by that date. In the case of the two who were married to men of the nobility, they had no doubt been provided with ample dowries by Angelo. Also unmentioned in Franceschina's will were Micheleto and Zani Condulmer, to whom Angelo had left 200 ducats' worth of *prestiti* each on the condition that they not ask for recognition. They may also have been his sons by Pasqua but were more likely children of a woman of even lower social status than Pasqua, whose sons he had indeed recognized.

Cristina Condulmer, daughter of Angelo and stepdaughter of Franceschina, identified herself in her will as the wife of the nobleman Pietro Diedo, whose father, Vettore, had been assessed at 5,500 ducats (second decile among nobles) in the 1379 *Estimo*. Pietro Diedo was active in governmental affairs as an advocate in various courts and as an official in charge of the silk cloth woven with gold threads that was one of the most prestigious of Venice's exports; he would sue his brother-in-law Simoneto Condulmer in 1412 as the result of a much earlier business transaction involving the bank of Pietro Benedetto.[22] Cristina did not, however, designate her noble husband among the executors of her 1396 will; in addition to her mother and mother-in-law, she named her sister Ursia and her brother Gabriele. She specified the tithe of her estate at 130 ducats, suggesting a total wealth of about 26,000 ducats. She was probably pregnant at the time of her 1396 will as she gave contingencies for the birth of a daughter or a son. If it was a daughter, she was to be given a dowry of 500 ducats at age fourteen; if she died before then, the sum would be divided, with half to go to her husband and sixths to her brothers Simoneto and Gabriele and her sister Ursia. If the daughter chose to become a nun, she would get an oblation of 300 ducats and 200 ducats would go to Cristina's mother, that is, to Pasqua. If the child was a boy, he would get the 500 ducats. The residue of her estate would go to her husband. As no further documentation of her or of any offspring has been found, she may well have died in childbirth.

Santuza Condulmer identified herself in her 1397 will as a widow as well as the wife of Antonio Ravagnan. Her second husband was from a non-noble family, one of whose members was unsuccessful in his bid to join the nobility at the time of the War of Chioggia and another of whom was assessed 1,000 ducats (fourth to fifth decile) in the *Estimo*.[23] Antonio Ravagnan witnessed the 1407 act whereby his brother-in-law Gabriele renounced his share of his inheritance to Simoneto and testified on behalf of another brother-in-law Giacomo Erizzo against Simoneto in a suit concerning trade in Egypt in the period from 1404 to 1411.[24] In addition to her mother Pasqua, Santuza Condulmer named her sister Madaluza and her husband as executors. She left 50 ducats to her mother; 3 ducats to her sister Madaluza's husband, Nicolo Trevisan, to reimburse pocket money supplied by him over the years; 50 ducats to the monastery of Corpus Domini for the sustenance of another sister, Lola, who was a nun there; and the residue of her estate to her husband, Antonio. As in the case of her sister Cristina, nothing is known of Santuza Condulmer after this will. Nor is there any documentation of the nun Lola outside of her sister's will.

Ursia Condulmer, a fourth stepdaughter of Franceschina, was married to Giacomo Erizzo, who was from a small house with noble and non-noble members; the only Erizzo who appeared in the 1379 *Estimo* was the non-noble

Andrea, with an assessment of only 500 ducats (decile 9 to 10). Giacomo
Erizzo was agent for his brother-in-law Simoneto Condulmer in Alexandria,
and like Cristina's husband Pietro Diedo, found himself opposed to Simoneto
in a court case resulting from that enterprise as well as in one resulting from
the 1405 collapse of the bank in which Simoneto was a principal.[25] Erizzo
stepped in as noble sponsor for the entrance of Ursia's very distant, noble
relative Antonio Condulmer, when he filed his Balla d'Oro petition to enter
the Great Council as a young man.[26] As no will of Ursia has been found, there
is nothing further known of her family or estate.

The fifth stepdaughter of Franceschina was Madaluza, who made out
three wills successively between 1434 and 1444, more than three decades
after those of her sisters.[27] In her second and third wills, she identified herself
as the daughter of the late Angelo Condulmer and widow of Nicolo Trevisan, using terms that indicate that her husband, like her father, was non-
noble.[28] Her first will named as sole executor the Procurator of San Marco
Leonardo Mocenigo, her third named the Procurators of San Marco *de Citra*
(inexplicably her second will, of 1441, named no executor); the choice of an
institutional executor was no doubt occasioned by the long-term provisions
in her will.[29] Her first will estimated her tithe at 150 ducats' worth of *prestiti*,
her second at 200, and her third at 350, suggesting a personal fortune that
might have risen from 30,000 to 70,000 ducats in the course of a decade,
if the half-percent tithe of Nicoleto Condulmer cited in Chapter 1 can be
taken as a guide. In the 1441 and 1444 wills, she left 6 ducats to Cataruza,
widow of Giovanni Condulmer, who was the brother of the money changer
Vielmo in the San Tomà branch of the house. Madaluza's home parish was
in San Marcuola in Cannaregio, and most of her pious donations were to
the abbess and nuns of the nearby hospice of San Girolamo, including the
furnishings of her house, except for two beds and their fittings. Those she
left to her niece Cristina, daughter of her oldest brother, Leonardo, who had
been married in 1429 to the noble Francesco Querini, a member of one of
the largest and wealthiest Venetian noble families.[30]

In addition to receiving beds, Cristina was the principal beneficiary of the
estate of her aunt Madaluza in all of her wills, including the inheritance of a
house that Madaluza owned in the parish of San Cancian. In the 1434 will,
the bedclothes were specified, and a warning was given that if Cristina or her
husband should seek more from the executors, they and their heirs would be
barred from any inheritance. A sum of 300 ducats was to be put into *prestiti*
for Cristina's daughter Agnesina for an eventual dowry, and Cristina was to

receive income from the remaining *prestiti* for life, with the income to pass to Agnesina at her death; after the death of both, the residual was to be divided between gifts to the poor and the convent of San Girolamo. In the 1441 and 1444 wills, the dowry for Agnesina was set at 1,000 ducats, which had to be matched by her father Francesco Querini; she would have the option of 500 ducats for oblation as a nun. Cristina was to get the proceeds from the rest of the *prestiti* for life, succeeded by Agnesina. The 1441 will maintained the earlier provisions for the estate after Agnesina's death, but in the 1444 will, the estate was to be divided into three parts rather than two, with the third going to any sons of Cristina that there might be. It is evident that all three versions of Madaluza Condulmer's wills were written to guarantee a prosperous future for one daughter of her brother Leonardo, in whose noble husband she seems to have had little faith, and for that niece's daughter.

Franceschina's Daughters

Three of Franceschina's own daughters married nobles, in compliance with the dowry provisions in the will of their father, Angelo. Fiornovella married Nicolo Marcello, a member of a ducal family with eleven members in the *Estimo*. In her will of 1402, Fiornovella named her mother, Franceschina, and her uncle Nicolo Lombardo as her executors and gave them each 100 ducats as a bequest.[31] In the paragraph dealing with the residue of her estate, Fiornovella sought to control the future lives of her survivors by making extraordinary provisions that, in essence, would have her mother Franceschina take her own place in their lives. She was acting no doubt from fear that her own noble husband would remarry another woman with a large dowry and neglect the children he had with her. The residue of Fiornovella's estate was left to her sons and daughters equally on the condition that they stayed in the house with her mother, Franceschina, until the boys reached the age of twenty and the girls married; neither sons nor daughters were allowed to marry without the permission of their grandmother Franceschina. If any of these children disregarded these provisions, their share of her estate would go to the others; if all disobeyed her will, the entire estate would go to Franceschina. Fiornovella's husband, Nicolo Marcello, was to make provision for food and clothing for their surviving children from his own funds; if he failed to do so, all of their children would be deprived of their legacy, and the whole estate would go to Franceschina. Fiornovella died in 1413, but two of her sons are known to have survived her; the elder, Angelo Marcello, registered to enter the Great Council in 1427 at age eighteen.[32]

The second of Franceschina's daughters, Elena, chose not to marry; in her will of 1400, she described herself as "not willing to marry or become a nun" and "by defect of my person I wish to maintain my chastity."[33] In accordance with the provisions of her father's will, she set out her bequests, naming her mother, Franceschina, and her uncle Nicolo Lombardo as her executors. Then to her four sisters she left 100 ducats each, to her uncle Nicolo 300 ducats, with the residue to go to her mother, clearly the focal member of her family and probably the support for her rare decision to remain unmarried.

Nothing further is known about Cataruza, the third daughter, or Angelica, the fifth daughter, who was absent from her father Angelo's 1394 will but present in Franceschina's of 1397 and that of her sister Elena of 1400; they may have died before reaching the age of marriage.

Polisena, the fourth of five daughters of Franceschina, seems to have been the one who inherited her mother's position as the matriarch of the family after Franceschina's death in 1431. Like her sisters, she was eligible for an enormous dowry of 2,500 ducats from the 1394 will of her father, Angelo, on the condition that she marry into the nobility, and she was bequeathed 80 ducats' worth of *prestiti* from the 1397 will of her mother, Franceschina, to be kept in trust until she married. She also received 100 ducats from the 1400 will of her sister Elena and was the only sister to be included in Fiornovella's 1402 will, with an additional 100 ducats toward her dowry.

In 1411, Polisena married the nobleman Nicolo Barbo. The Barbo family had ten heads of household assessed in the 1379 *Estimo*, including the famous statesman Pantaleone, who had an assessment of 18,500 ducats (in the top decile), and two others with assessments of 6,000 ducats each (in the second decile). The marriage contract between Polisena and Nicolo was accompanied by an extraordinary contract between the bride and Nicoleta, the mother of the groom, in which Nicoleta pledged to give the couple half of her own dowry of 115 ducats (3,000 lire a grossi), which she had recently received back on the death of her husband, Paolo Barbo.[34] She also relinquished the right to stay in the Barbo palace that she had been granted in her husband's will and pledged to give to the couple half of any other bequest that she should receive in the future from any individual. Though Franceschina is not listed as a party to this agreement between her daughter and her son-in-law and his mother, her strong hand can be seen in this provision of the marriage contract, which ensured that Polisena was not only marrying a nobleman but one with significant funds of his own. As the dowry of the groom's mother, Nicoleta, had been only 115 ducats while that of Polisena was 2,880 ducats, it is clear that the marriage arranged by Franceschina was of a very rich, non-noble bride to a relatively poor, noble groom.

Seven years later, in 1418, Polisena expelled everyone from the room when she wrote out her will in her own hand, folded it up, and had the notary sign it on the outside, with the result that it was not included among those that the notary probated (*roboravit*) in his protocols and made available for public use.[35] In it, she identified herself as daughter of Angelo Condulmer and wife of the noble Nicolo Barbo and named the Procurators of San Marco as her executors, along with her mother, Franceschina, and her stepsister Ursia. She left 100 ducats to her mother to reimburse her for what she had contributed toward her dowry. She instructed the executors to call back her dowry from her husband (as was the normal practice) as quickly as possible after her death and invest it in *prestiti*, with interest to accrue every six months. She instructed that 500 ducats' worth of *prestiti* be bestowed on each of her three daughters, Maria, Isabeta, and Pantalea, for dowries. She left the residue to her sons upon turning twenty-five; until then they would benefit from the income of the *prestiti*. She does not name these sons, but we know that Paolo had been born two years earlier, in 1416, and Pietro in 1417.[36] When Paolo turned eighteen and applied to join the Great Council, his father, Nicolo, had died, and it was his mother, Polisena, who testified to his age, while one of his pledges was Pietro Diedo, the husband of Polisena's half-sister Cristina.

Polisena seems to have had a strong tie to her half-brother Gabriele, Pope Eugene IV, that took her well out of the circle of Venetian women of her era. In 1436, while the pope was in Florence setting up the council that would bring the Byzantine emperor to Italy for the unification of the churches, Polisena visited him, a phenomenon that caught the eye of a chronicler in Bologna, where she stayed in the course of her journey; no mention is made of her having been accompanied by any male relative.[37] For a Venetian woman to travel on the mainland to visit a relative, even the pope, was an extraordinary act for Renaissance Venice, where women's activities in the public sphere were narrowly limited.[38] As we shall see, Gabriele repaid her attention with support of her son Pietro, putting him on a path to the papacy as Paul II.

CHAPTER 5

Simoneto Condulmer, Venetian Banker and Merchant on an International Scale

The Benedetto-Condulmer Bank

It was Angelo Condulmer's two illegitimate sons, Simoneto and Gabriele, who were to become noteworthy figures in Venice in the early decades of the fifteenth century. With a *cittadino* father, wealthy as he may have been, and a mother of obscure birth and not married to their father, they had no pretensions of belonging to the nobility, but they nevertheless rose to social prominence in Venice and beyond. Simoneto became a leading banker in the city, and Gabriele became the pope, whose policies and actions presented never-ending challenges to the Venetian state.

Simoneto Condulmer was the middle son of Angelo by Pasqua; when Angelo made out his will in 1394, Simoneto was younger than his emancipated brother, Leonardo, but older than his other brother, Gabriele. As he was younger than twenty according to the will but old enough to be named an executor in it, he was probably born between 1373 and 1379. Virtually no private papers survive from Simoneto; we do not even know the first name of his wife, whom we infer to be from the noble da Mosto family as two of his daughters name Gasparino da Mosto as their mother's brother in their wills.[1] He is best known from his frequent appearances in the Court of Petitions, seeking funds, often from his former business partners, to repay his debts resulting from the 1405 failure of the bank in which he was a partner.[2]

By the end of the fourteenth century, banking in Venice had reached a stage that would be familiar to modern readers in the form of the "script" bank.[3] Script banks took in deposits for which they set up accounts for individuals and corporate entities. Depositors could write notes to transfer these

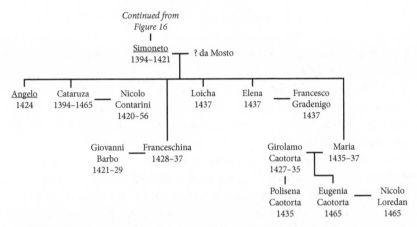

Figure 19. The family of Simoneto Condulmer. Underlined names are for people featured in this chapter. No last name is given for Condulmer. Years are of documents in which each is mentioned; † for year of death.

funds to others, who could then take these notes to the same bank or to an affiliated one to receive cash or have the sum credited to their own accounts. Unlike modern checks, these notes transferring credits were not on a standard form; they were written by the individual payer, sometimes with the confirmation of a notary, and might even have taken the form of just simultaneous entries in the account books of the two individuals involved in the transfer. A similarity to modern banks is that the amount of money generated by a given banking establishment could exceed that which was on deposit to it, in physical specie or in other assets that could be immediately liquidated, leading to the possibility of bank failure should a sudden demand exceed assets on hand. One difference from modern banks is the lack of limited liability in regard to the assets of the bankers; the individual partners could be held personally liable for the debts of a failed bank. In some cases, as in that of Simoneto Condulmer, the liability for such debts could devolve on their children or even grandchildren.

There were few script banks in late fourteenth-century Venice. The principal one was that of Gabriele Soranzo, which took over dominance after the failure of that of Giacomo Zanchani in 1374.[4] In about the same period, Pietro Benedetto began to appear in documents as a banker.[5] Simoneto's father, Angelo Condulmer, was a customer of the bank of Pietro Benedetto; he appeared before the Court of Petitions in 1393 to sue Nicoleto Rizzo for the repayment of a loan that he had made to Rizzo at the Benedetto bank.[6]

In this period, Simoneto was an agent of the Benedetto bank; a court case brought in 1412 by Pietro Diedo charged that on April 26, 1397, Simoneto had failed to transfer 80 ducats that Diedo had in the bank of Pietro Benedetto to a certain Belforto de Napoli.[7]

On September 29, 1400, the noble banker Pietro Benedetto, who had been assessed for 5,000 ducats in the *Estimo*, was dying of plague and had his "nephew" Marco Condulmer write down the provisions of his will.[8] On the next day, the will was written out by a Venetian notary, but when word of his illness caused a run on his bank, Benedetto declared his desire to add provisions on the future of his bank and took the will back from the notary. In the meantime, his creditors, mainly Florentine merchants, got the Merchant Consuls of Venice to examine the ledgers of the bank; these officials declared that the assets of about 55,000 ducats would satisfy all of the creditors and still leave 15,000 to 20,000 ducats for his estate. Pietro Benedetto died on October 2, and two days later, on October 4, his will was confirmed with signatures of the Doge Antonio Venier, four of the ducal counselors, and the ducal chancellor.

Benedetto named among his executors Marco Condulmer and his son-in-law Jacobello Zane; he added at the end of this provision that his "nephew" Simoneto Condulmer should also be an executor.[9] Marco was the son of Andriolo Condulmer (who was first cousin to Simoneto's father, Angelo) and had in February 1389 become a partner in a company with Jacobello Zane and Pietro Benedetto's son Zanino, which was dissolved three months later.[10] Simoneto and Marco were second cousins; the exact nature of their relationship to Pietro Benedetto is not certain. The word *nievo* could mean grandson as well as nephew, but it is unlikely that these adult men were the sons of one of Benedetto's daughters. Simoneto could not have been the son of one of Benedetto's sisters, as his mother was the obscure and surely not noble Pasqua; his wife from the da Mosto family might have been a niece of Benedetto. However, it is possible that the word *nievo* was used by Pietro Benedetto for Simoneto and Marco more broadly, perhaps as a term of endearment for his apprentice bankers.

The paragraph that Pietro Benedetto added to his will of 1400 instructed his executors to set up a new bank to succeed the one in his and Marco Condulmer's names, having as its four partners his estate as a whole, plus Giacomo Zane, and Marco and Simoneto Condulmer; it was popularly referred to as the "Benedetto estate bank." The four partners were characterized by a Florentine merchant in Venice as "gran ricchi."[11] The new bank opened on October 4, 1400, two days after Benedetto's death, and promised to pay all debts that were called. Assets flooded in and established the new bank as sound. The partnership that operated the bank had also been charged in Benedetto's will to continue its support of two silk shops operated in Venice by merchants from Lucca.

In a 1403 case regarding the disbursal of funds from the new bank to the estate of a depositor named Enrico della Piazza, the plaintiffs were represented by Marco Condulmer, characterized as a *campsor* (literally a money changer but a term also used for bankers) who appeared as one of the executors of the estate of Pietro Benedetto and on behalf of the new bank's other partners, including Simoneto.[12] The court supported the transfer of about 515 ducats from the della Piazza estate to the bank. By the end of 1404, the bank in which Simoneto was partner had become the leading one for foreign bills of exchange.[13] However, there were concerns that the bank was overextended, perhaps because of commercial investments made by the principals. In November 1404, the Senate debated a bill that called attention to the situation that bankers of script were making foreign investments with funds in their bank, endangering the accounts of their depositors.[14] By a very small margin, it passed a resolution limiting the amount that bankers could invest abroad or at home to one-and-a-half times the patrimony assessed on the *Estimo* as the basis for their mandatory purchase of *prestiti*.

In January 1405, the failure of the Foscherari bank of Bologna caused a run on the Benedetto-Zane-Condulmer bank in Venice when it was learned that they had guaranteed 12,000 ducats held by the Bolognese bank.[15] The bank posted liabilities of 110,000 ducats and assets of 40,000 ducats in real estate; 45,000 ducats in good debts plus gold and silver at the mint; 13,000 in the silk workshops; and an unspecified amount in merchandise overseas. As these assets, some potential, fell below its liabilities, the bank was forced to liquidate, with a repayment plan for creditors set up stretching until May 1407.

Marco Condulmer, cousin and partner of Simoneto in the failed bank, appears in a court case concerning a shipment of worked gold and silk that he had sent to Alexandria in 1405 to Stefano Benedetto, son of the late banker Pietro, who was to sell it and distribute the 2,500 ducats it would fetch among four individuals, including Leonardo and Giovanni Zane.[16] In November 1405, Marco Condulmer turned over the management of his affairs, including those relating to the bank, to a mercer named Astrasano and to Andrea Bon.[17] He must have died soon thereafter, as a reference to money raised from Simoneto's business associates to pay for a sepulcher for Marco appears in a later court case concerning transactions that took place around 1408.[18]

After this period, responsibility for settling the debts of the failed bank appears to have fallen exclusively on the shoulders of Simoneto Condulmer.[19] Within the administration of the Venetian state, jurisdiction over the bankruptcy process was uncertain and contested. In February 1405, the ducal counselors ordered that all of his goods and merchandise be subject to a payment of 3 percent to the officials charged with the bank's dissolution (the *Estraordinari*).[20] On April 29, 1405, the Merchant Consuls got the Council of Forty to give them authority over all of Simoneto's property and business transactions up to that day.[21] That summer, the Senate made mention of a grant that had been made to Simoneto and Marco Condulmer for the suspension of taxes.[22]

The process of the bank's liquidation is illustrated in a series of court cases brought by Alberto da Ca' da Monza against Simoneto for the return of his money deposited in the bank. In a case before the Court of Petitions filed on September 1, 1407, Alberto alleged that he had deposited 2,000 ducats in the bank on behalf of Gasparoto Bacacorno of Piacenza, for which he had a receipt in the hand of Simoneto Condulmer as principal, subscribed by Marco Condulmer, "formerly a banker of script in Rialto," in his name and that of his bank.[23] Alberto claimed that he was still owed 750 ducats of this sum. Simoneto responded that he had promised to the Merchant Consuls to pay the 750 ducats in installments rather than in its entirety. The judges found against Simoneto and ordered him to pay the 750 ducats plus court expenses. On February 14, 1408, Alberto returned to the court to complain that he had not yet been paid. In testimony, he noted that Simoneto had promised on April 29, 1405, to pay in full within one year, a pledge entered in the bank's accounts on May 20, after its failure.[24] He testified that Simoneto participated in the debt of the bank along with the heirs of Pietro Benedetto and Marco Condulmer, all of whom were relatives and brothers (*consanguine, germani*). This case, like the earlier one, appears canceled in the records of the appeals court, in accordance with a ruling on June 1, 1408, by the Lesser Council that the Merchant Consuls had jurisdiction over the repayment plans of the bank, so the judgments of the Court of Petitions were moot.[25] In 1411, the Court of Petitions ordered Simoneto to abide by an arbitration carried out by the Merchant Consuls favoring the estate of Cataruzo Anzoli.[26]

Even the action of Simoneto's brother Gabriele in 1407, transferring to him all of his assets except his interest in the family palace, did not satisfy Simoneto's liability to his creditors from the bank's failure.[27] The liquidation of the bank continued for many years; an act of the Great Council of July 7,

1418, authorized the processing of land forfeited by Simoneto Condulmer for a debt of the bank of Pietro Benedetto, of which he was said to have had a quarter share.[28] The debts of the bank would plague the Condulmer family for generations; in 1465, Eugenia Caotorta, Simoneto's granddaughter and wife of Nicolo Loredan, would bring suit for her share of the estate of her mother, Maria Condulmer, in which she enumerated her mother's debts, including one from 1454 for one-quarter of a payment demanded by the Merchant Consuls due to the obligation of Simoneto Condulmer for the bank of Pietro Benedetto.[29]

Simoneto Condulmer's Mercantile Activities During His Partnership in the Bank

In the years of Simoneto's partnership in the bank that succeeded that of Pietro Benedetto, he continued his active merchant activities in his own name. In fact, those that are revealed in a series of law cases show a level of business involvement stretching from Alexandria to Flanders that is little short of astonishing for a mid-level, non-noble businessman who was still younger than thirty. It is possible that some of Simoneto's merchant ventures were funded by the bank in which he appears to have been the most active partner and that the overextension of his investments may have played a role in the collapse of the bank in 1405. As far as can be determined from surviving documentation, Simoneto Condulmer never left Venice; he did not spend a period of his youth traveling to the various ports that traded with Venice and learning the practicalities of business abroad. Unlike noble Venetian youths at the beginning of their careers as merchants, he was not eligible to travel on the great merchant galleys as a "bowman of the quarterdeck," one of a couple dozen young nobles whose presence on the fleet was formally as archers but for whom such trips offered a practical introduction at the expense of the state to the network of Venetian commerce abroad.[30]

Simoneto had started his career as a merchant entrepreneur in a series of ventures with his younger brother, Gabriele, when both were about twenty years old, and he had continued it through his period as head of a major bank. The commercial relationship of Simoneto with his older brother, Leonardo, and with Gabriele was not a classic *fraterna* of shared investments between brothers. In 1398 and again in 1401, Leonardo vested full power over his affairs to Simoneto.[31] While Simoneto and Gabriele were the residual heirs of the estate of their father, Angelo, upon his death between 1394 and 1397, Leonardo did not share in this capital, presumably because he had been emancipated by Angelo with a substantial endowment and hence was considered the head of his own branch of the family. As we shall see in Chapter 6, Gabriele maintained his own commercial relationships in the period before 1407, sometimes but not always explicitly including his brother Simoneto in his affairs. Perhaps a reason for this lack of shared business identity was to shield Gabriele (and Leonardo) from the risk that Simoneto ran as head of a script bank.

In addition to ventures with his brothers, Simoneto worked closely with his second cousin Marco Condulmer, a participant along with Simoneto in the bank of Pietro Benedetto and fellow partner in the successor bank. Simoneto also had frequent business relationships with two of the noble husbands of his sisters. Pietro Diedo was married to his sister Cristina; we have already seen that in 1412, Pietro would sue Simoneto over a transaction of 1397 concerning the Benedetto bank. Another of Simoneto's brothers-in-law was Giacomo Erizzo, married to his sister Ursia; he would be the object of a suit brought in 1412 by Simoneto for his actions as Simoneto's agent in Alexandria in 1405.[32]

According to the particulars in a case that was settled in court in 1410, in 1396 the brothers Simoneto and Gabriele Condulmer sent forty sacks of cotton weighing 12,625 pounds to Flanders.[33] Simoneto (who had by 1410 taken over Gabriele's business interests) brought suit for a sum of 914 ducats that was supposed to be credited to their agent there, Antonio de Mercadeli, by their brother-in-law Pietro Diedo. Part of Diedo's defense was that he had passed on part of the proceeds to Giacomo Zane, Pietro Benedetto's son-in-law and a partner with Simoneto in the successor bank. The case was decided fourteen years after the transactions by a team of three appeal judges that included Leonardo Zane, brother of Giacomo. The judges put both Diedo and Simoneto under oath, but Diedo was not able to produce his account book supporting his version of the transactions. The court found in favor of Simoneto and ordered Diedo to pay him 726.5 ducats less some payments credited in 1399 and 1400, plus about 17 ducats in expenses.

Letters in the Datini archives in Prato give further information on the commercial activities of Simoneto and Gabriele Condulmer before Simoneto took over responsibility for the Benedetto bank. In July 1396, the brothers jointly sent a letter to enlist the aid of the Datini firm of Prato in the sale of 15 bales containing 230 wool cloths worth about 5,000 ducats that had been brought from Flanders, probably on the same voyage cited in the 1410 suit but, instead of being sold in Maiorca, had been brought to Livorno.[34]

Three entries concerning Simoneto's business activities in Egypt appear in the very fragmentary records of the Council of Twelve in Alexandria, accounting for three of the ten cases they considered in 1401 and 1402. In all three cases, Simoneto was represented by Leonardo Zane, the brother of Giacomo Zane, Simoneto's partner in the bank. In the first of the Alexandria cases, on March 20, 1402, Leonardo Zane, speaking on behalf of Simoneto, charged that of 283 barrels (*carateli*) of honey that Simoneto had sent on the ship of Vettore Fiolo on behalf of his older brother Leonardo Condulmer, only 278 were unloaded in Alexandria.[35] The council found in favor of Simoneto and ordered Fiolo to pay 32 ducats for the missing barrels. Three weeks later, Zane joined the noble Vettore Marcello in a suit against Fiolo concerning 79 pounds of pepper and other spices and 10 carats of ginger that Simoneto Condulmer and two others had sent to Methone, a Venetian entrepôt on the Peloponnesus, on behalf of Marco Condulmer; in this case, Zane was ordered to pay the extra shipping costs.[36] That August, Zane appeared before the consuls in a case involving a ship that Teodorino Zuchato had leased to Simoneto Condulmer for 355 ducats, of which Zane was to pay 150 in Alexandria and Simoneto the balance in Venice.[37] Zane countered that the lease had allocated 150 ducats to Zuchato for buying salt, but since Zuchato had not bought any salt, he should be absolved from the debt; the council ordered Zane to pay the 150 ducats for the freight charges but made Zuchato pay the expenses of the trial. At the same time, Simoneto added to his network of trade relationships by setting up Andrea Polo of Scutari as his representative in Dalmatia, Croatia, Slavonia, and Albania, and with his cousin Marco establishing Antonio Bartolomeo of Venice as their factor in Apulia.[38]

Also in 1403, a ship that Simoneto had chartered got involved in the war between Venice and Genoa in the Adriatic, leading to two court cases. Simoneto lost both cases, but the court records give a vivid view of commerce in the period and the scope of his operations.[39] On January 19, Simoneto charged that he had rented a small sailing ship piloted by Marino de Michele on which he was supposed to load wine and other commodities in Crete and travel from there directly to "Neapolis" in Apulia (Polignano a Mare), where he was to unload the wine and load the ship with new cargo and bring it to Venice. Instead, Simoneto charged, Marino brought the wine directly to Venice; Simoneto insisted that Marino be required to take it to Apulia and exchange its cargo as contracted. Marino responded that the original contract had called for Marino to take the ship to Francavilla al Mare in Abruzzo and load oil there, head to Corfu and add whatever commodities Simoneto's agent there wished to load, and then bring the whole cargo to Alexandria, where it would be unloaded by Leonardo Zane as agent for Simoneto and for which a freight fee of 400 ducats would be paid. Marino was then to take the ship to Crete and contact Simoneto's agent there, Bernardo de Mezzo. If de Mezzo had merchandise for him, he was to take it to Apulia for a freight fee of 400 ducats, and if not, he would receive only 25 ducats.

When they learned of the additional destination, Marino's sailors rose up and demanded two months' pay, which the Venetian administrator (*regimen*) of Crete upheld. While the ship was being loaded, word came of threats from Genoese ships in the Adriatic, and the regimen held Marino's ship for six days in Crete and sent it to Methone. Once in Methone, the sailors refused to go to Apulia for fear of falling into Genoese hands, so Marino took the ship to Corfu, where the Venetian representative (*bailo*) told him to take the ship directly to Venice rather than to Apulia. In finding in favor of Marino de Michele, the judges of the Court of Petitions noted that Simoneto had received the merchandise without complaint, and they remarked that all of the Venetian officials cited had confirmed that Marino had intended to pursue the contracted voyage but could not do so without willing sailors.[40]

Simoneto's commercial activities in Francavilla in Abruzzo in 1403 are documented in more detail in a case that he brought to the Court of Petitions fourteen years later.[41] In it, Simoneto sought a total of 233.5 ducats from his agent there, Antonio Dotto, for not having accounted payments from his debtors, among whom was a certain Giovanni Condulmer, probably the son of Alvise, brother to the ennobled Jacobello of the San Tomà branch of the house. In his defense, Antonio noted that he had sold about 30,000 ducats' worth of goods for Simoneto and had accounted for them properly, and that Simoneto had not challenged his accounts for fourteen years. He then proceeded to respond to each of the charges made against him; the judges held Antonio accountable for about 40 ducats and absolved him of the rest.

Six months later, in 1404, the Venetian Andrea de Cristoforo brought suit against Simoneto, saying that he, Andrea, had sent fourteen bales of paper (*ballas cartarum de papiro*) to Apulia on behalf of Simoneto the previous April, which he delivered to Antonio Angi, Simoneto's agent there. Antonio sold the paper with a profit of 122 ducats, which he said he spent on behalf of Simoneto.[42] Andrea claimed that when he returned to Venice, Simoneto and Marco Condulmer refused to reimburse him for the paper; the court found against Simoneto, ordering him to pay Andrea the 122 ducats plus court costs.

Simoneto's Merchant Activity After
the Dissolution of the Bank

In 1412, Simoneto brought suit against his brother-in-law Giacomo Erizzo concerning Simoneto's activities in Alexandria in the years around 1405.[43] In this suit, Simoneto noted that all of his transactions before his bank's failure on April 29, 1405, had been ordered to be within the jurisdiction of the Merchant Consuls but that those carried out since then should be rendered to him. He reported that about two years earlier, in 1410, Giacomo had left Alexandria but "neither love nor petition" had been able to get him to render his accounting for all he had carried out there on Simoneto's behalf since 1405. Simoneto reported that there were twenty-seven posts in the accounts after the cut-off date, beginning with two sacks of silk sent to him from Rhodes in 1405 and continuing to the arrival of eighty crates of soap sent by him from Venice in 1408. Simoneto calculated the amount owed him at 17,300 ducats. Giacomo defended himself by saying that he had sent to Simoneto no fewer than three sets of accounts in the years in question and that finally, when he arrived back in Venice in 1409, he had brought his own account book to his brother-in-law Antonio Ravagnan, who also happened to be the husband of one of Simoneto's sisters, Santuza. In explanation of the money for the sale of pepper that Simoneto claimed from him, Giacomo said that Simoneto had instructed him to spend a capital of about 14,000 ducats on pepper, estimated to be about 60 *sportas*, equivalent to about 12,900 kilograms. Giacomo recounted that in September 1407 he had received a letter from Simoneto while he was in Cairo instructing him to leave Cairo and go to Alexandria where the cog of Nicoleto Rosso would be bringing olive oil sent by Simoneto from Seville and to sell about a thousand jars (*jadrie*) of the oil and buy ninety to a hundred measures (*sportas*) of pepper. Giacomo sent the order to his agent Claro Arcangeli who had remained in Cairo to buy the pepper, but when he heard that the Venetian galleys were due in Alexandria sooner than expected, he wrote to Claro not to buy any pepper in Cairo, and he bought the balance himself in Alexandria. However, Claro had already bought the pepper, which he shipped to Alexandria too late to be loaded on the galleys, resulting in a large loss. The judges of the Court of Petitions reviewed the relevant documentation and found in favor of Giacomo Erizzo, absolving him of the payments sought by Simoneto and holding Simoneto responsible for court fees.

At about the same time, a merchant of Ancona named Giovanni Domenici brought charges in the Court of Petitions in Venice on behalf of himself
and Michele Pacis of Ancona against Simoneto Condulmer for about 30,000
liters of oil for lighting (*multarum sucendarum*).[44] Giovanni claimed that he
had had to pay 36 ducats to Jewish money lenders as interest for six months
on the 600 ducats Simoneto owed to him, an interest rate of 12 percent a year.
Simoneto responded that he had also sent to Giovanni and Michele 65,446
pounds of worked iron (*ferixi*) which had been stolen when the door and
walls of the storehouse had been broken. The judges awarded to Domenici
327 ducats for the unpaid balance of the accounts and ordered Simoneto to
pay the court costs.

In 1417, as part of a series of lawsuits he brought against various of his agents,
mostly for transactions the previous decade, Simoneto brought suit against the
nobleman Andrea Corner, of the extremely wealthy family that dominated
trade with Cyprus, and against Andrea's agent Pietro Michiel.[45] He charged that
in the accounts he had rendered, Andrea had included debits to Simoneto for
transactions carried out in Seville equivalent to around 135 ducats, including
damage to a shipment of the purgative *cassia fistula* and the loss of a canary
that was supposed to have been sent to Venice but never arrived, valued (rather
exorbitantly) at about 11 ducats. Simoneto also charged that Andrea had told
him that vair skins were highly prized in Seville and that he could get a profit of
16.6 percent, but of the two thousand vair backs and two thousand vair bellies
that Simoneto shipped, worth 180 ducats, he claimed he was still owed about 68
ducats. Simoneto also charged that he had sent 15,374 pounds of lead in sheets,
which were accounted below what should have been the sale price; the total that
Simoneto sought for these shortfalls was 250 ducats. In a detailed, point-by-
point defense, Pietro Michiel rebutted each of the complaints of Simoneto with
the exception of the missing canary, which he conceded was just. The judges
considered the relevant account books and gave Pietro three days to produce
the receipts for certain specific transactions, which he failed to do. They then
sentenced him to pay about 80 ducats from the funds of Andrea Corner and
about 33 ducats for the shortfall on the vair skins as well as the court expenses
but absolved him from all of the other claims.

The last document referring to Simoneto as living is the will of his aunt
Isabeta (the sister of his father, Angelo) of 1421, which includes him among
her executors, along with her other nephew Francesco, son of her brother
Marco.[46] As Simoneto appears to have been born between 1373 and 1379, he
would then have been between forty-two and forty-eight years old.

A Posthumous Court Case Involving
Simoneto's Son and Brother

Simoneto is cited in a document of 1424 as deceased and the codefendant with his son and heir Angelo in a dispute regarding a transaction of oil in Ancona that took place a few years earlier.[47] The plaintiff was Pietro Marcello, son of Bartolomeo, with the respondent identified as Angelo Condulmer on his own behalf and as the heir of his father, Simoneto. Marcello testified that he had made a contract with Angelo Condulmer to purchase in Ancona 150 measures of unclarified oil (*oio mosto*), that is, 2,610 liters weighing about 2,100 kilograms, for which he would pay 1,800 ducats.[48] He gave him 2 bails (*balli*) of pepper and 150 marks of silver and ingots of copper and a crate (*cassa*) of wax for the value of 1,120 ducats toward the purchase of the oil; he left 600 ducats in the hands of Giovanni Mantello, the captain of the boat, which was due to arrive in Ancona from Venice on February 14. The captain asked Angelo's agents which of them was in charge of the oil, and they responded that "the cardinal" would give them part of the oil within the time specified in the contract. However, when he got to Ancona, Mantello received only 23 barrels within the time allotted. He wished to draft a formal protest but was unable to find a notary because they were all allied with the cardinal, so he had to write out the protest himself as best he could. The cardinal who was so involved in the provision of oil on behalf of Angelo Condulmer was none other than Gabriele Condulmer, Simoneto's brother and Angelo's uncle, who, as we shall see in the next chapter, was in this period pursuing a career in the ecclesiastic hierarchy. Gabriele had been named titular Cardinal of San Clemente in 1408 and was appointed papal legate in Ancona after the beginning of October 1418; as Ancona was considered part of the Patrimonio of Saint Peter's, it was theoretically under papal authority, but the legate contested actual control with the communal government.[49]

According to his testimony, Captain Mantello announced that he was due to depart on February 26 and was summoned to the cardinal's presence and told to pay for the twenty-three barrels of oil on the ship. The captain refused, saying that 1,500 ducats had already been paid for it and the rest would be paid for when it was received, either in Venice or in Ancona. The cardinal then had Mantello seized and imprisoned him for twenty-two days. Mantello immediately had a notary write out a formal protest with four witnesses, which he sent by land to Pietro Marcello in Venice asking to have him released. Marcello took the protest along with the original contract he had made with Simoneto and

Angelo to the Merchant Consuls and obtained an agreement whereby Simoneto and Angelo would write out a directive to have the captain released from
prison and be given the remainder of the oil. When the cardinal received this
message, he sent men to the ship and had them open the coffers and seize silver
and pepper from it, to which Mantello made another formal protest.

Finally, the cardinal let Mantello out of prison and told him to proceed
to Monte Santo (Porto Potenza Picena) and San Lopido (Porto Sant'Elpidio),
both on the Adriatic coast south of Ancona, to pick up the rest of his cargo. By
April 15, Mantello had received a total of 115 barrels of oil from Ancona and
Monte Santo and another 65 barrels at San Lopido. As the season for sailing
to Constantinople had passed, the captain refused to take on more oil and
wrote up another protest; he set sail finally on April 25. Marcello reported that
because of the delay in sailing, he had been able to sell the oil in Chios for only
26 ducats per barrel rather than 32, because other ships had arrived before his.
He asked for compensation of 800 ducats for the loss of profit from the oil and
an additional 200 ducats' compensation for the shortfall of oil plus expenses
connected with the delay of the voyage for a total of 1,338 ducats.[50]

Angelo Condulmer responded to the court on behalf of his late father,
Simoneto, and himself. He denied that they had been part of the original
appeal to Marcello to bring oil to Romania and confirmed that the original
contract had been for 150 measures of oil in Ancona for an immediate payment of 1,500 ducats. He blamed the disagreement on Marcello and denied
that neither his father nor his uncle Gabriele, the cardinal, had instructed
the *podestà* of Ancona to hold Mantello there. He said that Mantello had
refused payment for the 23 barrels he had received there and that the *podestà*
of Ancona had him imprisoned, while the cardinal had played the role of
intermediary. As for the loss Marcello claimed to suffer because of the delay,
Angelo said that the higher price paid in Chios was for clear oil, while that
of Marcello was unrefined and was paid for in Turkish ducats, which were
5 percent lighter than Venetian ducats. The judges considered the original
contract between Simoneto and Marcello and various letters including one
from Gabriele registered in the papal curia; they ultimately found in favor
of Marcello, placing Angelo Condulmer in debt for 400 ducats and for court
expenses but absolving Angelo of all other charges, for which Marcello was
to pay court costs. There is no explanation in the brief finding as to how the
amount of compensation was decided upon nor which aspects of the charges
brought against Simoneto and Angelo Condulmer were valid, but it seems
that the court did consider the dealings of the father and son in the matter to
have brought some degree of loss to one of their business associates.

An Overview of Simoneto's Merchant Activities

Thanks to this series of detailed court cases, we can reconstruct Simoneto Condulmer's mercantile enterprises to an extent offered for few Venetian merchants of the period. Much of his commercial activity was in partnership with members of his extended family, including the noble husbands of his sisters. His earliest documented activities were as an executor of his father's will beginning in 1394 (when he was younger than twenty), along with his older brother, Leonardo. As early as 1396, he had entered into a partnership with his younger brother, Gabriele. In 1397, he gave temporary power of attorney to Leonardo and his second cousin Marco Condulmer, and in 1402 was a partner with Leonardo in the transport of honey to Alexandria. His partnership in the bank that succeeded that of the nobleman Pietro Benedetto from 1400 to 1405 was shared with his second cousin Marco and with the nobleman Giacomo Zane, Benedetto's son-in-law; the same three men represented a Florentine cloth merchant within Venice in the period.

Simoneto's own personal activity seems to have been restricted to Venice; his overseas transactions were carried out by agents, some of whom are known to have been working for him continuously in a single port over a span of years. In addition to an agent in Flanders, he did business there through his brother-in-law Pietro Diedo and also through Giacomo Zane. From 1402 to 1404, his agent in Alexandria was Giacomo's brother Leonardo Zane, who was later to serve on the appeals court that in 1410 awarded Simoneto more than 725 ducats in damages. Simoneto used Giacomo Erizzo, the husband of one of his sisters, as his agent in Alexandria from at least 1405 to 1410; Erizzo himself had an agent in Cairo. Simoneto also had an agent in Crete, one in Apulia, and one in Francavilla in Abruzzo.

Simoneto does not seem to have owned his own ships; he leased those of individuals and occasionally sent merchandise on the Venetian state galleys. The focus of much of his merchant activity seems to have been the trade in olive oil from the Adriatic coast of Italy, centered on Ancona and collected from surrounding ports south of there. He sent barrels of wine and honey to Abruzzo as well as saffron. In one venture, Simoneto had contracted with a private ship to go to Abruzzo and load oil, which he was to take to Corfu for merchandise to be brought to Alexandria. The ship was then to go to Crete for wine, which it was to bring to Apulia, with Venice as the final destination. He shipped bales of paper to Apulia. As early as 1396, Simoneto and Gabriele were in a joint venture to send almost 1,000 ducats' worth of cloth to Flanders on the state galleys that sailed through the Strait of Gibraltar. In 1407, Simoneto sent pearls on the same westbound voyage, which he sold to an agent in Cartagena in southern Spain, the source of some of his oil as well. His agent informed him that vair skins were highly prized in Seville, so he sent four thousand pelts there. Another commodity shipped there was sheets of lead.

Simoneto's activity in Alexandria from 1402 to 1404 is known from the survival of fragmentary accounts of the Council of Twelve as well as individual court cases in Venice. He sent to Egypt salt and soap from Venice; honey, probably of European origin; olive oil from southern Spain; and silk from Rhodes. His principal import from Alexandria was pepper, which his agent bought in Cairo, along with ginger and other spices, silk, and mastic. Though he was involved in trade with the Venetian island colonies of Corfu and Crete, as well as the Peloponnese colony of Methone and the island of Chios, Simoneto is not documented as having direct mercantile ties with the eastern Mediterranean ports of Cyprus, Syria, Asia Minor, Constantinople, or the Black Sea (Map 4).

We can be grateful to Simoneto Condulmer for his litigious nature; it is through the detailed charges and defenses in the lawsuits brought before the Court of Petitions that we know most about his mercantile activities. However, these cases raise certain questions about the course of his career. He was amazingly busy for a young man in the period leading up to the failure of his bank in 1405, but there is little documentation about his business activities in the following few years. In 1407, he received the fortune of his brother Gabriele, who had entered religious life. However, that does not seem to have been enough to cover his debts from the bank; beginning in 1410, he seems to have embarked on a campaign of lawsuits to recoup allegedly withheld funds from his business associates, many of whom were his own relatives. The courts sometimes found in his favor, sometimes against him, and sometimes split the decision. However, much energy must have been committed to dredging up the details of past transactions, and his reputation as a trustworthy and cooperative merchant could not have been improved by such attacks on his associates. He died between 1421 and 1424; as no will of his is known, there is little indication of the size or eventual disposition of what must have been an estate of sizable wealth but still burdened by liabilities for his bank's 1405 failure.

To contemporary Venetians, Simoneto was probably viewed as the nonnoble merchant who took over the successful bank of the noble Pietro Benedetto and was responsible for its collapse. The action of the Senate in 1404 limiting the amount that bankers could invest abroad was a last-minute warning about the possible insolvency of such a bank due to the overextension

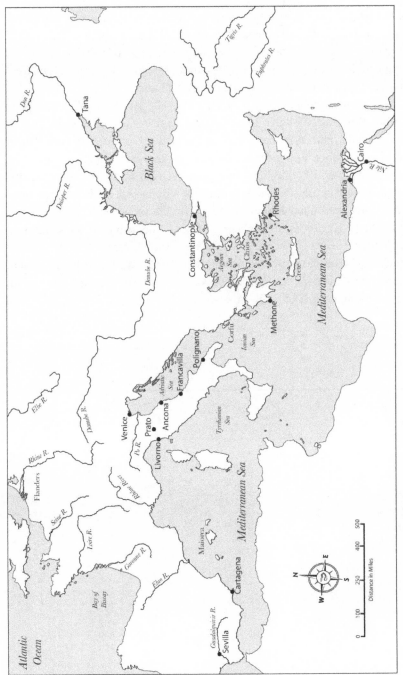

Map 4. The merchant network of Simoneto Condulmer.

of the assets by some bankers. The following year, the Condulmer-led bank failed, leaving in its wake depositors who would not be able to regain their assets for decades to come. With Simoneto's very public disgrace, the bad repute of the house of Condulmer must have become a widespread phenomenon in the opening decades of the fifteenth century.

Simoneto Condulmer had been viewed as a "great rich man" in the eyes of a Florentine observer when in 1400, less than thirty years of age, he became one of the partners in the bank that succeeded that of the noble Pietro Benedetto.[51] Throughout his life, his business associates were predominantly nobles, including those he employed as his agents overseas. Five years later, his bank failed because of funds it had guaranteed to a Bolognese bank, leaving him in a position of perpetual debt for the rest of his life and extending into the lives of his heirs. He continued his merchant investments but, at the same time, undertook a series of court cases against his former associates. The prestige that he had acquired both in Venice and throughout the Italian banking community must have vanished with the collapse of his bank, leaving him and his heirs with the stigma of being a perpetual debtor.

CHAPTER 6

Gabriele Condulmer, Also Known as
Pope Eugene IV

In his identity as Pope Eugene IV, who served from 1431 to his death in 1447, Gabriele Condulmer was one of the most consequential and complex figures of the early Renaissance, presiding over the papacy in the transition from the Western schism, through the battle over conciliar versus papal authority and the efforts to reunite with the Eastern Church, to the triumph of the monarchical papacy and the countervailing rise of Protestantism. The events of his entire reign are far too complex to be dealt with in this chapter, or even in a whole book, so we will concentrate here on his identities as a Venetian and as a member of the Condulmer family.[1]

Gabriele's Family and Early Career

As we have seen in Chapter 4, Gabriele was the son of Angelo Condulmer by a mother other than Franceschina, Angelo's only documented wife. He was probably the son of Pasqua, identified in the will of his sister Santuza as her mother and alive in 1397. The illegitimate nature of his birth appears to have led to the creation in his earliest biographies of a fictitious noble mother, Beriola Correr, sister to Pope Gregory XII. In addition to providing a legitimate and noble origin to Gabriele, it provided an explanation of his sudden rise in the ecclesiastical hierarchy. As we shall see, in his early career, Gabriele was indeed closely allied with Gregory XII and with Antonio Correr, one of the pope's nephews. Most contemporary documents name Antonio as a papal nephew and do not apply that term to Gabriele

Condulmer, but two contemporary foreigners did identify them both as the pope's nephews.[2]

Gabriele first appears in the archival records of Venice as the witness to documents of November 1393 concerning the receipt of a dowry of 2,200 ducats by Antonio Copo from the estate of Pietro Bembo, father of his bride, Maria; he is identified as "ser Gabriel, filius domini Angeli Condelmario."[3] In view of the epithet *Ser* and his status as a witness, he must have been at least a young man, which is inconsistent with the 1383 birth date given in early biographies, which would have made him only ten years old at the time.[4] In 1394, Gabriele appeared as an heir (but not an executor) in the will of his father, Angelo, along with his brother Simoneto and his half-sisters by his father's second marriage.[5] Simoneto was instructed in the will to give Gabriele 3,000 ducats when he (Simoneto) turned twenty, and the brothers were to receive the residue of the estate in the form of interest in *colleganze* arranged by the Procurators of San Marco, joint executors of the estate. It is clear that in 1394 neither of the brothers had been emancipated and neither was older than twenty. As Simoneto was made an executor along with their older, emancipated brother, Leonardo, and Gabriele was not, it is apparent that Gabriele was the youngest of the three sons. At the end of 1407, Gabriele was given a papal dispensation to become Bishop of Siena before the age of thirty, so he must have been born after the end of 1377.[6] In view of his identification as *Ser* in the 1393 dowry witnessing and his being younger than the under-twenty Simoneto in 1394, Gabriele Condulmer would then seem to have been born between about 1377 and 1381.

In 1396, Gabriele was named one of the executors and a beneficiary in the will of his sister Cristina, who identified herself as a daughter of the late Angelo and wife of the noble Pietro Diedo.[7] As Cristina apparently died in childbirth, Gabriele would have inherited 62.5 ducats that year in addition to half of the residue of the very large estate of his father, who had died between the 1394 date of his will and that of this one two years later. As a young man, Gabriele participated with Simoneto in several business ventures. He was a partner in a 1396 enterprise whose dispute with Pietro Rosso brought in arbitrators.[8] He was also a partner of his brother in the 1396 shipment of forty sacks of cotton to Flanders, as recounted in a suit that was not adjudicated until 1410, and in a series of transactions with the Datini firm of Prato concerning bales of wool brought from Flanders to Livorno in the same year.[9]

Merchant and Itinerant Cleric

By 1400, when he was around twenty, Gabriele added a religious identity to his merchant activities. In a document dated February 23, 1400, and drawn up in Rialto (that is, Venice itself) by the notary Enrico Salomon, who would follow him around the lagoon for the next few years, he identified himself as a son of the late Angelo and a subdeacon residing in the Camoldensian monastery on the island of San Michele, between Venice and Murano.[10] In this document, Gabriele and Giovanni de Restoro undertook a commercial venture to the southern Italian Samnite region with funds received from a bank and from individuals; it was Gabriele who would make the actual trip. In another document dated the same day, Gabriele made Restoro his general agent for the duration of his absence.[11] On July 12 of that year, in a document drawn up on Murano in the home of Stefano, dean (*plebano*) of the diocese of Torcello, Gabriele acknowledged that Restoro had fulfilled his duties as factor during his absence, including some transactions with Simoneto.[12]

That October, Gabriele set up a consortium for handling the proceeds he would be receiving from his father's estate through executors: the Procurators of San Marco and his brother Simoneto.[13] The members of the consortium comprised his agent Giovanni de Restoro; the venerable priest Giovanni da Pozzo, archdeacon of the Greek colony of Negroponte; and the brothers Donato and Giovanni Corner. Da Pozzo later would be appointed Bishop of Citta di Castello in Umbria by Pope Gregory XII between 1407 and 1408, but this office was not officially recognized due to the schism; in this capacity he would entrust his nephew Simone I Bona De and Giovanni Corner with transactions including the estate of his mother.[14] The Corner brothers were members of a large and prominent noble family [not to be confused with the Correr], which included two of the most highly assessed individuals in Venice.[15] Both had been purchasers of silver ingots from the money changer Vielmo Condulmer in 1399, using each other as pledges.[16] The consortium set up by Gabriele was renewed the following March.[17] In August 1401, Simoneto and Gabriele, residual heirs of their father, gave executive power to the Venetian noble Fantino Querini, a merchant in Trani, to procure for them proceeds from an estate there due to their father.[18]

In this period, Gabriele began acquiring *commenda* at outlying ecclesiastical establishments. *Commenda* were titles to offices in ecclesiastic institutions such as monasteries, which gave regular income to their holders with no obligation to perform services or even visit the institution.[19] On November 7, 1401, Gabriele Condulmer made a procuration (power of attorney) document in which he gave Antonio Correr, identified as deacon of the church of Corone, power to collect his *commenda* income as prior of the Monastery of Sant' Agostino of Vicenza.[20] Both men were described as living in Venice (Gabriele in the parish of San Lunardo). The non-noble Gabriele was characterized as "venerabilis et circumspectus vir" (respected and circumspect man), while the noble Correr was "reverendum ac providum" (revered and notable man), conveying the difference in their civil as well as ecclesiastical status. This document constitutes the first attested connection between Gabriele and the Correr family. Antonio Correr had been ordained a deacon in 1396 by his uncle Angelo (then titular Patriarch of Constantinople) and was a priest in 1400 when he received a benefice from the canonical chapter of the Venetian colony of Corone.[21] Antonio's uncle Angelo had been Bishop of Castello (Venice) in 1379 before becoming Patriarch of Constantinople in 1390; his office of Apostolic Collector granted by Pope Urban VI in 1387 included jurisdiction over Vicenza.[22]

In April 1402, Gabriele, identifying himself as deacon and having his home and location (*domicilium et stacium*) in the Benedictine monastery of San Nicolo on the Lido, gave a receipt to Giovanni de Restoro for various transactions carried out and monies received on his own behalf and that of his brother Simoneto.[23] In September, Gabriele issued another receipt to Restoro but now identified himself as "presbiter," or priest, of the college of clerics of Sant' Agostino outside of Vicenza.[24] The document was made out at the station of Pietro dalla Spada, deacon of Santa Fosca in Venice; the witnesses to this document were the other members of Gabriele's consortium: Giovanni da Pozzo and Donato and Giovanni Corner.[25] On the same day, he named as his general agents Pietro Miani, deacon of Sant' Agostino, and Giovanni de Restoro.[26]

Gabriele would continue in his absentee role as prior of Sant' Agostino of Vicenza for several more years, as he held other ecclesiastical offices in Venice. On August 1, 1406, he entrusted the administration of Sant' Agostino to other Venetians.[27] He was identified as prior of Sant' Agostino in 1407, when appointed to papal office, but in that same year, he was replaced as prior by the Venetian Lorenzo Giustinian, who had been at San Giovanni Decollato of Padua and came to Vicenza with twelve secular canons.[28] Gabriele continued his claim on an income of 300 ducats a year from the priory, a claim settled finally in 1415 by Pope Gregory XII.

San Giorgio in Alga

On September 20, 1403, Gabriele (then aged between twenty-two and twenty-six) made a final receipt to Giovanni de Restoro for three years' worth of transactions on behalf of himself and his brother Simoneto; this would also be his last act notarized by Enrico Salomon.[29] In it, he identified himself as the priest Gabriele Condulmer, at present inhabitant of the monastery of San Giorgio in Alga, an institution that would be closely associated with him for the rest of his life. A Benedictine monastery had been in existence for centuries on the small island of Alga (algae) in the Venetian lagoon, near the mainland settlement of Mestre. Its prior had received gifts of land in Padua in 1203 and again in 1219.[30] In 1343, the Avignon pope Clement VI confirmed the prior of the monastery as head of the Augustinian order of Venice.[31] In March 1397, the Venetian Senate held a competition among candidates for the office of prior of San Giorgio in Alga with the intention of sending their recommendation for approval by the pope. The choice of the Senate was a brother Giacomo, prior of San Clemente; in third place among the nine candidates was the Venetian noble Ludovico Barbo "studens in artibus."[32] However, Boniface IX, pope of the Roman branch of the schismatic church, chose Barbo for the priorate; in his request, Barbo estimated that the annual proceeds of the monastery did not exceed 2,000 gold ducats.[33]

In September 1404, Barbo appealed to Pope Boniface to reform the rules of the monastery of San Giorgio in Alga, which he said had lapsed.[34] A new set of rules was approved for the congregation, the most important being that after Barbo left his position as prior, the members would elect on an annual basis a new leader called a secular prior or rector with no interference from outside. Barbo would continue to receive personally one-third of the revenues until his departure, but thereafter all revenues would be held by the chapter in common. No one could become a canon before the age of eighteen and only after a year of probation; admittance was by a vote of the chapter. Members of the congregation would be required to sleep in common dormitories, eat together in a refectory, and not leave the monastery without permission of the rector. To keep the members from being distracted from their religious duties, outsiders older than the age of eighteen and unmarried people could be brought in to do manual labor. It may be at this juncture that the congregation adopted the blue cloaks over white tunics that would give them the nicknames of Azurini and Celestini.[35] San Giorgio in Alga would remain the Venetian center of the Augustinian order; when the monastery of

Sant' Agostino was reformed in Vicenza in 1419, it adopted the Augustinian rule of the canons of San Giorgio in Alga.[36]

The 1404 papal act lists Gabriele Condulmer as one of seven priests received into the monastery of San Giorgio in Alga; it is evident from his notarized document of September 1403 cited above that he was already a member of the community. He was not, however, moving far from the world in which he had grown up. Among the other men listed as enrolled in 1404, there were two other members of the Condulmer house, neither of whose relationship to Gabriele is clear: Michele Condulmer, who became a deacon of San Giorgio in Alga, and Marco Condulmer, who became a subdeacon. Michele had been the witness to the February 1400 document in which Gabriele made his first general quittance (receipt) to Giovanni de Restoro; he is identified there along with Gentile Avonal as "both clerics and close associates (*confines*) of Gabriele."[37]

Gabriele Condulmer was not a member of the noble branch of his house; it is unknown whether Michele or Marco Condulmer were noble.[38] All of the other Venetians listed as becoming canons of the reformed San Giorgio in Alga were, however, members of noble houses and in some cases among the most prominent.[39] Antonio Correr, listed as a priest, was from one of the more modest noble houses, with only three households in the *Estimo*, none rising above an assessment of 600 ducats, placing them in the bottom two deciles. We have already encountered Antonio as the agent authorized by Gabriele in 1401 to collect his income from Vicenza; he was the nephew of Angelo Correr, who as Pope Gregory XII confirmed the reform of San Giorgio in Alga in 1407.

In September 1405, Gabriele appeared as a witness to a document in the court of Pope Innocent VII in Viterbo along with Antonio Correr, his fellow priest in San Giorgio in Alga.[40] In December 1405, the Venetian Senate took up the election of an abbot for the monastery of Santa Giustina of Padua. Thirteen men applied for the position, among whom were "Dominus Gabriel Condolmario, quondam domini Angeli" and "Venerabilis vir dominus frater Ludovicus Barbo, prior Sancti Giorgi de Alga."[41] Apparently both the prior Barbo and the new canon Gabriele Condulmer were seeking to move up to the role of abbot of a major monastery in the newly conquered mainland possession of Venice. The Senate took no vote on the appointment; the whole section is canceled with a large X on the page, and the notation in the margin states that it was canceled by an act passed by the Senate.[42]

A New Pope and New Opportunities

On November 30, 1406, a conclave of cardinals in Rome elected Angelo Correr as pope to replace Innocent VII, who had died two weeks earlier; he chose the name Gregory XII.[43] Gregory was the first Venetian ever to hold the papal office. In this period, the Catholic Church had been in a state of schism for three decades, with competing claimants to the title of pope centered in Rome and in Avignon in France.[44] At the time of the death of Innocent VII, a representative from France was in Rome seeking an end to the schism; he entered into an agreement with the Roman cardinals that they would choose a new pope who would vow to abdicate at the same time as the Avignonese pope did in favor of a universally recognized new pontiff.[45] Giordano Orsini, the cardinal who proposed the seventy-year-old Angelo Correr, declared that he did so for the specific intention of his renunciation of the office, as he was otherwise unqualified to rule the Church; the other cardinals followed suit.[46] As Pope Gregory XII, however, Angelo Correr turned out to be mainly interested in promoting his own financial interests and those of his family and supporters. Gregory kept the benefices of his prepapal titles, Patriarch of Constantinople and Bishop of Corone; in October 1407, he reserved for himself the title and benefices of the Archbishopric of Crete.[47] The total revenues of these offices were around 7,000 ducats a year.[48] In the end, he proved reluctant to cede his office.

Antonio Correr, son of the pope's brother Filippo, was to become his closest supporter. Gabriele Condulmer had named Antonio as his agent in 1401 to collect revenues from his *commenda* in Vicenza and had been his fellow priest at San Giorgio in Alga since 1404. Antonio became the papal treasurer in the court of his uncle in March 1407, a post he gave up that June for the office of papal chamberlain.[49] Antonio was considered to have so much influence over his aged uncle that he was popularly called the second pope.[50]

Gabriele Condulmer, who, as we have seen, was a business partner and brother priest at San Giorgio in Alga of the new pope's nephew Antonio, similarly benefited from Pope Gregory's patronage. On January 1, 1407, the newly elected pope issued a safe conduct to Gabriele to join him in Rome.[51] Just before leaving Venice, on January 20, 1407, Gabriele broke his commercial partnership with his brother Simoneto, who as we have seen in Chapter 5 had recently incurred huge liabilities from his failed bank, and ceded to him his rights over the unmovable goods of their shared patrimony, retaining only title to the family palace in Rio Marin.[52] On February 25 of that year, Gabriele was named clerk of the papal chamber and on June 13 took on the office of papal treasurer.[53] After Gabriele left Venice in 1407, he is recorded as having returned only once in the remaining four decades of his life, in 1415, for a brief stay with his brother Simoneto on the way to the Council of Constance.[54]

The papal curia did not stay in Rome for long after Gabriele's arrival there in January 1407. In December 1406, soon after his installation, Gregory had written to his French rival Benedict XIII and the Avignon cardinals to propose a meeting to seek an end to the schism.[55] In February, Gregory designated his nephew Antonio Correr as one of the three ambassadors to go to Marseilles to set up the meeting; they met with the Avignonese pope on March 17 and agreed on the neutral territory of Savona on the Ligurian coast as the site of a meeting. In the meantime, Gregory sought funds for the great show of military pomp that such a mission entailed, both from the Venetian state and by pawning the papal tiara to Florentine merchants for more than 7,400 ducats.[56] One of Gabriele Condulmer's first official acts as clerk of the papal chamber was to sell off books from the papal library for about 500 ducats on the same occasion.

The Venetian Senate first received the requests of the pope for assistance to travel for the reconciliation of the schismatic branches of the Church on March 2, 1407, and appointed a commission to look into it.[57] After much debate, a majority voted in July to deny him the five galleys he sought for travel to Savona on the grounds that the activities of the Genoese fleet under the French commander Marshal Boucicaut had made travel along the Ligurian coast dangerous for Venetian ships.[58] On September 4, 1407, Gregory and his entourage, which included twelve cardinals, as well as Gabriele Condulmer and Antonio Correr, arrived overland in Siena, a commune within the sphere of influence of Florence and generally loyal to the Roman side in Italian politics (Map 5).[59] A few weeks later, Benedict and the French cardinals arrived in Savona; at the beginning of 1408, they moved to Porto Venere, within the Tuscan area of the Ligurian coast, and then on to Pietrasanta.

On December 30, 1407, Gregory XII appointed Gabriele Condulmer as Bishop of Siena, with a special dispensation because he had not yet reached the age of thirty.[60] Despite the reported unhappiness of the Sienese at the election of the young foreigner, Gabriele reached an agreement on March 14, 1408, with the monks of the Sienese monastery of All Saints that they would recognize his exercise of the pastoral office, with the actual governance of the church to be carried out by a local vicar, Bartolomeo da Torri.[61] However,

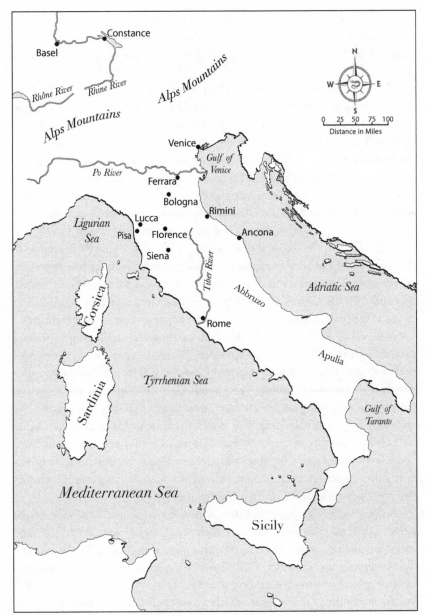

Map 5. Principal places in the life of Gabriele Condulmer.

within a month, Gabriele joined Gregory and his party as they moved on to Lucca, and there followed several months of negotiations to bring the two popes closer together both physically and in terms of cooperation to end the schism.

The situation was made more complicated when Ladislas of Durazzo, the young king of Naples and Sicily, attacked Rome in the spring of 1408, and Gregory recognized him as vicar of Rome in exchange for a remittance of 20,000 ducats to the papal treasury.[62] The alliance with Ladislas pushed the pope away from settling with his Avignon rival and alienated the cardinals who were with the pope in Lucca, most of whom were from prominent Roman families. In the meantime, there was a constant movement of representatives, official and unofficial, between the camps of the two popes, seeking to bring them together. One of the proposals that was brought to light in later testimony at the Council of Pisa was purportedly made by Leonardo of Arezzo, one of Gregory's secretaries, who proposed locking two representatives of each side in a room, with the presumption that Gabriele Condulmer and Antonio Correr, who had been monks, were used to abstinence and physical deprivation and would thus outlast any representatives of Benedict.[63]

In April 1408, frustrated by the lack of progress and fearing a further extension of the influence of Ladislas, the Florentine government proposed that both popes meet in Pisa. Antonio Correr and Gabriele Condulmer ultimately bore the blame among French and German critics for the refusal of Gregory to respond positively to the invitation.[64] On May 9, Gregory created four new cardinals, despite a vow at the time of his election not to do so.[65] One of these new cardinals was Gabriele Condulmer, Bishop of Siena and Clerk of the Papal Chamber, who became titular Cardinal Bishop of San Clemente; another was the pope's own nephew Antonio Correr, previously Bishop of Bologna, now Cardinal Bishop of Porto.

Immediately after the appointment of these new cardinals, nine of the twelve cardinals who had come to Lucca with Gregory abandoned him and met near Livorno with the cardinals who were simultaneously abandoning the Avignon pope Benedict XIII. These two groups of renegade cardinals began negotiations toward finding a third way out of the schism.[66] The following September, Gregory named nine new cardinals to replace those who had abandoned him, among whom were the Venetians Angelo Barbarigo and Pietro Morosini.[67] In this period, Gregory and his party, including Gabriele Condulmer, came under the protection of another patron: Carlo Malatesta, who exercised power in Milan and Mantua as well as in his ancestral lands of the Marches and Romagna.[68] Malatesta invited Gregory and his remaining followers to relocate from Lucca to Rimini on the Adriatic coast, where they arrived in November 1408.[69] From Rimini, Gregory sought to remove the Patriarch of Aquileia, a move opposed by Venetian senators, who singled out the malign and disloyal influence on the pontiff of the pope's nephew Antonio Correr ("nepos domini pape") and Gabriele Condulmer ("ille de cha' Condolmario" [that one of the house of Condulmer]).[70] It would appear that, at least in the eyes of Venetians, these two former monks were exerting controlling influence over the aged pope. In January 1409, Gregory appointed Gabriele vicar of the church of Constantinople, another title with no actual responsibilities but presumably significant income.[71]

The Council of Pisa

At the same time, the cardinals who had abandoned both popes met in Pisa, in what was to be the first ecumenical council of the Western Church not summoned by a pope. The Council of Pisa opened on March 25, 1409, and immediately sent envoys to the two recalcitrant popes seeking their participation.[72] Getting no response, they ordered that both popes and their respective supporters be held in contumacy against the church. An offer was made to the one old cardinal who remained with Gregory to join the council, but the four created recently by Gregory, who included Gabriele Condulmer, were not invited, as their promotion was regarded as null and without issue.[73] Meanwhile, the two rival popes negotiated in secret an arrangement that they would each continue to claim the title during their lifetimes, and when one died, the other would be recognized by all.[74]

Carlo Malatesta acted as an intermediary on behalf of Gregory and succeeded in getting approval from the cardinals at Pisa that should Gregory enter into an agreement with them, his nephew Antonio would remain a cardinal and even chamberlain. However, they balked at extending the same recognition to Giovanni de Domenico and Gabriele Condulmer, whom they characterized as "pessimos viros" (the worst of men) and dedicated to destroying the union of the church.[75] Gregory then rejected Malatesta's attempts to reach reconciliation with the Council of Pisa and instead called his own council, which ultimately met in Cividale, in Friuli, northeast of Venice, in June 1409.[76] In that same month, the Council of Pisa declared unanimously that both rival popes were schismatic and should be excluded from the Church and from the papacy and that the cardinals of the council should elect a new pope.[77] They then proceeded to elect Peter Phillarges of Candia in Crete, who had been named cardinal in 1405 by Gregory's predecessor Innocent VII, as the new pope, with the title of Alexander V.[78]

The new pope, Alexander, was from the island of Crete, a colony of Venice, so like Gregory a Venetian subject. This left Venice in a position of having to choose which claimant to the papacy to support, while taking into account all of the international ramifications of siding with one or the other. Venice sent an embassy to Pisa to meet with the cardinals in council there and maintained a dialogue with Carlo Malatesta, acting on behalf of Gregory and his followers in Rimini. In May 1409, as Gregory was sailing from Rimini to Friuli, the Senate considered a motion to send a delegation to meet him on the island of Torcello within the Venetian lagoon, but they voted it down.[79] Finally, in August 1409, the Venetian Senate voted on a motion to recognize Alexander V, chosen by the Council of Pisa, and to withdraw its support from Gregory; this was opposed by a motion to wait and see what sides the other major powers would take.[80] After a series of forty-one ballots over three days, the decision was made to abandon the Venetian Gregory XII (Angelo Correr) in favor of the Cretan Alexander V (Peter Phillarges).

Other than the six cardinals Gregory brought with him to Cividale, few other participants showed up at his council. Disguised as a merchant, Gregory soon fled to Gaeta, in the southern Italian lands controlled by Ladislas, where he was joined in January 1410 by Antonio Correr and Gabriele Condulmer.[81] On May 3, 1410, Alexander V died, and the Roman Baldassare Cossa was elected pope and took the name John XXIII. At this point, Ladislas abandoned Gregory in favor of the new Roman pope, in exchange for recognition of himself as king of Naples and ruler of the lands he had taken in the former papal states.[82] This left as Gregory's only possible ally Carlo Malatesta of Rimini, who was seeking to broker an arrangement that would finally end the schism, which now saw three claimants to the papal tiara.

In May 1411, Gregory issued a bull from Gaeta excommunicating his two rivals and their supporters and naming Carlo Malatesta rector of the papal province of Romagna.[83] In 1411, Sigismund of Luxembourg was elected German king and Holy Roman Emperor over the Bavarian claimant who had been an ally of Gregory, and in 1412 he extended recognition to John XXIII.[84] On October 30 of that year, Gregory XII left Gaeta, traveling with his remaining cardinals Antonio Correr, Gabriele Condulmer, and Angelo Barbarigo on two Venetian merchant ships and, facing pirates and bad weather in the

Adriatic, came to the Malatesta court in Rimini by way of the Corfu and the Dalmatian coast, arriving at court on Christmas Eve.[85]

Despite the setback to his career occasioned by remaining loyal to a pope abandoned by most of the rest of Christendom, including the government of Venice, Gabriele Condulmer's personal fortunes received a significant advance in this period. In March 1409, his brother Simoneto received on his behalf a total of 6,500 ducats deriving from their father's estate upon the deaths of three of their sisters.[86] In 1410, the Venetian courts adjudicated a case that the two brothers brought against their brother-in-law Pietro Diedo for transactions in 1396, awarding their joint fraternal company about 1,000 ducats.[87] In 1414, Gabriele sought the reinstatement of a payment of 300 ducats a year, compensation he had received in 1407 for the renunciation of his *commenda* of Sant' Agostino of Vicenza; Gregory XII sent a letter to the current rector of San Giorgio in Alga and to Lorenzo Giustinian asking for the money on Gabriele's behalf.[88]

The Council of Constance

The schism of the three popes was finally ended by the Council of Constance, summoned in November 1414 by King Sigismund. Carlo Malatesta acted as an intermediary between the camp of Gregory XII and the organizers of the council. The council opened in the Swiss city in November 1414, and on May 14, 1415, it deposed John XXIII, who had succeeded the pope chosen by the Council of Pisa.[89] Two weeks later, the council dealt with Gregory's wish to have the cardinals appointed by him (including Gabriele Condulmer) recognized as part of negotiations on his possible voluntary abdication.[90] On July 4, 1415, Malatesta conveyed to the council the intention of Gregory to abdicate.[91] Gregory himself informed his retinue in Rimini of his renunciation on July 9, saying that as he had been their father, he would henceforth be their brother.[92] The council then decided that the deposed former pope Gregory should be accepted as a cardinal and partake in the election of a new pope, along with those he had appointed as cardinals, including Gabriele, titular Bishop of San Clemente.[93] Carlo Malatesta directly addressed Antonio Correr and Gabriele in a letter that August, seeking their participation in the council.[94] In September 1415, Gabriele Condulmer stopped in Venice on his way to join the council, as did the other three Venetian cardinals of Gregory; he is noted as having stayed with his brother Simoneto in the family palace.[95] He appears first in the records of the Council of Constance on November 21, 1415, among the lists of cardinals in attendance as "Gabriele tituli sancti Clementis dicto Senensi."[96]

In January 1416, Sigismund carried on negotiations with Benedict XIII, the Avignonese pope, seeking his abdication and thus clearing the way for the election of a new, solitary pontiff. Gabriele Condulmer was among the cardinals who approved the report of these negotiations; he was present for most of the convocations throughout that year.[97] The Council of Constance finally declared the Avignon pope Benedict XIII schismatic and excommunicated in 1417. With all three claimants to the papacy removed, it was time to elect a new pope. In May 1417, while the other cardinals were in conclave for the papal election, Antonio Correr and Gabriele Condulmer were with King Sigismund, but in September they joined with the cardinals from the three previous obediences.[98] On May 26, Gabriele sent a letter from Constance to his brother Simoneto in Venice informing him of his and Antonio Correr's participation in the council's deliberations; the letter was distributed within the city and was copied into the chronicle of Antonio Morosini.[99] Sigismund arrived at the Council of Constance on November 4 with a plan for conducting the election and was met by opposition from Correr and Condulmer for not including any of Gregory's followers in the committee he proposed.[100] Though he participated in the sessions approving the rules for the papal election and accepting the selection, Gabriele Condulmer was not listed among the actual electors in the conclave of November 11, 1417, which selected Oddo Colonna as the new pope with the title of Martin V and thus ended the schism that had riven European Christendom for four decades.[101]

Gabriele Condulmer During the Papacy of Martin V

Martin V was from the prominent Roman Colonna family, which had held the papacy in the early Middle Ages and had competed with other local families for the papal tiara in the centuries before the schism. Though his election appeared to mark a return to an earlier era of dominance of the papacy by competing Roman families, the situation turned out not to be so straightforward. On the one hand, his papacy was soon challenged by a new Avignon pope, Clement VIII (1423–29), claiming the office with support of the Aragonese crown. More significantly, the Councils of Pisa and Constance had set a precedent for the growing power of ecumenical councils to challenge papal authority in the setting of church dogma and management of its political policy.

Throughout the reign of Martin V, from 1417 to 1431, Gabriele Condulmer played little if any role in the central administration of the papacy. In the *Book of Officials of Martin V*, he appears only in a listing of the cardinals who took part in the conclave that elected the pope.[102] Gabriele's only documented activity in the ecclesiastical world in this period is in the patronage of the constitution issued by Martin V on January 1, 1419, which set up a new congregation joining the monasteries of Santa Giustina of Padua, Santa Maria of Florence known as the Badia, San Giorgio Maggiore of Venice, and Santi Felice e Fortunato di Aimoni in the diocese of Torcello.[103] In 1430, he became commendatory (that is, nonresident) abbot of the merged monastic community, an office and income that he retained for the first decade of his papacy.[104]

Gabriele Condulmer did serve Martin V in the secular administration of the Papal States, areas of the Italian peninsula that had been under the political rule of the papacy before the schism and that Martin endeavored to return to papal obedience. Gabriele began this diplomatic service as a papal intermediary in a truce signed in Florence on June 5, 1419, between the town of Norcia and Rodolfo di Varano, lord of Camerino.[105] Gabriele's papal service under Martin V was mainly as papal legate to the cities of Ancona on the Adriatic coast of Italy and Bologna in the center of the peninsula; his presence in those cities alternated within the span of 1419 through 1424. Both cities were subject to claims of political domination by the pope as a secular lord but, at the same time, had deeply ingrained traditions of local governance by communal bodies and by families of local potentates. They were also caught up in an involved power play among various other forces in the peninsula, including the Kingdom of Naples to the south of Rome, increasingly coming under Aragonese dominance, and the city-states of Florence, Milan, and Venice. Moreover, Sigismund of Luxembourg, king of Germany and Bohemia, had taken an active role in Italian affairs, seeking papal recognition as Holy Roman Emperor with at least theoretical sovereignty over Italy.

Another threat to papal dominance in central Italy in this period was posed in the person of Braccio da Montone, a *condottiere*, or leader of an independent mercenary army, who sought to establish his own rule in the area. On August 17, 1419, Martin V instructed his legate in Bologna and the March of Romandiola to observe the truce made between Bologna and Braccio da Montone as worked out by "dilectum filium nostrum Gabrielem tituli sancti Clementi" (our dear son Gabriele, titular bishop of San Clemente), as cardinal and papal vicar in the March of Ancona.[106] When he arrived in Ancona as legate in March 1420, Gabriele proceeded to call a parliament, bringing together representatives of all of the towns in the district, at which he published a series of reforming constitutions.[107] However, the struggles of the local families of the Marches and the ambitions of the leading Ancona family of the Ferretti led to a breach between Gabriele and his sponsor, Pope Martin V.[108] On New Year's Day in 1421, Martin issued Francesco Ferretti a papal grant of safe conduct for himself and members of his family directed specifically against his own legate Gabriele.[109] Gabriele considered the Ferretti family a threat to his own power and ordered the imprisonment of several of the family members in Ancona. On January 13, the pope reacted to the breach of his grant of safe conduct by ordering Gabriele to free them and to leave the Ferretti family in peace.[110] A document of March 1421 that settled disputes between the Ferretti family and two other local families was signed by Gabriele as Bishop of Siena, Legate of the Marches of Ancona, sitting as tribunal in the episcopal palace in which he lived.[111]

Much of the work that Gabriele did as papal legate was routine, such as the confirmation of the rights of patronage of the church of San Giorgio of Fabriano over that of Santa Caterina of the same city, issued in Recanati on September 1, 1421.[112] This large formal document, issued in the name of Gabriele as Cardinal Priest of San Clemente, Bishop of Siena, and Papal Legate to the March of Ancona, bears his seal in red wax attached at the bottom (Figure 20). The unpublished seal depicts the Last Judgment at the top and has the Condulmer arms visible on the right side of the bottom. The closest published seal is, perhaps not surprisingly, that of Antonio Correr, Gabriele's former business and monastic partner, whose seal depicts the Ascension rather than the Last Judgment, perhaps displaying a difference in temperament between the two former close associates.[113]

As we have seen in Chapter 5, Gabriele used his control of the prison in Ancona in support of the commercial interests of his brother Simoneto in the 1423 dispute over oil in Ancona, where his role as papal legate put him in a position to favor his family's interests.[114] One of his positive contributions to Ancona was his efforts to repair the city's port, in the course of which he met a young citizen serving on the commune's committee, Ciriaco d'Ancona, who would become famous for his accounts of his travels and the Greek and Roman antiquities he observed on them.[115] Gabriele was recalled from the position as Legate to the Marches in the summer of 1423; Ciriaco, who had already completed significant travel in Greece, followed Gabriele to Rome and stayed at his house for forty days while surveying Roman antiquities.[116]

Figure 20. The seal of
Gabriele Condulmer as Papal
Legate to Ancona, John
Hinsdale Scheide Manuscript
Collection, Document 7788,
Ancona, 1421, Princeton
University, Princeton, NJ.
Published with permission
of the Princeton University
Library.

In 1425, Gabriele brought charges before a papal commission in Rome that he had not been fully paid his salary for his time in office in Ancona.[117]

One lasting result of Gabriele's stay in Ancona is that he appears to have learned some Greek during this time. Immediately after Gabriele's election to the papacy, Ludovico da Cividale, a monk in Zara on the Dalmatian coast, wrote a dialogue on papal power in which he asserted that he had stopped in Ancona on his way to Greece and spent four months as a guest of the papal legate Gabriele Condulmer, during which time Ludovico instructed his host in "Grecas literas," playing the role of Socrates to Pericles and of other ancient teachers of rulers.[118] Though the dialogue includes such rhetorical elements as a dream of the papal election the night before the news arrived, there is no reason to doubt the account of the earlier instruction in Greek. As the detailed minutes of the later Council of Ferrara-Florence are lost, there is no record of Eugene having spoken Greek with members of the visiting Byzantine delegation or in the public sessions, but such linguistic ability would certainly have been an asset in these negotiations.

Gabriele's activities as legate to Bologna were intermittent episodes in his ongoing position as legate to Ancona. In June 1420, he wrote to Simoneto from the region of Modena to inform his brother, and presumably the rest of Venice, of the recent events of the war between Bologna and Braccio da Montone.[119] Braccio had seized the town of Orvieto from Bologna, and Gabriele served as papal emissary in arranging a truce among all parties. On July 21, Gabriele Condulmer made a triumphant entrance into Bologna as papal legate there.[120] A month later, Martin V sent Cardinal Alfonso Carrillo as his permanent legate to Bologna, and Gabriele returned to Ancona.[121]

In 1422, however, Carrillo proclaimed an open alliance with the Visconti of Milan, and Gabriele was called back by the pope to Bologna. Gabriele was openly pro-Florentine, and in September, the papacy concluded a defensive league with Florence and disavowed the league to the Visconti.[122] After another papal legate to Bologna fled the city because of the plague, Martin again recalled Gabriele to the post. In January 1424, Gabriele's nephew, Angelo, son of Simoneto, had a commercial document drawn up in Bologna, in the "palace of the cardinal," presumably the quarters that Gabriele maintained there.[123] It appears that Gabriele drove a hard bargain to be recalled to this plague-ridden problem spot. According to Florentine sources, Alfonso Carrillo's salary as legate in Bologna in 1420 had been 650 florins a month, but Condulmer is said to have bickered over the amount offered him, which the Florentines reported to have been 4,000 florins a year against his demand of 6,000, still less than that given to his predecessor.[124] In June 1424, Braccio da Montone was killed in a siege of Aquila. With the greatest threat to peace in the papal states removed, Martin again recalled Gabriele Condulmer from Bologna, replacing him with the papal chamberlain, the pro-Milanese Lodovico of Savoy.[125] At this point, Gabriele returned to Rome, leaving both of the posts as papal legate in which he appears to have concerned himself mainly with secular affairs.[126] In 1425, he took part in the restoration of the Roman church of San Paolo fuori le Mura, and in 1426 he sponsored the petition of his relative Marco Condulmer to continue to receive his commendatory income as deacon and canon of Patras while pursuing his studies.[127]

On September 28, 1425, Martin V charged Gabriele with reform of the Benedictine monastery of Santa Giustina of Padua.[128] Since 1419, when Martin had taken a leadership role over other northern Italian congregations, Santa Giustina had risen to be a major center of reformed monasticism thanks to the leadership of Ludovico Barbo, who had been abbot of San Giorgio in Alga in Venice when Gabriele joined it in 1404. In 1430, Gabriele became commendatory abbot of San Giorgio Maggiore in Venice, within the orbit of Santa Giustina, probably an honorary title with accompanying remuneration, a position he held through most of his papacy, until 1441.[129] On February 22,

1431, two weeks before his papal election, Gabriele received 333 ducats at the death of his stepmother, Franceschina.[130]

All told, Gabriele Condulmer was in service as a troubleshooter in the political affairs of the papal state from 1419 to 1424, that is, only during the first half of the fourteen-year reign of Martin V. His service was marked by conflicts with the pope both in the matter of the Ferretti family of Ancona and the relationship of Bologna with Milan and Florence, respectively. For the remaining seven years of Martin's pontificate, Gabriele seems to have been in Rome, attending to local and family business and living off his inheritance and the income from his benefices.

The Election of Gabriele Condulmer as Eugene IV

Martin V died in Rome of a stroke on February 20, 1431, at the age of sixty-two. His successor would be the first pope elected in Rome under traditional circumstances in over a century; preceding elections had either taken place in Avignon, in Rome but with competing claimants abroad, or through council meetings in Pisa and Constance. Election to the papacy was traditionally, as it still is today, the purview the College of Cardinals, churchmen appointed by preceding popes to mostly honorary (suffragan) positions as heads of various churches in Rome. At the time of the sudden death of Martin V, there were twenty-five living cardinals recognized as legitimate.[131] The senior cardinal and undoubted favorite papal candidate at the time was Giordano Orsini, who had been elevated by Innocent VII in 1405 on the same occasion as the naming of three cardinals who had subsequently become pope: Angelo Correr, who became Pope Gregory XII in 1406; Peter Phillarges, who became Alexander V in 1409; and Oddo Colonna, who became Martin V in 1417.

As Martin's death was sudden and in winter, there were only fourteen electors in Rome for the conclave that began ten days later on March 1, 1431, in the church of Santa Maria sopra Minerva, a Dominican monastery built atop a pagan Roman temple. According to a Bolognese chronicle, at the beginning of the conclave, the Romans sealed all of the gates of the city out of fear of violence.[132] On March 2, the cardinals who were present issued a public memorandum stating their conception of the Church and the pope they were electing. It was a manifesto of papal monarchy with the consent of the cardinals, proclaimed in defiance of the conciliar sentiment developed at

Pisa and promulgated at Constance that sought to give powers to a broader representation of church leaders who attended the councils and participated in their theological and political pronouncements, as well as in their selection of popes.[133]

On March 3, Gabriele Condulmer was elected pope and took the name Eugene IV.[134]

The election of Gabriele as pope might seem unlikely, as he had neither family background nor a reputation for piety or theological learning; his recent stints as a political representative of the papacy in Bologna and Ancona had resulted in mixed success at best. As the deliberations were secret, there is no record of the proceedings of the conclave, so our knowledge of the election of Gabriele Condulmer as pope relies on secondary reports, especially the correspondence of the Sienese ambassador Pietro Antonio de' Micheli, who was present at the conclave.[135] According to Micheli, peninsular politics were at play in the election, as were local loyalties. Milan was in favor of someone supporting King Sigismund, while Venice and Florence sought a "Guelf" candidate, that is, one opposed to imperial and Milanese forces. Giordano Orsini had the advantage both of his seniority and of belonging to a cohort of cardinals that had already produced three popes; he had the liability of being from a powerful Roman family that was a longtime rival of the Colonna family of Martin V. His candidacy was opposed by adherents of the Carthusian monk Nicolo Albergati, who had the support of the Colonna faction (which included Gabriele's former close associate Antonio Correr), but as Albergati had not made it to Rome in time for the conclave, his supporters switched to Alfonso Carillo, the candidate of Milan and Siena. Neither Orsini nor Carillo got the required two-thirds of the votes on the first two ballots, and in the end the Orsini faction switched its support to Gabriele Condulmer. Perhaps it was his longtime relationship with the pro-Colonna Antonio Correr, reaching back to their business and monastic relations over the past three decades, that made him seem the best compromise candidate.

There is no obvious reason for Gabriele's selection of Eugene IV as his papal name; the previous pope Eugene had been a twelfth-century Cistercian from Pisa, who was a promoter of Crusading ventures. It may be that the notion of the involvement of the papacy in the revival of military actions against Muslims, in this case Turks, was on Gabriele's mind at the time of his election, a preoccupation that would result in the disastrous Crusade of Varna thirteen years later. Another possible explanation for the choice of name is the Greek meaning of the word εὐγενής (well born) for a pope who wished to escape the stigma of his illegitimate and non-noble birth.

Pope Eugene and Venice

Eugene IV was the second Venetian pope, or the third if one includes Alexander V, Peter Phillarges of the Venetian colony of Crete, who reigned as the choice of the Council of Pisa from 1409 to 1410 in opposition to Gregory XII. The reign of Gregory had been tumultuous, and he had soon lost the support of the Venetian government. Gabriele—unlike Gregory, who was from the noble Correr family—was from a non-noble branch of the Condulmer house, another branch of which had been admitted into the nobility only a half-century earlier. In the sixteen years of his papacy, Eugene never visited his home city but maintained a continuous stream of interaction with it, ranging from the closely collaborative to the openly confrontational. This communication was generally through the actions and letters of Venetian ambassadors or more properly spokesmen (*oratores*), usually drawn from the highest ranks of the government, who maintained a residence with the papal court for a year or two at a time and regularly presented reports to the Senate, either through letters or brief return visits. Through the registers of Senate deliberations, we can follow not only the evolving relationship between the pope and his home city but, especially in the instructions to new ambassadors, discern power dynamics within the papal curia.

News of Gabriele's election reached Venice on March 8, 1431.[136] On March 9, even before his formal investiture, the Senate selected eight ambassadors to go to Rome, supplying each with 100 ducats for a new velvet robe and funds for a contingent of eleven men to accompany each ambassador.[137] Among this party was Pietro Diedo, the husband of Gabriele's sister Cristina. We encountered Pietro earlier as the respondent to a suit brought by Gabriele's brother Simoneto in 1410 (in which Gabriele was also a plaintiff of record) and plaintiff against Simoneto two years later.[138] On Sunday, March 11, there was a torch-lit procession of the Venetian clergy and members of the lay confraternities, bringing their relics to the Piazza, followed by a solemn mass in San Marco.[139]

The first sign of friction between Venice and the new pope was in June 1431, when the Senate grudgingly recognized Gabriele's personal claim to the *commenda* of the Monastery of San Giorgio Maggiore, which he had received a year earlier, with the stated understanding that it would remain a chapel of San Marco, itself technically the ducal chapel.[140] In July of that year, Eugene, facing a famine in Rome, sent two representatives to Venice to ask for assistance in the form of two galleys to bring grain from Ancona to Rome; these representatives were the Venetians Giovanni Diedo and Antonio Condulmer, his very distant relative from the noble branch of the house.[141] As an "oblation" gift for the new Venetian pope, the Senate granted this request by a virtually unanimous vote (there was one abstention among 131 ballots). The expedition ended the following February, and the two galleys, commanded by Antonio Condulmer and Alvise Bembo, then joined the regular Venetian guard fleet.[142]

The election of Gabriele to the papacy had left only one Venetian cardinal, his old associate Antonio Correr, who was rumored to be in very poor health.[143] In September 1431, Eugene appointed another Venetian to the Curia: Francesco Condulmer, reputed to be his nephew.[144] This was to be one of only three cardinals he would name in the first eight years of his pontificate. In the same period, word came to Venice that Eugene had brought another member of his family into his inner circle in Rome, Marco Condulmer, said to be the son of his late brother.[145]

Soon after coming into office, Eugene issued a set of instructions to his chamberlain, Francesco Condulmer, to revive the minting in Rome of gold ducats resembling those of Venice ("secundum ducatos venetos") as had been done in the past.[146] The undated Roman ducats of the fourteenth century had been issued by the Roman Senate in close imitation of those of Venice, with Saint Peter substituted for Mark and the kneeling pope substituted for the doge; there had been no gold coins issued in the name of earlier Roman popes of the fifteenth century. The first issue of ducats of Eugene followed the same format as those of the previous century but added a small shield with the Condulmer arms below the staff of the banner on the obverse (Figure 21a). At some point in the reign, the Condulmer arms under a papal tiara took over the obverse of the coin, with Eugene's name and title displayed around them; the image of Peter was moved to the reverse, and Christ disappeared completely (Figure 21b). A third issue added the papal keys between the Condulmer arms and the tiara (Figure 21c).

In 1432, in a secret session of the Venetian Senate, instructions were given to the ambassador to Rome, Andrea Dona, to bring to the pope's attention its concern over a matter involving the personal honor of Gabriele that could damage his reputation—the presence in his bedchamber staff of a certain

S. PETRVS |SEN|ATOR VRBIS   ROMA CAPVT MVNDI SPQR

Figure 21a. Papal gold ducat of Eugene IV, mint of Rome, 1431–1447. Reproduced courtesy of Künker & Co. Osnabrück.

EVGENIVS.PP.QVARTVS   S.PETRVS BONONIA

Figure 21b. Papal gold ducat of Eugene IV, mint of Bologna, 1431–1447. Reproduced courtesy of Künker & Co. Osnabrück.

+EVGENIVS. PP.QVARTVS   S.PETRVS . ALMA ROMA

Figure 21c. Papal gold ducat of Eugene IV, mint of Rome, 1431–1447. Reproduced courtesy of Künker & Co. Osnabrück.

Pietro di Monza.[147] Though the concerns were couched in terms of the possible employ of Pietro by the Duke of Milan, a papal enemy, the expanded repetitions several months later of the warnings against the continued familiarity of the pope with this attendant and the doubts and perils that the relationship might raise about the pope's "person," coupled with the recommendation that the young man be given a canonate in Verona, suggest that the concern over the scandal caused by the relationship might have been more personal than

political.[148] In the meantime, Eugene went against the Venetian policy of having the state oversee religious institutions in the city by instructing the Bishop
of Castello and two other church officials to perform regular visitations of
all Venetian monasteries, enunciated in a bull that the Senate sought to have
changed.[149]

As part of its legacy, the Council of Constance had established a precedent for ongoing conciliar meetings; at the time of the election of Gabriele
to the papacy, such a council was meeting in Basel.[150] The struggle between
the pope and the ongoing Council of Basel over their relative competencies
in the governance of the church posed the greatest potential source of stress
between Eugene and the government of Venice, as it did to much of Christendom in general. This situation came to a head in 1432, with the travel to
Basel of Cardinal Antonio Correr, Gabriele's old colleague of three decades
standing. In March, Correr told the Senate that he was contemplating going
to Basel with their approval; they told him to seek such approval from the
pope.[151] A month later, the Senate communicated to the pope that Correr
had left Venice for Basel a few days before.[152] Antonio Correr appears in the
records of the Council of Basel as having arrived there on April 2, 1433, and
having celebrated a Christmas mass that year attended by King Sigismund;
at the council, he was given responsibility over a reform of the calendar
on the basis of his expertise in astronomy.[153] In July 1433, it became public
knowledge in Venice that Cardinal Antonio Correr had left the court of Pope
Eugene "with great confusion and little honor."[154] In August, the Venetian
Senate was informed that Correr had been working against the pope in Basel
and withdrew its support of him.[155] On September 20, 1433, Antonio Correr
left Basel to rejoin the pope.[156]

For a brief moment in 1433, Eugene seemed to put the opposition forces
at bay with his coronation of King Sigismund of Luxembourg as emperor;
such an imperial coronation was one of the few powers that all sides agreed
was exclusively papal. Eugene took full advantage of this prerogative, sum-
moning Sigismund to Rome in May 1433 for a lavish ceremony that he hoped
would establish his own primacy in the public eye.[157] Venice issued a special tax levy to support the subsidy that it sent to the pope for the emperor's
expenses, but when the pope sent word that he would like to accompany the
emperor on his visit to Venice, the Senate turned him down, decreeing that
Sigismund was welcome to come alone.[158]

Eugene's moment of glory was fleeting. Soon after the coronation of Sigismund, a popular uprising in Rome, urged on by agents of the Duke of Milan

and the Colonna faction (whose support had allowed him to be elected three years earlier) and proclaiming itself as acting in the name of the Council of Basel, made the pope's life in Rome so problematic that he asked the Venetian ambassador to seek aid in his fleeing the city.[159] The Senate offered him the use of three Venetian galleys currently in the Tiber but expressed its opinion that the best way for him to put an end to the opposition from the Council of Basel would be for him to appear there personally.[160] In May 1434, a mob of Romans seized Cardinal Francesco Condulmer, the pope's kinsman and chief adviser, made him climb on horseback, and held him prisoner first in the church of Santa Maria Oracieli, then in the Campidoglio, and finally in the Castel Sant'Angelo; this attack was reported to have been led by Angelo Fusco, a Roman whom Eugene had named cardinal at the same time as Francesco.[161] The pope fled to Florence, from whence he issued an order on July 12, 1434, dropping all charges against eight Romans arrested in the uprising in exchange for the liberation of Francesco Condulmer.[162] Pope Eugene IV would not return to Rome for almost a decade.

The Council with the Greeks

Shortly after fleeing Rome, Eugene appointed Cristoforo Garatone as apostolic nuncio to travel to the East to pursue unifying the Armenian church with that of the West and meeting with whatever other prelates he might encounter there.[163] In November, Eugene wrote to the Council of Basel about his plans for a union of all Christian churches, an effort that was to be the signal initiative of his reign.[164] The Byzantine emperor had sent his emissaries to Basel, seeking western support against the encroaching Turks; they had arrived there in July, just as the pope was leaving Rome. An agreement in principle was worked out at Basel in September 1434, which the pope signed onto the following month.[165] In August 1435, Eugene sent Garatone back to Constantinople to work out a meeting between the emperor and the Council of Basel that would be more advantageous to his own position.[166] The emperor responded to him in November, after meeting with Garatone (who spoke Greek), with agreement to the general principles, noting that his representatives in Basel had given a list of places that would be suitable for him; given the age of the Byzantine patriarch Joseph II, these would have to be easily accessible by ship.[167] A division arose within the Council of Basel on the question of the location of the meeting with the Byzantines, with one faction securing ships from Nice with the support of Savoy and Genoa to send an embassy to Constantinople and the other seeking Venetian support for their own representatives.[168]

Venice, not surprisingly, sought to make its own advantage of such an intervention in these proceedings. It was willing to advance the cost of four galleys for the transport of the Greeks to such a council plus two armed galleys and three hundred crossbowmen to protect Constantinople while the delegation was away.[169] The main request to the representatives from Basel in exchange for all of this was to have the meeting held in Friuli, a land that had long been contested between Venetian influence and that of surrounding powers to the north and east. At the same time, Venice extended its general treaties with Byzantium for another five years.[170] With the destination of the Greek visitors still unsettled, both parties prepared to set out for Constantinople in the summer of 1437.

By this time, Pope Eugene had taken a central role in the preparation of the Venetian convoy, assisted by various members of his family and his circle of favorites. In June 1437, the Venetian Senate acknowledged that the Council of Basel had refused to hold the meeting with the Byzantine emperor in Friuli and noted that the pope was Venetian and hence much more inclined to the honors and benefits of the homeland.[171] It agreed to supply him with a small galley for taking his representatives to Constantinople and then three great galleys for bringing the imperial party to Italy; the emperor and his retinue would sail on his own Byzantine imperial galley. The ships were to be outfitted at papal expense and provided with captains from among the Venetian nobility on the condition that the council be celebrated either in Venetian or papal lands. The Senate also approved a loan to the pope of 70,000 ducats if the council was held in Venetian territory.

Just before the Venetian ships arrived in Constantinople, however, Eugene issued a bull transferring the Council of Basel to Ferrara, dashing the Venetians' hopes for having it in their territory.[172] The move to Ferrara was accompanied by advantageous terms offered by its ruler, Nicolò d'Este, and may have been viewed by Eugene as a more neutral location than Venetian territory in terms of the political and military conflicts of northern Italy, and perhaps more likely to attract the recalcitrant members of the Council of Basel.[173] Venice grudgingly accepted the choice of Ferrara rather than Friuli for the new location on the condition that it not interfere with its ability to wage war in the region beyond the Po; the move, however, was viewed as a papal slap in the face to his home city, which had supplied the ships that made the emperor's presence possible.[174]

Nevertheless, Venice prepared a grand reception for the emperor and his retinue. In December, the Senate authorized 1,000 ducats for the preparation of the Venetian palace of the Marquess of Ferrara (known now as the Fondaco dei Turchi) as lodging for the emperor and that of the Veronese nobleman Ludovico dal Verme for the Byzantine patriarch, with other members of the delegation to be lodged at the Monastery of San Giorgio Maggiore.[175] The Greeks arrived in Venice on February 8, 1438, and were suitably impressed by their reception, their lodgings, and the riches of San Marco.[176] They stayed in Venice for three weeks, debating whether to proceed to Basel for the council there or to Ferrara, where the pope awaited them with those who had abandoned Basel. After a visit from the Venetian doge, the Greeks decided to join the pope in Ferrara, partly because it was much closer and also because Cardinal Giuliano de Cesarini, who had presided over the Council of Basel since it opened in 1431, had joined the papal side.[177] Eugene did not come to his home city of Venice to take part in the reception of his imperial guest; instead, he awaited him in Ferrara.

The Greek delegation arrived in Ferrara on February 28, 1438, where the council was already in session.[178] The council was later transferred from Ferrara to Florence in December 1438, ostensibly because of plague in Ferrara, but financial aid offered by Lorenzo de' Medici was probably also a factor in the move.[179] On July 6, 1439, an agreement proclaiming the union of the Latin and Greek churches was signed in Florence.[180] The Greek party arrived back in Venice on September 6, 1439, to discover that the emperor's personal galley had burned as the result of an explosion in the Venetian Arsenale and that the trade galleys on which they had planned to return to Constantinople had already departed.[181] While they waited in Venice, a mass in Eastern liturgy was celebrated in San Marco, which the Byzantine emperor supported in opposition to his recalcitrant clergy but did not himself attend.[182] Finally, on October 19, the Greek party left Venice on ships they had to charter on their own, with crews they believed to be unqualified Slavs and with accommodations they considered no more comfortable than those provided to enslaved Scythians being transported from the Black Sea.[183]

The Council of Ferrara-Florence was a signal success for the pope; the Council of Basel gradually lost influence over ecclesiastic affairs, though it officially deposed Eugene and appointed a replacement who took the name

Felix V.[184] Venice also received good publicity from the venture and cemented
its reputation as Europe's window on the Greek world, not least of all with
the welcome of Bessarion, Metropolitan of Nicaea, whose eventual gift of his
library would establish Venice as the center of Renaissance and early modern
Hellenism.[185] However, the ever-weakening military position of Byzantium in
the face of Turkish expansion would render the union of its church with the
Latin one moot and would also put Venice in the position of publicly favoring a losing side.

Pope Eugene and Venice After the
Council of Ferrara-Florence

While the council was meeting in Ferrara, word came to Venice that Pope
Eugene was planning to name his chamberlain and relative, Francesco Condulmer, to the recently vacated Bishopric of Verona, a mainland city that
had been resisting Venetian rule since its conquest three decades earlier.[186]
After several votes, the Senate conveyed to the pope its fervent desire that
this crucial office not be granted in *commenda* to an absentee holder, as had
become the practice with most of the principal monasteries in the region and
also with the bishoprics of many of Venice's maritime colonies. In December,
shortly before the council moved from Ferrara to Florence, Eugene sent word
to the Venetian Senate that he had indeed installed Francesco in the office,
and the Senate grudgingly accepted the appointment with the expressed
hope that Francesco would exercise the office in a manner that would please
the discontented Veronese populace.[187] Venice came into direct conflict with
Eugene in 1440, when Francesco, acting as Bishop of Verona, sought to exercise civil authority over Giovanni Memmo, a Venetian nobleman resident
there; the conflict was still unresolved six months later.[188]

   In this period, Pope Eugene became increasingly involved in the complex military and political struggles for territories in Italy among the cities of
Milan, Florence, Genoa, and Venice; the claimants for the throne of Naples;
and the various lords and *condottieri* who were contesting for military dominance. In this effort, Venice supplied half of the funding for two thousand
horsemen and a thousand foot soldiers toward Eugene's effort to reestablish
papal control over Bologna in the face of Milanese pressure.[189] This support
was explicitly offered in return for the pope's recognition of Venetian sovereignty over the territory of Ravenna, which like Ancona and Bologna, was

contested among the papacy, a local communal government, and a local patrician family.[190] In 1440, Eugene arranged a general treaty among Genoa, Florence, and Venice, which Venice objected to when it learned that one of the promises Eugene had made to Milan was to have Venice cede to it the cities of Brescia and Bergamo.[191] Nevertheless, the Venetian Senate continued its support of the papal army, now including the *condottiere* Francesco Sforza, with Venice agreeing to pay 12,500 ducats a month toward the support of three thousand horsemen and a thousand foot soldiers.[192] This alliance was threatened in 1442 when word came to Venice that Pope Eugene had suddenly made a concord with its enemy the *condottiere* Niccolò Picinini, who had captured Bologna.[193] The complex conflicts between the goals of Pope Eugene and those of Venice would not be resolved until after 1447, when Eugene's death was followed by that of Filippo Maria Visconti, leading to Francesco Sforza's inheritance of the Duchy of Milan.[194]

The Crusade of Varna

The final troubled interaction between Gabriele Condulmer and his home city occurred when Venice participated in the so-called Crusade of Varna, an effort of the pope to follow up his ecclesiastical alliance with Byzantium with a military defense of the Greek empire against the Turks. Venice, however, had established diplomatic relations with the Turks as well as the Byzantines; in 1436 a delegation from the Ottoman ruler had been received by the Senate and sent away with lavish gifts of clothing, cloth, and money to offset the expenses of their return.[195]

In January 1444, Pope Eugene entreated Venice to join an armada to prevent Turkish forces from crossing from Asia to Europe by blocking access to the Strait of Gallipoli, thereby controlling the entrance from the Mediterranean to the Sea of Marmora and the Bosporus.[196] The Senate gave instructions to arm its auxiliary galleys that were stationed at the various Venetian Aegean colonies and send them to its port of Negroponte (Chalkis in Euboea); these were to be joined by the main Venetian guard fleet under the command of the Captain of the Gulf. The Senate also summoned Francesco Condulmer, who was in his diocese of Verona, to come to Venice and take charge of the fleet. Francesco insisted that Alvise Loredan, the prestigious Procurator of San Marco, be made captain of the galleys in the name of the pope; Venice agreed.[197] Eugene pledged that 1,200 ducats of papal exactions from the clergy would be available to pay the extra wages of the sailors (*refusuras*) when the ten galleys returned, as well as 10,000 ducats from a general collection of tithes.[198]

In all, seven galleys armed by the pope, eight galleys and other ships of the Venetian state, and four of the Duke of Burgundy set out in July 1444.[199] The Venetian fleet stationed itself at Tenedos, at the mouth of the strait, awaiting the arrival of a land army from Poland and Hungary heading for the Bosporus. Supplies for the sailors began to run short by October.[200] In late October, the main Turkish army under Murad, which had earlier crossed into Asia Minor across the Strait of Gallipoli, returned to the European side unopposed by crossing the Bosporus above Constantinople rather than via the strait.[201] In November, the pope relayed a request from the land armies led by Cardinal Giuliano Cesarini and King Ladislas of Poland and Hungary for support from the Venetian galleys in the strait.[202] Nevertheless, the fleet remained at Tenedos in the strait rather than sailing north into the Bosporus to join with the land army. On November 10, 1444, the Christian and Turkish armies fought at Varna, on the Black Sea just south of the Danube Delta, with no support from the great fleet, which was still anchored at Tenedos. Though the results were uncertain for several days, the battle was in the end a decisive Turkish victory and both Cardinal Cesarini and King Ladislas were killed, though rumors persisted of the survival of Ladislas.

Even after the battle, the Venetian-papal fleet remained through the winter at Tenedos. Venice sent repeated messages to the pope telling of the hardships endured by the sailors and urging him to send the funds promised for their pay upon return.[203] The pope responded by promising to send 10,000 to 12,000 ducats to the ships for provisions, somewhat offending the Venetians by using Genoese bankers rather than their own.[204] By March, Venice was alarmed by the threats posed to its colony of Negroponte and to such areas of its influence as Albania and Rhodes by the tying up of its defense fleet in Tenedos.[205] Word came to Venice in April from the pope that Francesco Condulmer had decided to keep most of the galleys at Tenedos, allowing a few to return to Venice, at which point the Senate reminded him of the money promised for returning sailors.[206] Meanwhile, Venice wrote to Alvise Loredan, its captain of the fleet at Tenedos, instructing him to endeavor to make a treaty with the Turks for the benefit of its merchants, using gifts of from 500 to 600 ducats; if that failed, he was to bring back all of the galleys except that of Francesco.[207]

In May 1445, the galley captained by Antonio Condulmer, which had borne the papal emissary Cristoforo Garatone, arrived back in Ancona, with its captain dead and the ship in terrible condition; Venice asked the pope for the money to repair it and pay those of its sailors who had not fled in Ancona.[208] Nevertheless, Francesco Condulmer stayed in Constantinople with the remaining galleys, hoping to revive the crusade against the Turks; the Venetian Senate instructed Loredan that if he could not persuade Condulmer to return, he should bring back two more galleys and try to persuade the Burgundians as well to return before the onset of winter.[209] Finally, Francesco Condulmer and Alvise Loredan returned to Venice with the eight remaining galleys on January 10, 1446, and Francesco departed for Rome five days later.[210] A month later, Venice negotiated a treaty with the new sultan Mehmed II.[211] In Rome, where the pope had finally returned from exile in 1443, Eugene and Francesco began to make plans for a new crusade; the response of Venice called attention to the number of its sailors who had perished on the last such venture and the others who were in extreme poverty because of the failure of the pope to supply funds for their return payment.[212]

On February 23, 1447, Pope Eugene IV, born Gabriele Condulmer, died in the Vatican palace, at an age between sixty-six and seventy.[213] There was little reaction to the news in Venice. The first notice of this event in the records of the various Venetian governmental bodies was the instruction given on March 3 for a new ambassador to be sent to Rome and to meet with the cardinals in conclave there to get their approval for sending an envoy to the king of Aragon in support of the league between Venice and Florence.[214] On March 20, in response to a letter from the new pope, Nicholas V, the Senate unanimously authorized the sending to him of a letter with fulsome praise for his qualities and another one urging him to support the accords Venice had reached with his predecessor Eugene, along with letters to Francesco Condulmer and the Venetian cardinals Alvise Trevisan and Pietro Barbo seeking their support.[215]

Gabriele's Sexuality

It is difficult to form a complete picture of the man Gabriele Condulmer and the Pope Eugene IV. Until 1400, when he would have been between nineteen and twenty-three years old, he seems to have been a typical Venetian businessman, investing in various ventures abroad and at home, often in partnership with his brother Simoneto, who was at the time entering the economic elite as one of four principals of one of the few banks of the city. In commercial documents of the next few years, Gabriele identified himself successively as a subdeacon of San Michele, a deacon of San Nicolo of the Lido, and finally, in 1403, as a priest in the island monastery of San Giorgio in Alga, at which point he seems to have left commercial life; in 1407 he transferred all of his wealth to Simoneto, except for his rights to a house in Venice that he would never occupy.

There is no record of what brought Gabriele to a career in the Church. There was a practice among Venetian patricians to keep the patrimony together by having brothers live and do business together as a *fraterna,* or for the elder one to marry and the younger one to enter the Church.[216] This does not, however, appear to have been the practice of the wealthy non-noble branch of the Condulmer house: both of Meneghello's sons, Marco and Fiornovello, had set themselves up as the heads of family groups, as had Fiornovello's two sons Marco and Angelo, and Angelo's older sons (and Gabriele's brothers) Leonardo and Simoneto.

As he was well furnished by his father with an inheritance and as Simoneto's bankruptcy would not happen until 1405, after he had taken his vows, Gabriele seems to have chosen an ecclesiastical career in response to a genuine attraction to the religious life rather than to practical necessity. He gathered significant income from *commenda,* which he retained through his papacy, so it was clearly not a life of poverty that attracted him. Though early biographies praise his pious abstinence and humility, there is no sign of these qualities in the documentary record; the 20,000 ducats he donated to San Giorgio in Alga according to Vespasiano da Bisticci, one of his earliest biographers, appears to be just as fictitious as the mysterious hermit who appeared at his door at the monastery and predicted he would be pope.[217]

It may be that one of the attractions of monastic life—and religious life in general—for Gabriele was its all-male context, removed from the Venetian expectations of marriage and family relationships.[218] The island monastery of San Giorgio in Alga, with a dozen upper-class young men living under a relaxed rule, would no doubt have been attractive in this respect. The episode shortly after Gabriele became pope in which the Senate warned him of the scandal to his personal honor and reputation caused by his relationship with Pietro di Monza, one of the attendants of his bedchamber, suggests a preference for relationships with young men that went beyond the spiritual, as do the extended stays in his home of the young men Ciriaco d'Ancona and Ludovico da Cividale. It is, of course, possible that Gabriele's own remarkable rise within the Church was furthered by sexual relationships with senior clerics, the two most obvious being his longtime associate Antonio Correr or, in the more typical Renaissance pattern of the liaison between a rising young man and a powerful older man, with Antonio's uncle, Pope Gregory XII.[219]

Pietro di Monza left the pope's bedchamber staff soon after the relationship became notorious, but his position appears to have been taken up by a much longer-lasting favorite, known to history variously as Alvise Trevisan, Master Ludovico of Venice, and Ludovico Scarampi Mezzarota. In May 1432, the papal chamberlain ordered payments of 25 gold florins each to Pietro di Monza, Ludovico of Venice, and a third "cubicularius," or bedchamber attendant, for secret reasons on behalf of the pope.[220] In the course of 1433, Trevisan received a total of 3,400 florins from the papal treasury for unspecified reasons.[221] Trevisan traveled with Gabriele to Florence in 1434, where he appears to have entered into a close relationship with Cosimo de' Medici.[222] Alvise Trevisan proceeded through a series of papal appointments to ecclesiastical offices, as well as friendships with well-known humanists, serving as Bishop of Florence during the papal conference there and chief *condottiere* for the Florentine forces at the victorious battle of Anghiari; he ended up as Patriarch of Aquileia, the political as well as religious head of the fertile district of Friuli to the northeast of Venice that was crucial to Venetian international politics. In 1440, Eugene made him a cardinal.[223]

Perhaps the most willful, and remarkable, expression of Gabriele's affection for a young man is contained in an unpublished and apparently unstudied papal bull of 1435 in the Archivio di Stato of Venice.[224] In it, Eugene grants to his acolyte Giovanni, son of Stefano, "formerly Scaramelli, now Condulmer," the use of the name Condulmer and entry into the family. Adoption does not appear to have been a common phenomenon in late medieval Venice and would seem to have been out of the question in the case of a priest, let alone a pope.[225] Giovanni appears in papal documents the following year with the surname Condulmer.[226] Three years later, in 1439, when the pope was in Florence for the great council, Giovanni Condulmer, identified as his acolyte, sued a tailor in Florence for 5 florins he had given as a deposit for clothing he had not received.[227] In 1440, Eugene granted the vacant canonries of Padua and Verona, along with their annual benefices of 150 ducats and 100 ducats, to his acolyte Giovanni Condulmer.[228] Identifying himself as Doctor of Decretals and Canon of Padua and Verona, Giovanni Condulmer took part in the 1443 competition for the Bishopric of Treviso; he received only 6 of the 131 votes cast.[229]

Eugene's Legacy

Shortly after Gabriele's death, his cousin Francesco Condulmer commissioned the sculptor Isaia da Pisa to carve a monument to Gabriele for Saint Peter's Basilica in Rome; it was installed at the top of the north aisle by 1455 (Figures 22 and 23).[230] When Old Saint Peter's was demolished and replaced by the sixteenth-century building, the tomb of Eugene IV was moved across the remains of the nave and re-erected next to that of his nephew Paul II. In the final stage of the elongation of the nave, the monument was moved to the church of San Salvatore in Lauro, a Roman establishment of the canons of San

Figure 22. Isaia da Pisa, funerary monument of Eugene IV, 1455, Rome, Pio Sodalizio dei Piceni. Published with the permission of the Department of Visual Art, University of Bologna.

Figure 23. Isaia da Pisa, funerary monument of Eugene IV, detail, 1455, Rome, Pio Sodalizio dei Piceni. Published with permission of the Fondazione Federico Zeri, Bologna.

Giorgio in Alga. In the mid-nineteenth century, it was removed to the adjoining oratory of the Pio Sodalizio dei Piceni, a charitable foundation, where it currently graces a conference hall.

Images of Gabriele did remain on view in Saint Peter's, on the doors made by the sculptor known as Filarete (Antonio Averlino), which Eugene had commissioned in 1433 and that were finally installed in 1445, shortly before the pope's death.[231] These famous doors were among the few elements of the old church reinstalled in the new Saint Peter's in the sixteenth century: they were placed at the center entrance of the atrium of the basilica. In one of the large central panels, Gabriele Condulmer kneels before Saint Peter, who hands him the keys that will make him Pope Eugene IV, a scene analogous to that on Eugene's first papal ducat (Figure 24, cf. Figure 21a). On another, he crowns the kneeling Emperor Sigismund, the most successful moment of his reign (Figure 25). The image of the Byzantine emperor John VIII kneeling before the seated pope at Ferrara depicts an act that is not documented and scarcely credible (Figure 26). In a scene of the Council of Florence, both leaders are seated, but the pope is on the right side and seated on a platform,

Figure 24. Filarete (Antonio Averlino), bronze doors, 1445, Rome, Saint Peter's Basilica: Gabriele Condulmer receiving the papal keys from Saint Peter. Wikimedia Commons, public domain by Sailko.

so above the emperor (Figure 27). The depiction of Eugene in these images is rather generic, with an emphasis on his robes and tiara, but it does in general depict an individual with the same full face and deep wrinkles as that of the tomb effigy.

There are no monuments in Venice to Gabriele Condulmer or to other members of his house; his conflicts as pope with the Venetian state did not engender a positive reputation for him or his relatives in papal office. Gabriele Condulmer's affairs in Venice were handled after his death by Nicolo

Figure 25. Filarete (Antonio Averlino), bronze doors, 1445, Rome, Saint Peter's Basilica: Pope Eugene IV crowns Emperor Sigismund. Wikimedia Commons, public domain by Sailko.

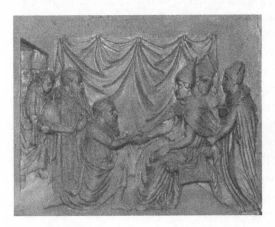

Figure 26. Filarete (Antonio Averlino), bronze doors, 1445, Rome, Saint Peter's Basilica: Byzantine emperor John VIII kneels before Pope Eugene IV. Wikimedia Commons, public domain by Sailko.

Figure 27. Filarete (Antonio Averlino), bronze doors, 1445, Rome, Saint Peter's Basilica: Byzantine emperor John VIII and Pope Eugene IV at the Council of Ferrara-Florence. Wikimedia Commons, public domain by Sailko.

Contarini, husband of Simoneto's daughter Cataruza, who in 1449 was ordered to pay 300 ducats that Gabriele had pledged in 1426 for the dowry of his relative Francesca Condulmer, daughter of Marco, who had married the Veronese nobleman Lotario dal Verme. Verme had died before the marriage could be consummated, but the debt for the dowry was upheld two decades later.[232]

A full assessment of Gabriele's papacy is hampered by the lack of a complete publication, or even a register, of his bulls and other pronouncements; even his speeches at the crucial council of Florence have not come down to us. Nor are there published sermons, treatises, meditations, or commentaries on sacred texts. His published bulls demonstrate a great interest in monastic reform, in the sense of providing existing monasteries, mainly those following the Benedictine rule, with a version of the rule of the Augustinian canons as practiced at San Giorgio in Alga. While in theory this reform would have actually loosened such vows as those of poverty, isolation, and physical labor, it is difficult to gauge how rigorous observance had been in the houses before his reforms. There is little record of his involvement in theological questions or in the church practices that were stirring up calls for reform among the followers of Hus and Wycliff; his opposition to and avoidance of the Council of Basel, which did seek to deal with such issues, seems to have been based primarily on the struggle for power within the Church between the papacy and the conciliar movement.

The aspect of church governance that Eugene IV seems to have responded to with the most enthusiasm was the pursuit of the political and military achievements of the papal state, in essence establishing it as a power on equal footing with the secular states of the age and placing himself on a footing with kings, counts, dukes, and marquesses. In these diplomatic and military engagements, he showed no favoritism to Venice or its allies. He particularly antagonized his native state by ignoring its wishes to hold the council for the union of the churches within Venetian territories, by appointing his relative and first assistant Francesco as absentee bishop of Verona counter to the explicit pleas of the Venetian Senate, and by leaving Venice uncompensated for the payments to the crews of the galleys supplied for his doomed crusade, which put Venice at a disadvantage relative to the Turks with which it was forming commercial and diplomatic ties.

CHAPTER 7

The Aftermath

After the distinctive and sometimes dramatic lives led by the members of the House of Condulmer in the decades following the Black Death, the family appears to have slipped into the ranks of those of the lower level of the nobility or the upper level of the *cittadinanza*, or more particularly those families with members in both social levels. The descendants of the various family members presented in this book lived, for the most part, lives with little drama or notoriety.

The Noble Descendants of Jacobello Condulmer

Jacobello's son Pietro Condulmer entered the historical record in an inauspicious way. In 1368 he was convicted of having snuck into the palace of Michele Dolfin three times to have sex with the enslaved Rubea; he was fined and paid 62.5 ducats.[1] He acquired personal wealth in 1374: the dowry brought by his bride Cristina was a very substantial 1,650 ducats.[2] In 1376, as the war with Genoa was brewing, he was captain of a cog that was captured by the Genoese.[3] Pietro must have been emancipated from his father by 1379, as he appears in the *Estimo* in his own right with an assessment of 1,000 ducats. As Jacobello's pledge for entry to the nobility included the participation of his sons Pietro and Zancolo in the war galleys, along with two servants, we can presume that he served in this capacity from 1379 to 1380. Jacobello's entrance to the Great Council entitled Pietro to be elected to offices reserved for nobles. He was elected as Supervisor of Malamocco, on the Lido, in 1384; in 1387, as captain of the coast guard squadron of the Marches; and in 1388, as Rector of Valmareno near Treviso and as general captain of small boats (*barcharum et ganzarolorum*) with a salary of 35 ducats a year.[4]

Pietro's wife, Cristina, died in 1380, leaving him no children; her family of birth is unknown. Her will shows her to have retained much personal wealth.[5] She made Pietro one of her executors and left him 350 ducats; another of her executors was an aunt Madaluza (married to Pietro, son of Minello Condulmer), to whom she left 250 ducats. Among her many generous benefactions was 30 ducats to the Hospital of Saints Peter and Paul, of which her father-in-law, Jacobello, had been a procurator.

In 1391, Pietro Condulmer, son of Jacobello, wrote out his will.[6] Pietro's will reveals him to have been in a very different position, personally and financially, from that of his father. He prefaced his bequest with a sad notice: "Note that I have dispensed many expenditures and labor for recovering the rights of my late mother, Agnesina, so that there does not remain much." He had not remarried after Cristina's death but had fathered three children by a woman named Costanza, to whom he left 40 ducats. He left the 350 ducats inherited from his wife and whatever other residue there might have been from his goods to these illegitimate children.

The other surviving son of Jacobello, Zancolo, was an original member of the Confraternity of Merchants founded by his father.[7] The 1370 will of his noble wife, Lena da Molin, left 30 ducats to their son Bernardo, who was then not yet sixteen.[8] Like his brother, Zancolo must have done galley service in the War of Chioggia. Zancolo was elected official of gold cloth in 1384, captain of the archers in Friuli and estimator of Grado in 1385, silver official in Rialto in 1386, and castellan of Belforte in 1387.[9] He was one of four residual legatees in the 1391 will of his brother Pietro to receive a share of the meager estate should all three of Pietro's illegitimate children predecease him.

Zancolo's son Bernardo Condulmer appears as a noble member of the confraternity of San Giovanni Evangelista in a listing dating from about 1387.[10] In 1388, he was elected as one of two supervisors of boats for the sestier of Cannaregio, an office held only by noblemen.[11] In 1394, the "nobilis vir" Bernardo Condulmer of Santa Croce successfully brought suit against Marco Filacanevo for an investment of 80 ducats.[12] In 1399, Ursia, Bernardo's sister and Jacobello's granddaughter, married the noble Paolo da Mosto with a substantial but far from extravagant dowry of 500 ducats.[13] In 1427, their son Giovanni was presented for membership in the Great Council by his mother, Ursia.[14]

The Heirs of Vielmo Condulmer

The 1421 will of the ostentatious money changer Vielmo provided lifetime income from bonds to his widow, his sister Isabeta, and his brother
Filippo. As instructed in Vielmo's will, the Procurators of San Marco sold
all of his possessions other than those left to his wife and put the funds in
state bonds. His widow, Clara, is not known from documents after Vielmo's death. His sister Isabeta continued to receive her payments from the
Procurators as late as 1456.[15] The residue of Vielmo's estate was to go to his
brother Filippo; if he died without heirs, the interest on the state bonds was
to be applied in perpetuity toward providing novitiate fees of young Venetian women entering convents. Filippo is described as a *sensèr*, a broker or
go-between, as a witness in a slave sale in 1429; according to the sixteenth-
century genealogical tables of Marco Barbaro, he had three sons and at least
two grandsons.[16]

The Progeny of Franceschina Condulmer

Franceschina Condulmer died in 1431. An entry in the account books of the
estate of her late husband, Angelo, who had predeceased her by thirty-five
years, records the dispersal of 1,000 ducats on that occasion.[17] One-third
went to two surviving daughters of her stepson Simoneto—Cataruza Contarini and Franceschina Barbo; one-third went to her daughter Polisena;
and one-third was recorded as going to her stepson "Pope Eugene, formerly
Cardinal Gabriele." As Gabriele was not to be elected pope until the beginning of the following month, it appears that Franceschina had died just a
few weeks short of seeing the greatest success among her children, and the
executors inserted his title into their account books after her death. It is
difficult to gauge the degree that the rise in social standing of the children
of the non-noble Angelo Condulmer was owed to his wife, Franceschina,
but the marriage of three stepdaughters and two daughters into the nobility
during her more than thirty-six years of widowhood, as well as the support
of the ecclesiastical careers of a stepson and grandson who became popes,
must have derived to a great extent from a concerted effort on her part
for the social mobility of the family that she had married into and made
her own.

The Successors of Simoneto Condulmer

Little is known of the activity of Simoneto's son Angelo beyond his appearance in court in the 1424 case involving oil transactions in Ancona. In the same year, he is mentioned as being in Bologna at the palace of the cardinal, that is, his uncle Gabriele Condulmer.[18] A genealogy inserted at an uncertain date in the estate record of Simoneto's father, Angelo, lists Simoneto's only son as Angelo, along with five daughters, four of whom continued the practice of the previous generation of his branch of the family by being married into noble families—the houses of Contarini, Gradenigo, Caotorta, and Barbo.[19]

In 1420, Cataruza, one of Simoneto's five daughters, married Nicolo Contarini, a member of one of Venice's most prestigious noble families, which had produced a recent doge.[20] Contarini was to serve as the executor in Venice for the goods of Simoneto's brother Gabriele after he became pope in 1431. In 1439, Nicolo Contarini represented Gabriele in the Court of Procurators in his successful claim for the palace in the parish of San Simeone Profeta that Simoneto's father, Angelo Condulmer, had left to his wife, Franceschina, after her death, and which Gabriele had retained a claim on when he ceded the rest of his Venetian assets to Simoneto in 1407.[21] In 1449, Cataruza was sued as the heir to her uncle Gabriele, the late pope, for claims on part of a dowry that Gabriele had promised in 1426 on behalf of his cousin Marco's daughter Franceschina.[22] In 1455, Cataruza brought claims to the Court of Procurators, who dealt with questions of inheritance, as sole heir of Gabriele against the estate of her sister Maria Caotorta, heir of Simoneto, for land that had belonged to the brothers' father, Angelo.[23]

In 1428, Franceschina Condulmer, daughter of the late Simoneto, married the noble Giovanni Barbo son of the late Paolo.[24] Little is known of Simoneto's daughters Elena and Loicha; on October 10, 1437, they went together to a notary to make out their wills.[25] Both named their mother's brother Gasparino da Mosto and their sister Cataruza as executors; Loicha also named all four of her sisters as executors, while Elena named her own husband, Francesco Gradenigo, and Cataruza's husband, Nicolo Contarini, as executors. However, Elena's husband, from a ducal family, remarried that same year, so she must have died soon after making out her will, as the unmarried Loicha may also have done.[26]

In 1435, Simoneto's daughter Maria made out her will in which she named her husband, the noble Girolamo Caotorta, as her executor and as residual executors her sister Cataruza and her husband, Nicolo Contarini, as well as two cousins in the noble Barozzi family.[27] In 1465, Maria's daughter Eugenia, represented by her husband, Nicolo Loredan, sued her aunt Cataruza for her share of her mother's estate.[28] Among the many expenses she enumerated in this very long court case were the payments she had made in 1454 to the creditors of her grandfather Simoneto as a result of charges lodged against her by the Merchant Consuls, resulting from the failure of the Benedetto-Condulmer bank a half-century earlier.

The Papal Nepotism of Gabriele Condulmer

Nepotism, the promotion of relatives (literally nephews) of the pope to important and well-paying positions within the church, was a well-established phenomenon by the time of the election of Gabriele Condulmer. We have seen how the first Venetian pope, Gregory XII, gave offices to his own nephew Antonio Correr as well as to Antonio's business associate and fellow monk Gabriele Condulmer, supposed by some contemporaries and modern scholars to have also been his nephew. The next pope, Martin V, had made one of his nephews, Prospero Colonna, cardinal before his death and had entrusted much of the papal treasury to other members of his family.[29] In the course of his papacy, Gabriele involved four members of his house in high papal office. In the cases of Francesco, Marco, and Antonio Condulmer, this may have been out of a sense of trust and familiarity or part of a general desire to promote his family name beyond his home city. In the case of his nephew Pietro Barbo, the result, if not necessarily the intention, was to initiate a papal dynasty.

Francesco Condulmer

The most visible other member of the Condulmer house in evidence in Rome at the beginning of the papacy of Eugene IV was Francesco Condulmer. Although sources, even some Venetian ones, identify him as Gabriele's nephew, he was in fact the son of Gabriele's first cousin Marco, son of Fiornovello and brother of Gabriele's father, Angelo.[30] He is identified as *protonotarius* of the Apostolic See in Venetian documents of 1429, so he must have come to Rome to fill this position in the later years of the pontificate of Martin V, when Gabriele was still a cardinal.[31]

Francesco is identified in papal documents as *protonotarius* and vice chamberlain within a month after Gabriele's election to the pontificate in March 1431; he soon took on the title of chamberlain (*camerarius*).[32] In August of that year, the Venetian Senate approved the granting in *commenda* to Francesco of the abbacy of the Benedictine monastery of San Pietro Rosazzo in Aquileia.[33] In September, Eugene appointed his first two cardinals (and the only two of his first six years in office), one of whom was Francesco Condulmer. He named Francesco Cardinal Priest of San Clemente, the suffragan church to which he himself had been appointed in 1408.[34] According to hostile testimony given later at the Council of Basel, Francesco had to be instructed in grammar at that point, as he had never learned Latin.[35] He retained his title of vice chancellor but was replaced in the office of *protonotarius* by Fantino Dandolo, who had been one of the ambassadors sent by Venice to welcome the new pope; there was consternation in Venice that Dandolo, grandson of the famous doge Andrea, was not himself named as a cardinal.[36] In November 1431, when Eugene issued a bull to dissolve the Council of Basel and replace it with one in Bologna, Francesco was one of four cardinals endorsing the measure (Antonio Correr, the old comrade of Gabriele, did not sign).[37]

In 1432, Eugene granted the Bishopric of Narbonne in France to Francesco; this absentee *commenda*, which paid an annual benefice of 9,000 florins, was revoked by the Council of Basel in 1436.[38] For the next two years, Francesco played a leading role in the diplomatic activities of the papacy, including the coronation of Sigismund as emperor and the negotiations for the succession to the kingdom of Naples.[39] In May 1434, an uprising of Romans, purportedly led by Cardinal Angelo Fusco (whom Eugene had named cardinal on the same occasion as Francesco), targeted Francesco as the most visible representative of papal power, capturing him and holding him in the Castel Sant'Angelo as a hostage in exchange for the transfer of that ancient building and papal stronghold to the communal government.[40] The pope refused to exchange the freedom of his relative and administrator for the castle and fled to Florence; Francesco was freed and joined the papal party only in December.[41] He immediately resumed his role as papal diplomat, involved in the question of Sicilian succession, the papal pact with the Malatesta, as arbiter in a dispute with the Este, and as participant in the negotiations between Venice and Emperor Sigismund over the status of Friuli.[42] As a reward, Eugene granted him further distant benefices: the Bishopric of Amiens in 1436 and the Archbishopric of Besançon in 1437.[43]

On March 4, 1438, Francesco Condulmer was one of four cardinals des-ignated to receive the Byzantine emperor and his retinue on their arrival in Ferrara.[44] He delivered the papal payments for the expenses of the legates to Constantinople, including those who had defected from Basel, such as Nich-olas of Cusa, and to the captains of the galleys that had carried the Greeks, including Antonio Condulmer.[45] For the next year and a half, Francesco took care of the finances of the council, first in Ferrara and then in Florence, cater-ing to the demands of the often discontented Greeks, and finally paying a Florentine goldsmith for the four lead bulls that sealed the Decree of Union of the Churches.[46] On October 1438, as we have seen, Eugene appointed him Bishop of Verona, an office he held until his death. In that year, he also became vice chancellor of the Church, that is, head of the pontifical chancellery.[47]

Francesco Condulmer's most important role in world history, and the greatest test of his talents, came with his leadership of the fleet that Eugene and Venice sent in 1444 to protect Constantinople against the Turks. Our best account of Condulmer's actions in the crusade comes from the chronicle of Jean de Wavrin, who was on the Burgundian fleet that accompanied the Vene-tians.[48] He reports that while the Burgundians were in the Bosporus trying to keep the Turks from crossing, Francesco was in Constantinople urging the emperor to send a land army to support the Hungarians.[49] After the battle of Varna, Francesco heard a rumor that the king of Hungary had survived the battle, was assembling a new army, and would return to Greece in the sum-mer. He led a few of the Venetian ships along with some of those of the Bur-gundians to try to sail up the Danube to support this rumored new Hungarian army. When the small fleet was at Silistra, about three hundred miles up the Danube, the Venetians took down their sails and refused to attack the city. The Burgundian captain attributed the delay to Condulmer's cowardice and said, "When you appoint a priest leader in war, no good can come of it." According to Wavrin, however, the truth was that Condulmer had received word that the town was heavily garrisoned by Turks and his decision was credited by the chronicler with avoiding a massacre of the European forces.[50] Nevertheless, it was a fool's errand in search of a phantom king; after going aground where the river became shallow, the galleys had to row back down the Danube to the Black Sea. They arrived in Constantinople in November 1445, with just enough time to get back to Venice before another winter set in.

Francesco arrived back in Rome via Venice on February 15, 1446, where he was given the title of Cardinal Priest of Porto and Santa Rufina.[51] He was present at the death of his patron and cousin Gabriele in February 1447 and took part in the conclave that elected his successor Nicholas V.[52] In 1449, he left Rome for two months to stay at the spa of Puteoli and then joined the Curia of the new pope in Spoleto.[53] He died in Rome on October 30, 1453, in the house built for him on the ruins of the Theatre of Pompey.[54]

Marco Condulmer

Another "nephew" of Gabriele who enjoyed papal favor during the reign of Martin V was Marco Condulmer, who first appears in documents in 1420 as deacon and canon of the Latin church in Patras, a Greek city under Venetian control; in 1426, he was given permission by Martin V to keep the income from these offices while serving Gabriele or attending university.[55] His actual relationship to Gabriele is uncertain; according to the Morosini Chronicle, he was the son of a late brother of Gabriele, probably Leonardo.[56] In hostile testimony at the Council of Basel, Marco was said to have been an apothecary before becoming a cleric.[57] In 1429, Marco was sent out of Patras to meet with a Byzantine delegation seeking to take over the city; the fact that he and the Venetian official were accompanied by an interpreter suggests he may not have been fluent in Greek at this time.[58]

Upon Gabriele's election in 1431, Marco Condulmer joined the papal service in Rome as castellan of the Castel Sant'Angelo.[59] In January 1432, Eugene appointed him to fill three vacancies in southern France simultaneously: the rectorate of the Comtat-Venaissain, the general vicariate for the Comtat and Avignon, and the Bishopric of Avignon.[60] In the face of local opposition, Marco had to leave the Comtat and find refuge in Provence; the states of the Comtat later removed themselves from obedience to him, without prejudicing their fidelity to Eugene.[61] In 1433, the pope made Marco legate to Bologna, his own office under Martin V, and soon transferred him from the see of Avignon to that of the Tarantaise in Savoy, where he became archbishop.[62] Marco went to Bologna in February but was imprisoned by local uprisings in May and again in June.[63] He represented the papacy before the Venetian Senate in the period from 1434 to 1437.[64]

In 1437, Marco Condulmer was appointed to his most significant role, as head of the delegation sent by the pope to Constantinople to arrange for the presence of the Byzantine emperor and the patriarch for the council leading to the union of the Latin and Greek churches.[65] He was also given extraordinary powers to minister to communities of Greeks who might choose to follow Latin rites.[66] En route to Constantinople, he encountered the chronicler Phrantzes, who recalled having met him eight years earlier at Patras.[67] In his account of the voyage to Venice, Sylvester Syropoulos credited Cristoforo Garatone as the artisan of the future union, but reported that Marco Condulmer, the legate, defended the Venetian navigators during a calm by crying out to the passengers in Greek that the navigators could not produce a suitable wind from their own lungs.[68] Once the party had arrived in Venice in February 1438, Marco rushed to Ferrara to report to the pope.[69] That same month, he was inducted as Patriarch of Grado and in May would be made exempt from all papal taxes because of his role in the union of the churches.[70] Marco was the eleventh Latin prelate to sign the document of the union of the churches in July 1439, the second noncardinal (the first was the titular patriarch of Jerusalem).[71]

Marco Condulmer was again called into service in the East for Eugene's papacy on the occasion of the galleys sent to Constantinople for the Crusade of Varna. In May 1443, he came to Venice as the papal representative for collecting the tithes for the fleet to Constantinople; the Senate agreed to the levy but directed that all the Venetian funds be held toward the cost of outfitting the galleys.[72] In December 1444, Eugene appointed Marco nominal Patriarch of Jerusalem at the death of the previous patriarch, Giovanni Vitelleschi, a former papal *condottiere*.[73] In January 1445, as the depleted crews of the disastrous mission to Gallipoli were on their way home, Eugene designated Marco as the supreme leader of a new crusade against the Saracens and charged him with raising an army to protect Greece and Cyprus from the Turks.[74] This idea of a crusade died with Eugene two years later; Marco stayed on in papal circles for another fifteen years, dying around 1460.[75]

Antonio Condulmer

By virtue of being great-grandson of Jacobello, who entered the Great Council in 1381, Antonio Condulmer was a member of the nobility, unlike any of the members of Gabriele's branch of the house.[76] He was presented for admission to the Great Council in 1413, so he was probably born around 1395.[77] As his father, Bernardo, was apparently already dead by this point, his nomination came from Giacomo Erizzo, the noble husband of Gabriele's sister Ursia. The only civil office he held was as one of the three heads of the Council of Forty in 1428, an office commonly held at the beginning of a young man's political career.[78] His professional life was as the owner and captain of a cog, a sailing vessel whose activity was outside the control that the state exercised over its commercial and military galleys (that is, ships powered by oarsmen as well as sails). He is documented as being the captain of cogs to Syria in 1421, 1426, 1427, 1428, and 1430; to Valencia in 1422; and to Flanders in 1429–30.[79] In 1425, he captained an armed sailing ship that accompanied other merchant vessels to Constantinople in the face of the threat of attack by Genoese ships aiding the Turks.[80] As a member of the Great Council, he was eligible for election to Venetian offices, in his case the most important being patron (that is, captain) of a state galley, but before Gabriele's election as pope in 1431, he had not succeeded in the auctions for patronage of the state commercial galley nor been appointed captain of one of the military galleys.

In July 1431, Antonio Condulmer (identified as a noble) appeared before the Senate on behalf of the pope, asking for two Venetian galleys to be provided to him to bring grain to Rome; the Senate agreed on the condition that the expenses of fitting out the galleys be paid by the pope.[81] A papal order of safe conduct for this expedition names Antonio as a papal shield-bearer (scudiero).[82] In February 1432, two Venetian galleys captained by Alvise Bembo and Antonio Condulmer, were fitted out at the expense of the pope and set out to join the Venetian military fleet; the fleet returned to Venice in October.[83] These expeditions at papal expense appear to have opened up for Antonio regular service to the Venetian state. In January 1433, he was elected patron of one of the cogs of the commune.[84] The next year he succeeded in the auction of patronage of one of the commercial galleys to Flanders, paying 616 ducats, the largest pledge of the six patrons; as travel in the western Mediterranean was especially dangerous in this period, the 1434 Flanders fleet was given a subsidy of 5,000 ducats.[85]

Antonio Condulmer entered world history in 1437 as the captain of the fleet sent by Venice under papal patronage to bring the Byzantine party to the council for the union of the churches. For this he received a payment of 5,000 florins from the papal treasury, paid out over the next two years.[86] Syropoulos reports that when the representatives from the Council of Basel arrived in Constantinople two weeks after the papal galleys, Antonio Condulmer tried to physically block their disembarkation and was personally reprimanded by the Byzantine emperor.[87] During the council, he was in Ferrara, although a power of attorney he drafted with a Venetian notary listed his residence as Bologna.[88] For the return voyage after the council, the fleet consisted of a new imperial galley (built to replace the one that had burned in Venice during the council), two state galleys of the Romanian type, and a pilgrim galley owned by Andrea Gritti; all were under the direction of Antonio Condulmer as captain.[89] The account book from the flagship of this fleet (one of the only extant

Figure 28. Account book of the ship carrying the Byzantine delegation back to Constantinople in 1439. The cover shows the papal arms of Eugene IV. ASVe, Spirito Santo, Pergamene, B.4. Published with permission of the Archivio di Stato, Venezia.

medieval Venetian ship's accounts) bears on its cover the papal Condulmer arms in full color (Figure 28).[90]

In March 1444, Antonio Condulmer returned to service for both the pope and Venice as the lead captain of the fleet that was sent to Gallipoli to support the Byzantine emperor.[91] The battered "galea condolmaria" was one of the earliest to leave the straits, returning to Ancona in May 1445, bearing the papal legate Cristoforo Garatone and the body of its captain Antonio Condulmer, who had perished at age fifty during the voyage.[92] His relationship to his distant, non-noble relative Gabriele appears to have been based on personal devotion, as well as, perhaps, professional advancement: he named a son Gabriele, born in 1430, a year before his namesake's papal election, and another son, born three years later, Eugenio.[93]

Pietro Barbo

Pietro Barbo was born in 1417; as we have seen, he was the son of Polisena Condulmer, half-sister of Gabriele, and the brother of Paolo, who was one year older.[94] In 1434, Eugene granted a fief in the diocese of Aquileia to the brothers Paolo and Pietro, and in the following few years, Paolo pursued a career as a cavalry soldier.[95] The younger brother, Pietro, seems to have spent the next decade in the papal court of Eugene, serving as *protonotarius*. He accompanied his uncle during the stay of the papal court in Bologna, from 1426 to 1438, and was named archdeacon of Bologna in 1437, earning the scorn of the Bolognese for his association with Gabriele, whose period as legate there was remembered with acrimony.[96] He was made cardinal by his uncle in 1440, at age twenty-three, and succeeded Antonio Correr in 1440 as absentee holder of the Bishopric of Cervia.[97] He was given a *commenda* of a monastery in Friuli in 1441 and one in the district of Padua in 1445.[98] By this time, he was papal chamberlain and was present at Eugene's death in 1447.[99] He became Bishop of Vicenza in 1451 but had other ecclesiastics administer the office, which he held until his election as pope in 1464 when he took the name Paul II.[100]

The House of Condulmer into the Modern Age

The grandson of the noble ship captain Antonio Condulmer, also named Antonio, was to play an important role in Venetian history with his diplomatic service and correspondence relating to the complicated relationship of Venice with the France of Louis XII in the first years of the sixteenth century.[101] Perhaps the member of the Condulmer family best known to modern readers is Elisabetta Condulmer, the illegitimate daughter of Girolamo, another grandson of the noble captain Antonio, whose will and inquisition postmortem of 1538 illustrate the lifestyle of an upper-tier courtesan.[102] In 1653, another branch of the Condulmer family bought its way into the nobility with a gift of 100,000 ducats toward the War of Candia.[103] By the end of the Venetian Republic, in the closing decades of the eighteenth century, there were fifteen male heads of household in the various branches of the Condulmer house.[104]

A palazzo built on the Rio dei Tolentini in the eighteenth century for a member of the Condulmer family currently serves as the seat of the Austrian consulate.[105] The chief presence of the Condulmer name today is in the Golf Club Villa Condulmer in the region of Treviso, whose clubhouse was built as a villa of a branch of the family at the end of the seventeenth century on the ruins of a fourteenth-century monastery.

NOTES

Chapter 1

1. Archivio di Stato di Venezia (hereafter ASVe), Senato Secreti, R. 3, f. 129, 12/8/1408, published in Dieter Girgensohn, *Kirche, Politik und adelige Regierung in der Republik Venedig zu Beginn des 15. Jahrhunderts*, Veröffentlichungen des Max-Planck-Instituts für Geschichte 118, 2 vols. (Göttingen, 1996), 479–80, #56; 483–84, #58. It is also noteworthy that the word for *house* written in the records is given as *cha'*, in the Venetian form, the language in which the debate took place, rather than as *casa* in the Latin in which the chancellor recorded the rest of the proceedings.

2. Elisabeth Crouzet-Pavan, *"Sopra le acque salse": Espaces, pouvoir et société à Venise à la fin du Moyen Âge*, Istituto Storico Italiano per il Medio Evo, Nuovi Studi Storici 14 (Rome, 1992), 383–409.

3. Dorit Raines, *L'invention du mythe aristocratique: L'image de soi du patriciat vénitien au temps de la Sérénissime*, Istituto Veneto di Scienze, Lettere ed Arti, Memorie, Classe di Scienze Morali, Lettere ed Arti 113 (Venice, 2006), 486–94.

4. ASVe, Avogaria di Comun (hereafter AC), Balla d'Oro, R. 162-1, f. 52v, 9/1/1413.

5. See Chapter 7, below.

6. Elisabeth Crouzet-Pavane, *Venice Triumphant: The Horizons of a Myth*, trans. Lydia G. Cochrane (Baltimore: John Hopkins University Press, 2002), 184–226.

7. Philip Jones, *The Italian City-State: From Commune to Signoria* (Oxford: Oxford University Press, 1997), 333–485; Daniel Waley and Trevor Dean, *The Italian City-Republics*, 4th ed. (London: Routledge, 2013), 170–83.

8. The classic exposition of this framework is Marc Bloch, *La société féodale* (Paris: A. Michel, 1939–40).

9. David Herlihy, "Three Patterns of Social Mobility in Medieval Society," *Journal of Interdisciplinary History* 3 (1973), 625; Jones, *Italian City-State*, 299–311; Giuseppe Petralia, "Problemi della mobilità sociale dei mercanti (secoli XII–XIV, Italia e Mediterraneo europeo)," in *La mobilità sociale nel medioevo*, ed. Sandro Carocci (Rome: École Française de Rome, 2010), 266; Sergio Tognetti, "Businessmen and Social Mobility in Late Medieval Italy," in *Social Mobility in Medieval Italy (1100–1500)*, ed. Sandro Carocci and Isabella Lazzarini (Rome: Viella, 2018), 211–12.

10. For the most detailed history of this process, see Giorgio Cracco, *Società e stato nel medioevo veneziano (secoli XII–XIV)* (Florence: Olschki, 1967). For an argument that

this amounted, in fact, to an expansion of the council and of the nobility, see Frederic C. Lane, "The Enlargement of the Great Council in Venice," in *Florilegium Historiale, Essays Presented to Wallace K. Ferguson*, ed. J. G. Rowe and W. H. Stockdale (Toronto: University of Toronto Press, 1971), 237–74; rpt. in Lane, *Studies in Venetian and Social History*, ed. Benjamin G. Kohl and Reinhold C. Mueller (London: Variorum Reprints, 1987).

11. Stanley Chojnacki, "La formazione della nobiltà dopo la serrata," in *Storia di Venezia: Dalle origini alla caduta della Serenissima*, vol. 3: *La formazione dello Stato patrizio*, ed. Girolamo Arnaldi et al. (Rome: Istituto della Enciclopedia Italiana, 1997), 641–725.

12. Chojnacki, "La formazione," Table 1-A, 655; Dennis Romano, *Patricians and Popolani: The Social Foundations of the Venetian Renaissance State* (Baltimore: Johns Hopkins University Press, 1987), 28–29.

13. Chojnacki, "La formazione," 662–64.

14. Sergio Tognetti, "Businessmen and Social Mobility in Late Medieval Italy," in Carocci and Lazzarini, eds., *Social Mobility*, 211–12.

15. Stanley Chojnacki, "Kinship Ties and Young Patricians," in *Women and Men in Renaissance Venice* (Baltimore: Johns Hopkins University Press, 2000), 206–26

16. For a detailed breakdown of governmental institutions, see Giuseppe Maranini, *La costituzione di Venezia*, Vol. 2: *Dopo la serrata del Maggior Consiglio* (1931; rpt. Florence: La Nuova Italia, 1974).

17. Monique O'Connell, *Men of Empire: Power and Negotiation in Venice's Maritime State* (Baltimore: Johns Hopkins University Press, 2009), 43–45.

18. Romano, *Patricians and Popolani*, 7–8, 29.

19. Romano, *Patricians and Popolani*, 36–37.

20. Sandro Carocci, "Social Mobility and the Middle Ages," *Continuity and Change* 26:2 (2011), 369–70.

21. Wladimiro Dorigo, *Venezia romanica: La formazione della città medioevale fino all'età gotica* (Venice: Istituto veneto di scienze lettere ed arti, 2003), 1, 58. The parish was located at the end of the physical region of Cannaregio but belonged administratively to the Santa Croce sestier, or urban sixth, into which the city was divided. Most of it is covered by the modern railroad station: Crouzet-Pavan, *"Sopra le acque salse,"* Carte 5.

22. Raines, *L'Invention du mythe*, 406, 894. For Gondolmero, see below; the spelling Glomdomero appears in a 1310 document concerning the dowry given to Giacomo Condulmer, who wrote his will in 1295: ASVe, Procuratori di San Marco, de Ultra, B. 96 (carta Condulmer Nicoletta ved. Giacomo dal conf. S. Lucia), parchment.

23. ASVe, S. Maria della Misericordia o della Valverde, R. 1 (Mariegola), f. 15. The list is dated and discussed in Marco Pozza, *"Marco Polo Milion:* An Unknown Source Concerning Marco Polo," *Mediaeval Studies* 68 (2006), 285–301, 286, n.12. The name appears as "Menegelo Gondolmero Stazonero" in an undated but apparently earlier list of members on f. 8 of the same manuscript.

24. Roberto Cessi, ed., *Deliberazioni del Maggior Consiglio di Venezia, 3 vols. (Bologna:* Accademia Nazionale dei Lincei, 1950, 1931, 1934), 1, 269–362.

25. ASVe, Libri Commemoriali, R. 1, f. 22v–23, #56; summarized in R. Predelli, ed., *I libri commemoriali della repubblica di Venezia: Registri,* 1. *Libri I e II,* Monumenti Storici, ser. 1, vol. 1 (Venice, 1876), 1, 21, I, #83, February 130[2]; his name appears as Meneco Condulmero in this Latin document.

26. Among the many discussions of this rebellion, see most recently Fabien Faugeron, "L'art du compromis politique: Venise au lendemain de la conjuration Tiepolo-Querini (1310)," *Journal des Savants* (2004), 2, 357–421.

27. Lorenzo de Monacis, *De gestis, moribus et nobilitate civitatis Venetiarum,* ed. Flaminio Corner, as *Chronicon de rebus gestis* (Venice, 1758) [composed c.1421–28], 274–77.

28. Marin Sanudo, *Vite dei duchi di Venezia,* in *Rerum Italicarum Scriptores,* 22, ed. Lodovico Antonio Muratori (Milan, 1733), c. 591; Giovanni Giacomo Caroldo, *Cronaca,* ed. Şerban V. Marin, as *Istorii Veneţiene* 2 (Bucharest, 2009), 119.

29. Simone was one of three members of the Balduin family named as participants in the conspiracy; he and his brother, the priest Nicolo, were imprisoned for *lesa majestas (lèse-majesté),* while Marco Balduin went into exile in Fermo: Ferruccio Zago, ed., *Consiglio dei Dieci, Deliberazioni miste,* 1 *Registi I–II (1310–1325),* Fonti per la Storia de Venezia, sec. 1 (Venice, 1962), 1, 28–29, #32, 11/21/1319; Vittorio Lazzarini, "Aneddoti della congiura Quirini-Tiepolo," *Nuovo Archivio Veneto* 10 (1895), 81–96.

30. ASVe, Libri Commemoriali, R. 1, f. 158v, 12/15/1310; the summary in Predelli, *Libri commemoriali,* 1, 106, I, #465, incorrectly identifies him as the former Procurator of San Marco, a position limited to members of the nobility, with a well-documented list of holders.

31. Faugeron, "L'art du compromis politique," 357–421.

32. ASVe, Libri Commemoriali, R. 1, f. 245–46, #643; Predelli, *Libri commemoriali,*1, 157–58, I, #694, which dates this undated document to May 1316.

33. Zago, *Consiglio dei Dieci,* 1, 81, #200, 12/3/1320.

34. Zago, *Consiglio dei Dieci,* 1, 94, #242, 7/29/1321.

35. Zago, *Consiglio dei Dieci,*1, 104–5, #274, 2/25/132[2].

36. This provision was amended the following week to allow the Condulmer property to be leased to Guercio di Montagnana or another factor of Jacopo da Carrara, the ruler of Padua who was a consistent ally of Venice: Zago, *Consiglio dei Dieci,*1, 105–6, #277–78, 3/3/1322.

37. Zago, *Consiglio dei Dieci,*1, 137, #370, 2/9/132[3].

38. ASVe, Libri Commemoriali, R. 2, f. 182–83v, #433; summarized in Predelli, *Libri commemoriali,* 1, 270–71, II, #457, 1/17/132[6]. Sums in documents expressed as *lire di grossi* are rendered in this book in ducats at the rate of 10 ducats per lira; though this equivalence became fixed only around 1328, it was pretty close to this rate since the beginning of the century: Frederic C. Lane and Reinhold C. Mueller, *Money and*

Banking in Medieval and Early Renaissance Venice, vol. 1, *Coins and Moneys of Account* (Baltimore: Johns Hopkins University Press, 1985), 333.

39. ASVe, Cassiere della Bolla Ducale, Grazie, R. 3, f. 3v, #43, 7/10/1329.

40. ASVe, Cancelleria Inferiore, Notai, B. 73 (Ermolao pievano of San Marco), #17, parchment 19. This document is a plea entered by Anzosia Condulmer in the ducal court of Venice on May 14, 1349, to recognize the 1336 will produced by a foreign notary thirteen years earlier.

41. ASVe, Procuratori di San Marco, Misti, Pergamene, B. 20, parchment 7, 9/2/1338. I am grateful to Reinhold Mueller for bringing this document to my attention.

42. ASVe, Libri Commemoriali, R. 3, f. 61v, #103; summarized in Predelli, *Libri commemoriali,* 2, 35, III, #200. There is surprisingly little documentation for the background or activity of Fiornovello, whose branch of the family will figure prominently in Chapters 4, 5, and 6.

43. ASVe, Cassiere della Bolla Ducale, Grazie, R. 6, f. 34, 9/26/1334. Other family members named Giacomo and Benedetto also lived in the outlying parish of Santa Lucia: Giacomo: ASVe, Procuratori di San Marco, de Ultra, Commissarie, B. 96 (Nicoletta Condulmer ved. Giacomo dal conf. S. Lucia) parchment, 5/13/1310; Benedetto: ASVe, Cancelleria Inferiore, Notai, B. 136 (Nicolo, prete in S. Cancian), prot. 4, 2/10/1332. Other Condulmer men lived closer to the heart of Venice: Francesco, who died before 1323, and his son Pietro, identified as a fur merchant in 1338, lived in the more central Cannaregio parish of San Geremia; Bartolomeo Condulmer, listed as a member of the Confraternity of the Misericordia in 1319, lived in the parish of Santa Maria Formosa; Vettore Condulmer lived in San Silvestro as presumably did his father, Leonardo; and Nicoleto, identified in the modest will of his wife in 1321 as a spinner of hemp, lived in San Moise: Francesco and Nicolo: ASVe, Notarile Testamenti, B. 55a (Amizo, plebano di S. Moise), #163, 9/17/1323; ASVe, Cassiere della Bolla Ducale, Grazie, R. 8, f. 1v, 11/15/1338 (where Pietro is identified as living in San Tomà); Bartolomeo: ASVe, S. Maria della Misericordia o della Valverde, R. 2, Mariegola, f. 17 and f. 19v, 8/1/1319; published in Pozza, *"Marco Polo Milion,"* 301; Vettore and Leonardo: ASVe, Cancelleria Inferiore, Notai, B. 199 (Marco de Tocci), parchment, 12/28/1342; Nicoleto: ASVe, Notarile Testamenti, B55b (Amizo, plebano di S. Moise), #296, 6/6/1321. The home parish is not known for Marinello, who was one of sixty Venetians (mainly nobles) excommunicated in 1324 for trading with the Saracens and with Egypt: ASVe, Libri Commemoriali, R. 2, f. 155–156v, #392, 10/1/1324, summarized in Predelli, *Libri commemoriali,* vol. 1, 260–61, II, #415.

44. ASVe, Cassiere della Bolla Ducale, Grazie, R. 7, f. 23v, 5/12/1336; there is no marginal indication that the appeal was granted, but it is not canceled so was probably granted. Minello is an uncommon proper name in Venice or in Italy in general; it is probably the result of adding the diminutive suffix *-ino* to a name ending in M and then adding the additional diminutive *-ello* and dropping all but the M. The only proper name ending in *-mo* that appears among medieval members of the Condulmer family is Vielmo (the Venetian form of Guglielmus or William), so the original name could well

have been Vielmino; in any case the name appears only as Minellus in Latin and Minello or Minol in vernacular documents.

45. Raimondo Morozzo della Rocca, ed., *Lettere di mercanti a Pignol Zucchello (1336–1350)*, Fonti per la Storia di Venezia, sec. IV, Archivi Privati (Venice, 1957), 16–17, #3, 5/24/1340.

46. ASVe, Cassiere della Bolla Ducale, Grazie, R. 8, f. 78v, 11/28/1340.

47. ASVe, Cassiere della Bolla Ducale, Grazie, R. 9, f. 13, 7/8/1341.

48. Morozzo della Rocca, *Pignol Zucchello,* 68–71, #34, 10/7/1346.

49. ASVe, Avogaria di Comun, Raspe, R. 3642, part 2, ff. 20–20v, 10/23/1346.

50. ASVe, Notarile Testamenti, B. 763c (Nicolo Rosso, S. Simeone Apostolo), #83, 3/21/1346.

51. ASVe, Notarile Testamenti, B. 763c (Nicolo Rosso, S. Simeone Apostolo), #76, 7/27/1346.

52. ASVe, Cancelleria Inferiore, Notai, B. 114 (Marino, prete di San Tomà, plebano Ss. Gervasio e Trovaso, cancelliere ducale), R. 3 [no foliation in codex], #19, 5/20/1351, referring to a will of 6/15/1348.

53. ASVe, Cancelleria Inferiore, Notai, B. 18 (Andrea Bianco), protocol 2, ff. 19v–20, 3/18/1372.

54. ASVe, Cancelleria Inferiore, Notai, B. 114 (Marino, prete di San Tomà, plebano Ss. Gervasio e Trovaso, cancelliere ducale), R. 6, f. 11, 7/29/1377.

55. ASVe, Cancelleria Inferiore, Notai, B. 18 (Andrea Bianco), protocol 2, ff. 25–25v, 9/9/1372.

56. ASVe, Notarile Testamenti, B. 615 (Conte di Bertoldo), #115, 4/11/1380; ASVe, Cancelleria Inferiore, Notai, B. 114 (Marino, prete di San Tomà, plebano Ss. Gervasio e Trovaso, cancelliere ducale), R. 5, f. 60v, 8/21/1380. This Pietro was a son of the ennobled Jacobello: see Chapter 2.

57. ASVe, Procuratori di San Marco, de Ultra, B. 97 (Nicolo Condulmer di S. Cassiano), parchment (partially missing), 10/15/1339.

58. One of Nicoleto's brothers, Almoro, lived in the parish of Sant'Agnese, opposite the island of Giudecca. In 1333, he brought three silk veils to Venice and took them by ship with other merchandise to Apulia but was turned back by a storm and reimported them to Venice: ASVe, Cassiere della Bolla Ducale, R. 5 (= Grazie di Contrabanda 4), f. 19v, 2/12/133[3]. He then took the ship to Crete, where it was robbed by Genoese pirates. The Venetian authorities fined him for taking the silk to Crete, as it fell in the category of lightweight merchandise that could only be carried by the state galleys, but in view of his mishaps, the fine was forgiven. In 1346, Almoro's brother Vielmo, who lived in the parish of San Felice in Cannaregio, carried out a trade of 341 pounds of cloth worth 170 ducats with the nobleman Zufredo Morosini in the Rialto marketplace but ran afoul of the officials there and received a fine for which he was forgiven: ASVe, Cassiere della Bolla Ducale, Grazie, R. 11, f. 82v, 6/1/1346.

59. ASVe, Cassiere della Bolla Ducale, Grazie, R. 3, f. 34, 7/18/1329.

60. ASVe, Cassiere della Bolla Ducale, Grazie, R. 8, f. 7, 2/15/133[9].

61. ASVe, Cassiere della Bolla Ducale, Grazie, R. 8, f. 76v, 10/10/1340. The record of this plea has the term *nobiles viri* crossed out in reference to Nicoleto, Bianco Michiel (who was probably noble), and Tomaso Agostin (who was not).

62. ASVe, Cassiere della Bolla Ducale, Grazie, R. 9, f. 37v, 2/23/134[2].

63. It should be borne in mind that the Grazie registers contain records only of infractions for which clemency was sought and, for the most part, granted; the regular course of merchant activity in medieval Venice is not recorded in documents that have come down to us.

64. ASVe, Procuratori di San Marco, de Ultra, B. 97 (Nicolo Condulmer di S. Cassiano), R. 1, ff. 5–11, 5/31/1348.

65. For the relationship between the dowry proper and the trousseau (*corredo*), commonly worth about half as much, see Stanley Chojnacki, "From Trousseau to Groomgift," in *Women and Men in Renaissance Venice* (Baltimore: Johns Hopkins University Press, 2000), 82–86.

66. ASVe, Procuratori di San Marco, de Ultra, B. 97 (Nicolo Condulmer di S. Cassiano), estate accounts: R. 1, 1348–1360; R. 2, 1357–1415; R. 3, 1416–1534; R. 4, 1535–1596 (hereafter Nicoleto Condulmer estate accounts).

67. Nicoleto Condulmer estate accounts, R. 1, f. 5 and f. 9.

68. Nicoleto Condulmer estate accounts, R. 1, front cover and f. 5 v, reference to a decision of February 12, 1349.

69. ASVe, Procuratori di San Marco, de Ultra, B. 97 (Nicolo Condulmer di S. Cassiano) and ASVe, Procuratori di San Marco, de Ultra, B. 262 (Nicolo Condulmer and Paolo Signolo), parchments of Curia Procuratorum dated March 5, 1349; and March 9, 1349.

70. Nicoleto Condulmer estate accounts, R. 1, front cover, note dated June 13, 1349, citing a decision of June 4. In July, Fiorenza made a claim to the entire estate of Nicoleto as heir to Zanino; the procurators spent 2 ducats in attorneys' fees and about 15 ducats to send a priest to the town of Portogruaro on the mainland to investigate an aspect of her claim. In September, they gave 337 ducats to the state treasurer to pass along to her in accordance with a decision of the Court of Procurators of September 3, 1349, that she be entitled to the value of the estate of Zanino himself but not that of Nicoleto: Nicoleto Condulmer estate accounts, R. 1, f. 10v. Fiorenza received about 360 ducats as the return of her dowry; this was assembled from credits to two individuals and mainly investments in the Salt Office: Nicoleto Condulmer estate accounts, R. 1, f. 5v. In 1350, the estate got a judgment against Fiorenza for 250 ducats, which it received back over the next two years: Nicoleto Condulmer estate accounts, R. 1, f. 2.

71. Nicoleto Condulmer estate accounts, R. 1, ff. 1–2.

72. Nicoleto Condulmer estate accounts, R. 1, f. 4.

73. Nicoleto Condulmer estate accounts, R. 1, f. 1v.

74. Nicoleto Condulmer estate accounts, R. 1, ff. 2–3v.

75. Nicoleto Condulmer estate accounts, R. 1, ff. 2–2v. These accounts are kept in the *lira a grosso* rather than the *lira di grossi* system of accounting; there were 26.11 *lire*

a grosso to the *lira di grossi* (see Lane and Mueller, *Money and Banking,* vol. 1, 290–92). The capital of the holdings can be derived from the distributions of 430 *lire a grosso* on August 1355 (entered in January 1356), which are specified as being a profit of 2 percent of capital. Distributions were usually made twice a year at a return of 5 percent of capital per year; after disruptions attributed to the plague of 1348, regular distributions resumed in 1351.

76. Nicoleto Condulmer estate accounts, R. 1, f. 5. In the settlement of Venetian wills, the first payment was traditionally (and sometimes explicitly) the tithe, or general contribution to the church, paid to the bishop. While the tithe of most Italian regions was based on the value of landed property, this was often not a significant part of the wealth of Venetians. In Venice the amount to be paid as tithe is sometimes specified in the will; otherwise it was based on a general assessment of property: Catherine E. Boyd, *Tithes and Parishes in Medieval Italy: The Historical Roots of a Modern Problem* (Ithaca, NY: Cornell University Press for the American Historical Association, 1952), 198–99. As the total value of movable goods sold on behalf of the estate over the next decade was about 5,256 ducats, almost four times this amount, with the addition of 1,300 ducats worth of *prestiti* and 1,250 ducats worth of real estate, the entire estate was valued in excess of 7,500 ducats. It may well be that the basis of the calculation of the tithe was the value of his *prestiti*, the only value for which the Venetian state would have a readily available figure.

77. Nicoleto Condulmer estate accounts, R. 1, inside front cover. One-and-a-half years later the Procurators followed up with a payment of 4.5 ducats to the Officials of Extraordinaries, said to represent a levy of one-third of a percent, which appears to have been calculated on the basis of a value of 1,320 ducats as well: Nicoleto Condulmer estate accounts, R. 1, f. 5.

78. Two of the sons of Nicoleto's nephew Vielmo got 2.5 ducats each, and the 10-ducat bequest to the sons of his late nephew was divided among the two living ones, Giacomo and Alvise, and the estate of Rafaele. Cataruza della Rosa, his wife's sister, got 15 ducats at the convent of Santa Caterina dei Sacchi, where she was a nun; Fiorenza used her discretionary privileges to give an additional 5 ducats to the convent and chose its male overseer to receive the 15 ducats for the pilgrimage he made to Santiago for the soul of Nicoleto. In 1354, the Court of Procurators made the estate reimburse Fiorenza 20 ducats for the tomb of Nicoleto: Nicoleto Condulmer estate accounts, R. 1, ff. 8v–9v; parchment dated 7/13/1354.

79. For Moise as a merchant of pepper: ASVe, Giudici di Petizion, Sentenze a Giustizia, R. 4, f. 38v–39 (1376); as a lawyer: ASVe, Giudici di Petizion, Sentenze a Giustizia, R. 2, f. 22–22v (1366); ASVe, Segretario alle Voci (hereafter SV), R. 3, f. 8v (1383, 1387); as a judge: SV., R. 3, f. 8v and 14 (1384, 1386).

80. ASVe, Procuratori di San Marco, de Ultra, B. 97 (Nicolo Condulmer di S. Cassiano), parchment dated 5/14/1349.

81. Nicoleto Condulmer estate accounts, R. 1, f. 12.

82. Nicoleto Condulmer estate accounts, R. 1, f. 6v, R. 2, R. 3, R. 4.

83. Nicoleto Condulmer estate accounts, R. 1, f. 13v.

84. ASVe, Procuratori di San Marco, de Ultra, B. 262 (Nicolo Condulmer and Paolo Signolo), R. 5, ff. 2–4.

85. Vincenzo Zanetti, *Guida di Murano* (Venice, 1866), 117.

86. Mario Brunetti, "Venezia durante la peste del 1348," *Ateneo Veneto* 32:1 (1909), 289–311; 32:2 (1909), 4–42; Reinhold Mueller, "Aspetti sociali ed economici della peste a Venezia nel medioevo," in *Venezia e la peste, 1348–1797* (Venice, 1979), 71–76.

87. For the outlines of this debate, see Giuseppe Petralia, "Problemi della mobilità sociale dei mercanti (secoli XII–XIV, Italia e Mediterraneo europeo)," in *La mobilità sociale nel medioevo*, ed. Sandro Carocci (Rome: École française de Rome, 2010), 247–71. For the Black Death in general, see Nükhet Varlik, *Plague and Empire in the Early Modern Mediterranean World: The Ottoman Experience, 1347–1600* (Cambridge: Cambridge University Press, 2015), 17–54; for an "optimistic" view of the effects of the Black Death on Venetian trade, see James Belich, *The World the Plague Made: The Black Death and the Rise of Europe* (Princeton, NJ: Princeton University Press, 2022), 106–22.

88. ASVe, Procuratori di San Marco, de Ultra, B. 96 (Tutella figli minori di Alvise Condulmer); ASVe, Cancelleria Inferiore, Notai, B. 164, 1 (Francesco Recovrati), register of 1359, f. 1v–2: 1360 ducal probate of Alvise's 1348 will.

89. ASVe, Cassiere della Bolla Ducale, Grazie, R. 11, f. 82v; ASVe, Cancelleria Inferiore, Notai, B. 114 (Marino, prete di San Tomà, plebano Ss. Gervasio e Trovaso, cancelliere ducale), R. 1, April 11, 1350 (no foliation in codex).

90. ASVe, Cancelleria Inferiore, Notai, B. 114 (Marino, pr. di San Tomà, plebano Ss. Gervasio e Trovaso, cancelliere ducale), R. 3 (no foliation in codex), #43, 1/16/135[2].

Chapter 2

1. See Chapter 1 for a discussion of Nicoleto and the other Condulmer plague victims; see Figures 12 and13 for the interrelationships of the San Tomà branch of the family.

2. ASVe, Cancelleria Inferiore, Notai, B. 115 (Marino, pr. di San Tomà, plebano Ss. Gervasio e Trovaso, cancelliere ducale), R. 1, #167 [no foliation in codex], document of 9/6/1363 recording a document of 9/28/1332; ASVe, Cancelleria Inferiore, Notai, B. 164, 1 (Francesco Recovrati), register of 1359, f. 1v–2, 1/5/13[60], confirming a will of 2/10/134[8].

3. ASVe, Cancelleria Inferiore, Notai, B. 136 (Ognibene, pievano di S. Giovanni di Rialto, arciprete di Castello), protocol N, f. 10, 11/23/1355; ASVe, Procuratori di San Marco, de Ultra, B. 96 (Tutella e commissaria di Zanino Condulmer).

4. ASVe, Procuratori di San Marco, de Ultra, B. 97 (Nicolo Condulmer di S. Cassiano), parchment of 10/15/1339; R. 1, f. 8v, 12.

5. ASVe, Cancelleria Inferiore, Notai, B. 114 (Marino, pr. di San Tomà, plebano Ss. Gervasio e Trovaso, cancelliere ducale), R.1 (no foliation in codex), act of 4/11/1350.

6. ASVe, Procuratori di San Marco, de Ultra, B. 97 (Nicolo Condulmer di S. Cassiano), R.1, f. 8v, f. 14.

7. ASVe, Procuratori di San Marco, de Ultra, B. 96 (Giacomo Condulmer), parchment dated 5/16/1370; Procuratori di San Marco, de Ultra, B. 96 (Tutella e commissaria di Zanino Condulmer), parchments dated 8/12/1366, 11/9/1366, 2/19/1369, and 9/27/1371.

8. ASVe, Procuratori di San Marco, de Ultra, B. 96 (Tutella e commissaria di Zanino Condulmer), parchment dated 5/18/1381.

9. ASVe, Procuratori di San Marco, de Ultra, B. 96 (Tutella e commissaria di Zanino Condulmer), parchment dated 7/12/1381.

10. ASVe, Cancelleria Inferiore, Notai, B. 115 (Marino, prete di San Tomà, plebano Ss. Gervasio e Trovaso, cancelliere ducale), R. 1, #167 [no foliation in codex], document of 9/6/1363 recording sales on 9/28/1332 and 3/10/1361.

11. ASVe, Cancelleria Inferiore, Notai, B. 136 (Ognibene, plebano di S. Giovanni di Rialto, arciprete di Castello), protocol A, f. 118, 3/13/1353.

12. ASVe, Cancelleria Inferiore, Notai, B. 136 (Ognibene, pievano di S. Giovanni di Rialto, arciprete di Castello), protocol N, f. 10, 11/23/1355.

13. ASVe, Procuratori di San Marco, de Ultra, B. 96 (Giacomo Condulmer), parchment dated 11/22/1366.

14. ASVe, Procuratori di San Marco, Misti, Miscellanea Pergamena, 34, document of 10/2/1383. See Map 2, properties labeled 1 through 5, respectively.

15. Wladimiro Dorigo, *Venezia Romanica,* Istituto Veneto di Scienze, Lettere ed Arti, Monumenta Veneta 3 (Verona: Cierre, 2003), 901, 903; Piero Pazzi, *Lo Stradario di Venezia,* 3rd ed. (Venice: Piero Pozzi, 2001), 626–27.

16. Dorigo, *Venezia Romanica,* 847–48.

17. Dorigo, *Venezia Romanica,* 426, 819.

18. Dorigo, *Venezia Romanica,* 840.

19. ASVe, Cassiere della Bolla Ducale, Grazie, R. 12, f. 33, 1/9/13[50].

20. ASVe, Cancelleria Inferiore, Notai, B. 19, #7 (Benedetto Bianco), R. 2, f. 32v, 8/13/1360. I am grateful to Hannah Barker for this reference. Venice was a center of the market for enslaved people, importing them from the region to the north of the Black Sea via its colony of Crete. In the later Middle Ages, in Venice, as in most of Europe, enslaved people were used mainly for domestic purposes and were frequently victims of sexual abuse. See, in general, Hannah Barker, *That Most Precious Merchandise: The Mediterranean Trade in Black Sea Slaves* (Philadelphia: University of Pennsylvania Press, 2019).

21. ASVe, SM. R. 30, f. 96, 7/23/1362, published in Giovanni Cassandro, *Le rappresaglie e il fallimento a Venezia nei secoli XIII–XVI* (Turin: Lattes, 1938), 78–79, #30.

22. ASVe, Cancelleria Inferiore, Notai, B. 16 (Suriano Belli), register of 1364, f. 1, 3/1/1364.

23. ASVe, Giudici di Petizion, Sentenze a Giustizia, R. 4, ff. 54v–55v, 4/24/1376.

24. ASVe, Libri Commemoriali, R. 5, ff. 93v–94, #216, 5/5/1357; summarized in Predelli, *Libri commemoriali,* 2, 262, V, #230.

25. ASVe, Libri Commemoriali, R. 6, f. 134, #316, 4/30/1362; summarized in Predelli, *Libri commemoriali,* 2, 332, VI, #313.

26. ASVe, Senato Misti, R. 36, f. 3v, 4/9/1377.

27. Franca Semi, *Gli ospizi di Venezia* (Venice: Helvetia, 1984), 78–82.

28. ASVe, Libri Commemoriali, R. 7, ff. 93–94, #508, 1/2/137[6]; summarized in Predelli, *Libri commemoriali,* 3, 75, VII, #447.

29. ASVe, Libri Commemoriali, R. 7, f. 94, #509, 1/2/137[6]; summarized in Predelli, *Libri commemoriali,* 3, 122, VII, #789.

30. For the history of the church, see Vincenzo Zanetti, *La chiesa della Madonna dell'Orto in Venezia* (Venice: Visentini, 1870); Lino Moretti, Antonio Niero, and Paola Rossi, *La chiesa del Tintoretto: Madonna dell'Orto* (Venice: Parrocchia Madonna dell'Orto, 1994).

31. ASVe, Scuole piccole e suffragi, B. 406 (S. Cristofalo alla Madonna del Orto), Mariegola, f. 1.

32. The noble members are listed on ff. 22–23, the physicians on f. 24, and the *cittadino* brothers on ff. 25–77v. As is typical of such listings, the members are listed alphabetically by first name, with a cross added before the name as a member died and new members added below the original ones. The original noble members are considered to be those whose names are preceded by an S (for *Ser*), and, for the non-noble brothers, those whose names are entered in the continuous fine Gothic book hand are considered members of the original 1377 confraternity.

33. Romano, *Patricians and Popolani,* 77–118.

34. ASVe, Scuola Grande di S. Giovanni Evangelista, R. 4.

35. See Chapter 3 for Vielmo Condulmer as a member of the Scuola Grande of S. Giovanni Evangelista.

36. ASVe, Scuole Piccole e Suffragi, B. 410 (SS. Maria e Cristoforo dei mercanti, scuola alla Madonna dell'Orto, 1215–1806, pergamene 1350–1399), parchment dated 8/3/1377.

37. ASVe, Scuole Piccole e Suffragi, B. 410 (SS. Maria e Cristoforo dei mercanti, scuola alla Madonna dell'Orto, 1215–1806, pergamene 1350–1399), parchment dated 9/8/1377.

38. ASVe, Scuole Piccole e Suffragi, B. 410 (SS. Maria e Cristoforo dei mercanti, scuola alla Madonna dell'Orto, 1215–1806, pergamene 1350–1399), document dated 9/8/1377.

39. Burial at designated cemeteries on neighboring islands such as San Michele and the Lido was an introduction of the early modern age.

40. Wolfgang Wolters, *La scultura veneziana gotica (1300–1460)* (Venice: Alfieri, 1976), 32–39.

41. ASVe, Procuratori di San Marco, Misti, Commissarie, B. 51 (Andriolo Betin q. Marco, Santa Maria Formosa), quaterno 1371–1385, ff. 3v, 4v, 5v.

42. ASVe, Notarile Testamenti, B. 753 (Nicolo Leonardi), R. 1, ff. 8–8v, #30, 7/9/1384.

43. Lino Moretti, Antonio Niero, and Paola Rossi, *La chiesa del Tintoretto: Madonna dell'Orto* (Venice, 1994), 14.

44. See Chapter 6 for the Order of San Giorgio in Alga.

45. ASVe, Scuole piccole e suffragene, B. 406 (S. Cristofalo alla Madonna dell'Orto), Mariegola, ff. 17–21.

46. Peter Humfrey, "Competitive Devotions: The Venetian *Scuole Piccole* as Donors of Altarpieces in the Years Around 1500," *Art Bulletin* 70:3 (September 1988), 421–23.

47. Gastone Vio, *Le Scuole Piccole nella Venezia dei Dogi: Note d'archivio per la storia delle confraternite veneziane* (Costabissara, 2004), 526–29.

48. Marino Sanudo, *De origine, situ et magistratibus urbis Venetiae ovvero la città di Venetia (1493–1530)*, ed. Angela Caracciolo Aricò, Collana di testi inediti e rari 1 (Cisalpino: La Goliardica, 1980), 49–50.

49. Sanudo, *De origine,* 51.

50. Wolters, *La scultura veneziana gotica,* 1, 38.

51. Email from Lorenzo Lazzarini to Alan M. Stahl, October 18, 2011.

52. Francesco Sansovino, *Venetia citta nobilissima e singolare* (Venice: Giacomo Sansovino, 1581; rpt. Bergamo, 2002), ff. 59–59v.

53. The major source for information on the War of Chioggia is Daniele di Chinazzo, *Cronica de la guerra da Veneciani a Zenovesi,* ed. V. Lazzarini, Monumenti Storici, n.s. 11 (Venice, 1958); modern accounts are in Heinrich Kretschmeyr, *Geschichte von Venedig,* 3 vols. (1905–33; rpt. Aalen, 1964), 2, 230–42; Roberto Cessi, *Storia della repubblica di Venezia,* 2nd ed. (1968; rpt. Florence, 1981), 324–32; Frederic C. Lane, *Venice: A Maritime Republic* (Baltimore: Johns Hopkins University Press, 1973), 189–96; Giorgio Cracco, *"Un altro mondo," Venezia nel medioevo dal secolo XI al secolo XIV* (Turin, 1986), 143–48.

54. ASVe, Senato Misti, R. 36, f. 81, 7/7/1379.

55. Chinazzo, *Cronica de la Guerra,* 56–57.

56. The documentation relating to these bonds in medieval Venice is published in Gino Luzzatto, ed., *I prestiti della repubblica di Venezia,* R. Accademia dei Lincei, Document Finanziari, 3rd ser., vol. 1, pt. 1 (Padua: Draghi, 1929); Luzzatto's introduction, slightly revised, was republished as *Il debito pubblico della Repubblica di Venezia* (Milan: Varese, 1963). Other important discussions of the *prestiti* and the *Estimo* of 1379 are found in Roberto Cessi, "La finanza veneziana al tempo della Guerra di Chioggia," in *Politica ed economia di Venezia nel Trecento* (Rome: Edizioni di Storia e letteratura, 1952), 179–248; Frederic C. Lane, "The Funded Debt of the Venetian Republic, 1262–1482," in *Venice and History; The Collected Papers of Frederic C. Lane* (Baltimore: Johns Hopkins University Press, 1966), 87–98, translated from his appendix to Luzzatto, *Il debito;* Reinhold C. Mueller, "Effetti della Guerra di Chioggia (1378–1381) sulla vita economica e sociale di Venezia," *Ateneo Veneto* 19 (1981), 27–41; and Reinhold C. Mueller, *The Venetian Money Market: Banks, Panics, and the Public Debt, 1200–1500,* Money and Banking in Medieval and Renaissance Venice 2 (Baltimore: Johns Hopkins University Press, 1997), 488–96.

57. See Mueller, *Venetian Money Market,* 610–16, for a reinterpretation of the accounting used in the *Estimo* that reduces Luzzatto's widely cited but scarcely credible sum of 107 percent imposition of assessed wealth to 41 percent.

58. The document is published in Luzzato, *I prestiti*, #165, 138–95, with the date given as "1379 (?)," in the absence of archival documentation. It is based on texts in one sixteenth-century chronicle and one seventeenth-century one. Mueller, on p. 490 in *Venetian Money Market*, argues that at least part of it was completed by early spring of 1379.

59. Mueller, *Venetian Money Market*, 491.

60. See Mueller, *Venetian Money Market*, 610–17, for the argument that the *lira d'estimo* was equivalent to the ducat of account. The fact that both Jacobello and Pietro appear with the noble epithet *Ser*, as well as the other members of the Condulmer house, is an indication that the extant redactions of the *Estimo* were drawn up after Jacobello's admission to the Great Council in 1381. The inclusion of *Ser* for the non-noble members of the family is an error of the redactors.

61. See Chapters 4, 5, and 6 for the careers of Angelo, his wife Franceschina, and his sons Simoneto and Gabriele.

62. Cristina appears as an executor of Nicolo's will in ASVe, Giudici di Petizion, Sentenze a giustizia, R. 4, ff. 5–6, 10/23/1375.

63. There are actually sixteen nobles and eleven non-nobles with assessments of 100 to 250 ducats, but this seems to have been an exceptional level.

64. Alan M. Stahl, *Zecca: The Mint of Venice in the Middle Ages* (Baltimore: Johns Hopkins University Press, 2000), 276–77, 294.

65. ASVe, Senato Misti, R. 36, f. 86, 12/1/1379.

66. Chinazzo, *Cronica de la guerra*, 74–82.

67. "Ser Jacomo Chondolmer da San Tomado si offeri do so figliouli su la dita armada con do fameij a suo spexe. Et oltra questo se offerse de far vegnir stara mille de formento, possando quello vender in fontego."

68. Morosini Codex, in a section written in continuous hand to 1414, ed. M. P. Ghezzo, J. R. Melville-Jones, and A. Rizzi, as *The Morosini Codex* (Padua, 2000), 2, 86–87; and by Andrea Nanetti as *Il Codice Morosini: Il mondo visto da Venezia*, 4 vols. (Spoleto, 2010), 1, 128–32.

69. The chronicle of Giorgio Dolfin of 1458 includes Jacobello Condulmer in its chronological section in the listing of those making offerings for the war; a later hand in the manuscript notes that he was a gold merchant from Pavia: Giorgio Dolfin, *Chronicha dela nobil città de Venetia*, ed. Angela Carraciolo Aricò (Venice, 2009), 2, 97; Biblioteca Nazionale Marciana, MSS Ital, Cl. VII, 794 (8503), ff. 74–74v. An introductory section of the same manuscript concerning noble houses gives results of the voting in which Angelo Condulmer, son of Nicolo of San Geremia, is listed as being elected but with the notation that he had died and was replaced by his son Jacobello in the balloting: ff. 16–16v. In 1479, an inquiry was made by the Council of Forty, which reported that some names had been fraudulently added to the listing of offers for the War of Chioggia in the possession of the Armaments Office and produced a listing that the Forty claimed had been reconstructed accurately in view of official records from 1379: ASVe, Atti diplomatici, Miscellanea R. 127, as published in *Bilanci Generali della Repubblica di Venezia*,

R. Accademia Nazionale dei Lincei, Documenti Finanziari, I, 1 (Venice, 1912), 68–78, #78. In this document the offer made by Jacobello Condulmer is substantially the same as in earlier lists, but his sons are listed as Angelo and Pietro. There is also an entry for the bid made by Angelo Condulmer offering the interest on his government bonds and the pay of ten archers for two months. In the sixteenth-century *Lives of the Doges* by Marin Sanudo, Angelo's promise contains the salary of fifty archers rather than ten archers and fifty oarsmen, but Sanudo omits Jacobello Condulmer's offer entirely; in Sanudo's report on the results of the balloting, Jacobello appears as of San Marcuola and is said to have been elected because of the death of his father, Angelo: Marin Sanudo, *Vite dei duchi di Venezia*, in Rerum Italicarum Scriptores, 22, ed. Lodovico Antonio Muratori (Milan, 1733), c. 1012. The only listing of those elected to the Great Council and hence the nobility as a result of their 1379 offers that appears in a regular archival document is the list of the final thirty selected, but rather than being in the registers of the Senate, it is recorded in a compilation known as the *Commemoriali*, which preserves the texts of important treaties, court decisions, and other acts outside of the activity of the main legislative bodies: ASVe, Libri Commemoriali, R. 8, f. 42v, 9/4/1381; summarized in Predelli, *Libri commemoriali*, 3, 150, #95. The document in the *Commemoriali* gives the date of the election as September 4, 1381; it does indeed contain the names of thirty men, all of whom can be found on the various lists of the final voting but not all on that of earlier offerings. Jacobello Condulmer appears appropriately in this listing as having been elected to the Great Council and hence bearing noble status to be transmitted to his direct descendants; there is no mention of Angelo.

70. See Chapter 6.

71. See Donald E. Queller, *The Venetian Patriciate: Reality Versus Myth* (Urbana, IL, 1986), for a strongly argued presentation of this aspect of Venetian society.

72. ASVe, Procuratori di San Marco, de Ultra, B. 96 (Tutella e commissaria di Zanino Condulmer), parchments dated 5/18/1381 and 7/12/1381; ASVe, Giudici del Procurator, Sentenze a Legge, R. 1, ff. 96v–97.

73. In the September 4, 1381, listing in the *Commemoriali*, twelve of the forty names of those elected are preceded by a cross, indicating that they had died between the call for pledges and the acceptance of their election to the Great Council; as Jacobello's name is not preceded with a cross, he must have been alive on that date.

74. ASVe, Procuratori di San Marco, de Ultra, B. 96 (Giacomo Condulmer), parchment dated 10/30/1381.

75. ASVe, Giudici del Procurator, Sentenze a Legge, R. 2, ff. 24v–25, 11/22/1381.

76. ASVe, Giudici del Procurator, Sentenze a Legge, R. 2, ff. 134v–135, 8/1/1382.

77. ASVe, Procuratori di San Marco, de Ultra, B. 96 (Agnese Condulmer, rel. Giacomello, San Luca), parchment dated 8/9/1389.

78. ASVe, Procuratori di San Marco, Misti, Miscellanea Pergamena, B. 34, parchment of 10/2/1383.

79. ASVe, Giudici di Procuratori, Sentenze a Legge, R. 2, f. 61, 2/22/1382; ASVe, Giudici del Procuratori, Sentenze a Legge, R. 2, f. 75, 3/26/1382; ASVe, Giudici del

Procuratori, Sentenze a Legge, R. 2, f. 84, 5/10/1382; ASVe, Giudici di Procuratori, Sentenze a Legge, R. 2bis, ff. 43–43v.

80. ASVe, Procuratori di San Marco, de Ultra, B. 96 (Agnese Condulmer, rel. Giacomello, S. Luca), parchment dated 9/12/1403.

81. ASVe, Procuratori di San Marco, de Ultra, B. 96 (Agnese Condulmer, rel. Giacomello, S. Luca), parchment dated 4/13/1386.

82. ASVe, Procuratori di San Marco, de Ultra, B. 96 (Agnese Condulmer, rel. Giacomello, S. Luca), quaterno, front cover, note dated 9/25/1386 relating document of 7/4/1388.

83. ASVe, Procuratori di San Marco, de Ultra, B. 96 (Agnese Condulmer, rel. Giacomello, S. Luca), quat. ff. 1–2, 3/10/1389.

84. ASVe, Procuratori di San Marco, de Ultra, B. 96 (Agnese Condulmer, rel. Giacomello. S. Luca), parchment dated 5/31/1389.

85. ASVe, Procuratori di San Marco, de Ultra, B. 96 (Agnese Condulmer, rel. Giacomello. S. Luca), parchment dated 8/9/1389.

86. ASVe, Cancelleria Inferiore, Notai, B. 169 (Marco Rafanelli), R. 1, document dated 8/28/1392.

87. ASVe, Cancelleria Inferiore, Notai, B. 146 (Bernardo Panza, detto di Ghibellino), quaternus, f. 24, 9/4/1392.

88. See the references supplied for comparable data for Jacobello Condulmer, notes 66–69, above.

89. Giuseppe Gullino, "Garzoni, Francesco," in *Dizionario biografico degli italiani*, vol. 52 (Rome, 1999), 430–32.

90. Giuseppe Gullino, "Garzoni, Marino," in *Dizionario biografico degli italiani*, vol. 52 (Rome, 1999), 444.

Chapter 3

1. For the *cittadino* class and the other gradations of Venetian status, see Romano, *Patricians and Popolani*.

2. For the Balla d'Oro, see Stanley Chojnacki, "Kinship Ties and Young Patricians," in *Women and Men in Renaissance Venice* (Baltimore: Johns Hopkins University Press, 2000), 206–8.

3. For the performative value of self-representation as a factor of social mobility, see Sandro Carocci, "Social Mobility and the Middle Ages," *Continuity and Change* 26:2 (2011), 389–90.

4. Vielmo (the Venetian form of the name Guglielmo, or William) was the son of Nicolino Condulmer and the grandson of another Vielmo; Venetian men were almost never named after their fathers but frequently after their grandfathers. Nicolino was the nephew and modest heir of the Nicoleto Condulmer whose death from the plague was recounted in Chapter 1, and of Jacobello's father, Pietro. Nicolino's assessment in the *Estimo* of 1379 was 1,000 ducats, much less than his cousin Jacobello's 4,000 ducats but the same as that of Jacobello's son Pietro.

5. ASVe, Procuratori di San Marco, Misti, Commissarie, B. 182 (Guglielmo Condulmer, q. Nicolo), parchment dated 10/3/1383. Andriolo Novello appears in the *Estimo* of 1379 with an assessment of 500 ducats, putting him in about the same financial range as Vielmo's branch of the Condulmer family.

6. ASVe, Scuola Grande di S. Giovanni Evangelista, R. 4, ff. 13–13v. For a similar term, *popolo grande*, see Romano, *Patricians and Popolani*, 36–37.

7. ASVe, Procuratori di San Marco, Misti, Commissarie, B. 182 (Guglielmo Condulmer, q. Nicolo), will dated 7/6/1421.

8. ASVe, Cancelleria Inferiore, Notai, B. 170 (Marco Rafanelli, R. 1), document of 8/17/1402.

9. ASVe, Notarile Testamenti, B. 557 (Leone da Rovelone), protocol, ff. 84v–85, 4/18/1396.

10. ASVe, Cancelleria Inferiore, Notai, B. 225 (Angeletto da Venezia, f. Andreuccio da Bologna), ff. 64v–65 (6/28/1401).

11. ASVe, Giudici di Petizion, Sentenze a Giustizia, R. 7, ff. 40–40v, 3/21/1403.

12. ASVe, Cancelleria Inferiore, Notai, B. 226 (Angeletto da Venezia, f. Andreuccio da Bologna, fasc. 2, f. 323v (2/1/141[2]).

13. ASVe, Procuratori di San Marco, Misti, Commissarie, B. 182 (Guglielmo Condulmer, q. Nicolo), parchment dated 7/26/1421.

14. ASVe, Procuratori di San Marco, Misti, Commissarie, B. 182 (Guglielmo Condulmer, q. Nicolo).

15. ASVe, Miscellanea atti non appartenenti a nessun archivio, B. 28 (rent book of Donato Soranzo), ff. 30–31.

16. ASVe, Giudici di Petizion, Sentenze a Interdetti, R. 7, ff. 4v–5, 10/24/1404. }

17. Mueller, *Venetian Money Market*, 174–75; for Marco and Simoneto Condulmer, see Chapter 5.

18. See Stahl, *Zecca*, 321–323, for minor coins circulating within Venice in this period.

19. Stahl, *Zecca*, 126–67.

20. Vielmo Condulmer account book 1412–13, f. 41. The Venetian mark used to weigh gold and silver was equivalent to 238.5 modern grams: Stahl, *Zecca*, 19.

21. Alan M. Stahl, "The Mint of Venice in the Face of the Great Bullion Famine," in *Le crisi finanziarie: Gestione, implicazioni sociali e conseguenze nell'età preindustriale*, ed. Giampiero Nigro, Istituto Francesco Datini, Settimane di Studi 47 (Florence, 2016), 223–37. Vielmo Condulmer's account books are arranged by the stages in which bullion was treated, organized according to the Venetian calendar, which ran from March 1 to the end of February. For example, on folio 13v of the 1399–1402 book, he kept a running tally for the Venetian year of 1402 of the amount of silver he had in his hands, which ranged from 410 to 561 marks (about 100 to 134 kilograms), and the silver held in the mint in his account, from 1 to 20 marks. On the next two pages, he recorded the source of the bullion, either from himself or from other people; for 1402, the amount he processed on his own behalf was 541.5 marks (129 kilograms), sometimes specified as being in the form of coins, scrap silver, or his own ingots. On folio 16 of this account book, he

recorded the monthly totals for the silver that he took to the refinery and that which he received back refined to the official Venetian *de bulla* standard of 0.952 pure silver. A total of 1,076 marks of silver of varying fineness was brought into the mint, from which he received back 966.75 marks of refined silver, a loss of about 10 percent, probably the difference between the fineness of the coins, scrap silver, and foreign ingots he brought in and that of the official Venetian standard. On folio 18, he listed his deliveries of silver to the mint for minting into Venetian coins. This amounted to 183.25 marks, about 19 percent of the silver he had received back from the refineries. It would have represented the amount of the *quinto*, which required one-fifth of imported silver to be brought to the mint for coinage into petty coinage at an artificially low rate; see Stahl, *Zecca*, 176-79.

22. Alan M. Stahl, "Ingots and the Venetian Mint in the Later Middle Ages: The Accounts of Guglielmo Condulmer," in *Money and Its Use in Medieval Europe Three Decades On: Essays in Honour of Professor Peter Spufford*, ed. Martin Allen and Nicholas Mayhew, Royal Numismatic Society Special Publications 52 (London, 2017), 75-84. In 1402, such use was restricted to Venetians carrying on trade with the eastern Mediterranean by galleys; in 1407 the laws were liberalized in the hopes of attracting more silver to Venice, and from that time forward, Venetians could export silver by sea in any direction and foreigners could use ingots for trade only in the western Mediterranean. Vielmo sold 927.05 marks' worth of silver ingots (221.5 kilograms) ranging in weight from 21.1 to 27.9 marks (5 to 6.6 kilograms) each. The sale prices declined over the year from a high of 5.82 ducats per mark in March 1402 to 5.63 ducats per mark the following February. No such ingots are known today; they must all have been transformed into bullion at their destination.

23. ASVe, Procuratori di San Marco, Misti, B. 182 (Guglielmo Condulmer, q. Nicolo), account book 1399-1402, f. 14; for the Venetian systems of account in use at the time, see Mueller, *Venetian Money Market,* 610-25. On March 9, Vielmo bought 69.125 marks (about 16.5 kilograms) of silver ingots at the rate of 5.45 ducats per mark from one of his best customers, Martore di Zan Magno. These ingots, rather than coins or scrap metal he usually bought, were probably of the fineness of those of the Venetian mint. If this was typical of what he was paying for good silver and represented the base rate discounted for lower-quality silver, he would have paid 5,269 ducats for the silver he acquired in 1402 and sold it for 6,479.2 ducats.

24. Stahl, "Mint of Venice," 232-24.

25. ASVe, Senato Misti, R. 44, f. 138v, 1/15/1[400]; ASVe, Procuratori di San Marco, Misti, Commissarie, B. 103 (Gasparino Morosini), testament 1401, parchment dated 7/14/1402; ASVe, Senato Misti, R. 48, ff. 82-83v (6/18/1409); ASVe, Senato Misti, R. 49, ff. 31v-33 (6/13/1411); ASVe, Collegio Notatorio, R. 5, f. 90v (1/14/141[8]).

26. ASVe, Senato Misti, R. 46. f. 144 (7/11/1404); ASVe, Senato Misti, R. 48, ff. 150v-51v (6/9/1410); ASVe, Senato Misti., R. 41, f. 85 (6/4/1390); and ASVe, Senato Misti, R. 51, f. 139v (6/19/1416).

27. Alan M. Stahl and Louis Waldman, "The Earliest Known Medalists: The Sesto Brothers of Venice," *American Journal of Numismatics*, ser. 2, 5:6 (1993-94), 167-88.

28. *Bilanci Generali*, 1, 1, 68–78, #78.

29. Lorenzo is identified as the son of Marco di Garzoni in *Bernardo de Rodulfis: Notaio in Venezia (1392–1399)*, ed. Giorgio Tamba, Fonti per la Storia di Venezia, sec. 3 (Venice, 1974), 72–73, #65.

30. See Chapter 2.

31. Desanka Kovačević Kojic, "Serbian Silver at the Venetian Mint in the First Half of the Fifteenth Century," *Balcanica* 50 (2019), 58–71.

32. Alan M. Stahl, "Venice in the Transformation of Northern Bullion to Mediterranean Money," in *Bullion Trade in Medieval and Early Modern Europe: 3rd Prague Conference in Economic History*, ed. Roman Zaoral and Claudio Marsilio (Prague, forthcoming 2024).

33. Benjamin Ravid, "The Legal Status of the Jews in Venice to 1509," *Proceedings of the American Academy for Jewish Research* 54 (1987), 169–202.

34. Mueller, *Venetian Money Market*, 272, 276.

35. ASVe, Segretario alle Voci, 3, f. 42; ASVe, Notarile Testamenti, B. 364 (Basilio Darvisio), prot. ff. 54–55v, 10/4/1400.

36. ASVe, Procuratori di San Marco, Misti, B. 127a (Pietro Stornello q. Marco, test. 1392, d. 1394), quat., f. 2. For Stornello's business dealings, see Alan M. Stahl, "Where the Silk Road Met the Wool Trade: Venetian and Muslim Merchants in Tana in the Late Middle Ages," in *Crusading and Trading Between West and East: Studies in Honour of David Jacoby*, ed. Sophia Menache et al., Crusades—Subsidia 12 (London, 2018), 351–64.

37. Lane, *Venice: Maritime Republic*, 196–97. The best listing of long and short houses is that published by Heinrich Kretschmayr, *Geschichte von Venedig* (Gotha, 1920), 2, 653–54, n. 2, based on that of the late fifteenth-century annals of Domenico Malipiero (the misprint of "Doria" should be corrected to "Dona").

38. ASVe, Segretario alle Voci R. 3, f. 20v.

39. Stahl, *Zecca*,157–61.

40. ASVe, Senato Misti, R. 39, f. 124 (8/8/1385); Segretario alle voci R. 3, f. 47.

41. ASVe, Segretario alle Voci R. 3, f. 20v.

42. ASVe, Procuratori di San Marco, de Citra, B. 27 (Commissaria of doge Antonio Venier), original parchment dated 10/24/1400.

43. Procuratori di San Marco, Misti, Commissarie, B. 182 (Guglielmo Condulmer, q. Nicolo), parchment dated 7/26/1421.

44. Procuratori di San Marco, Misti, Commissarie, B. 182 (Guglielmo Condulmer, q. Nicolo), paper notebook of 16 folios, 110 × 300 mm. For a partial transcription and translation of this inventory, see Alan M. Stahl, "Vielmo Condulmer, a Moneychanger as Would-Be Noble in Medieval Venice," in *Cultures of Exchange, ed.* Susanna Barsella and Germano Maifreda (Toronto: University of Toronto Press, forthcoming 2024).

45. Richard J. Goy, *Venetian Vernacular Architecture: Traditional Housing in the Venetian Lagoon* (Cambridge, 1989), 129–35.

46. Stahl, *Zecca*, 152–61.

47. For example, Vettore Carpaccio, *Arrival of the Ambassadors,* 1496; cf. Patricia Fortini Brown, *Narrative Painting in the Age of Carpaccio* (New Haven: Yale University Press, 1988), 184–86.

48. B. Cecchetti, *La vita dei veneziani nel 1300,* part 3, *Le veste* (1886: rpt. Bologna, 1980), 36–37; Lisa Monnas, "Some Medieval Colour Terms for Textiles," *Medieval Clothing and Textiles* 10 (2014), 43–47.

49. See Chapter 6.

50. David Young Kim, "Gentile in Red," *I Tatti Studies in the Italian Renaissance* 18:1 (Spring 2015), 157–92, esp. 173–75.

51. Stahl, *Zecca,* 325-26.

52. Gerhard Dohrn-van Rossum, *History of the Hour: Clocks and Modern Temporal Orders,* trans. by Thomas Dunlap (Chicago: University of Chicago Press, 1996), 21–24, 48–52; I am grateful to Pamela O. Long for this reference.

53. Goy, *Venetian Vernacular Architecture,* 49–51.

54. Goy, *Venetian Vernacular Architecture,* 129–35.

55. See Patricia Fortini Brown, *Private Lives in Renaissance Venice* (New Haven: Yale University Press, 2004), for the elaborations of such *restelli* in the Renaissance.

56. Brown, *Private Lives in Renaissance Venice,* 13, 176–77. On the other branch of the Condulmer house, Cristina Gradenigo, wife of the non-noble Marco Condulmer who was the son of Fiornovello and brother of Angelo, owned at the time of her death a shawl embroidered in gold with the arms of her husband's family, the Condulmers, valued at 30 ducats; after her death, her brothers had this shawl reembroidered with the Gradenigo arms: ASVe, Giudici di Petizion, Sentenze a Giustizia, R. 32, ff. 107–108, 9/20/1413.

57. Horses were common within Venice through the mid-fifteenth century: Bartolomeo Cecchetti, *La vita dei Veneziani nel 1300,* part 1, *La città, la laguna* (1885; rpt. Bologna, 1980), 40–42.

58. On the non-noble side of the Condulmer house, that of Fiornovello and Angelo, one of Angelo's granddaughters, Cristina, would marry a Querini in 1429, eight years after Vielmo's death: ASVe, AC, Matrimoni Patrizi per nome di donna, 086/ter (A-L), 121.

59. ASVe, Procuratori di San Marco, Misti, B. 182 (Guglielmo Condulmer, q. Nicolo), parchment dated 7/9/1409.

60. ASVe, Procuratori di San Marco, Misti, B. 182 (Guglielmo Condulmer, q. Nicolo), parchment dated 7/14/1416.

61. Procuratori di San Marco, Misti, B. 182 (Guglielmo Condulmer, q. Nicolo), notebook of estate receipts, R. 1.

Chapter 4

1. Crouzet-Pavan, *"Sopra le acque salse,"* 2, Carte 5: "La géographie administrative de Venise à la fin du XIVème siècle."

2. See Chapter 2 for the *Estimo.*

3. Romano, *Patricians and Popolani*, 39–64, 119–40.

4. Stanley Chojnacki, "From Trousseau to Groomgift," in *Women and Men in Renaissance Venice: Twelve Essays on Patrician Society* (Baltimore: Johns Hopkins University Press, 2000), 83–84.

5. See Chapter 2, Figure 11.

6. ASVe, Notarile Testamenti, B. 435a (Nicolo Ferranti), #110, 12/18/1388.

7. For a discussion of the practices of dowry giving in Venice in this period, see Chojnacki, "From Trousseau to Groomgift," and "Getting Back the Dowry," in *Women and Men*, 77–94 and 95–111. To produce 25 ducats a year, the dowry would have had to have been at least 500 ducats at the 5 percent rate of return of *prestiti* and other safe investments in the period.

8. Stanley Chojnacki, "Dowries and Kinsmen," in *Women and Men*, 140–42.

9. ASVe, Atti Diplomatici, Miscellanea 127, as publ. in *Bilanci Generali*, I, 68–78, #78; Marin Sanudo, *Vite dei dogi, ed.* Giovanni Monticolo. Rerum Italicarum Scriptores, 2nd ed., vol. 22, part 4 (Città di Castello, 1900,, cc. 733–39.

10. Procuratori di San Marco, de Citra B. 83 (Angelo Condulmer q. Fiornovello); copy in Procuratori di San Marco, de Ultra 96, 9/9/1394.

11. Chojnacki, "Dowries and Kinsmen," Table 8, 138.

12. Stanley Chojnacki, "Measuring Adulthood: Adolescence and Gender," in *Women and Men*, 186–88.

13. I am grateful to Maarten Halff for pointing out this consideration.

14. See note 10, above. The phrase apparently forbids them to make further claims of paternity on him nor present themselves as cittadini.

15. ASVe, Notarile Testamenti, B. 466 (Giovanni Gazo), 7/12/1397.

16. There were at this time six Procurators of San Marco, each elected for lifetime. They were divided into three units of two each: the Procurators *de Citra*, who executed estates of individuals on the San Marco side of the Grand Canal; the Procurators *de Ultra*, who executed estates on the other side of the Grand Canal; and the Procurators *de Sopra*, who handled the affairs of the basilica of San Marco. Franceschinaʼs estate would normally have been executed by the current Procurators de Ultra; by specifying by name the Procurators de Citra, she was in effect making them executors as individuals.

17. Boyd, *Tithes and Parishes*, 198–99.

18. Chojnacki, "Dowries and Kinsmen," 141–42.

19. Giuseppe Del Torre, *Patrizi e cardinali: Venezia e le istituzioni ecclesiastiche nella prima età moderna* (Milan: FrancoAngeli, 2010), 137–38. I am grateful to Reinhold C. Mueller for calling this posthumously published book to my attention.

20. ASVe, Notarile Testamenti, B. 416 (Bernardo di Rodulfis), #5, 11/20/1396. Though "madona" is given the gloss of "suocera, madre del marito" (mother-in-law) in Giuseppe Boerio, *Dizionario del dialetto veneziano* (Venice, 1856), the more literal meaning of "my lady" must be meant here, as Cristinaʼs mother-in-law is the next executor named.

21. ASVe, Notarile Testamenti, B. 571 (Giorgio di Ghibellino), #205, 11/22/1397.

22. See Chapter 5; ASVe, SV, R. 3, f. 12v, 9/20/1383; ASVe, SV, R. 3, f. 18, 4/23/1387; ASVe, Giudici di Petizion, Sentenze a Giustizia, R. 22, f. 63, 6/1/1412.

23. ASVe, Atti diplomatici, Miscellanea 127, as published in *Bilanci Generali*, I, 68–78, #78.

24. ASVe, Procuratori di San Marco, de Ultra, B. 96 (Angelo Condulmer), quat. [sixteenth century? copy], ff. 6–9v, 1/20/140[7]; ASVe, Giudici di Petizion, Sentenze a Giustizia, R. 22, ff. 18–20, 1/23/141[2].

25. ASVe, Giudici di Petizion, Sentenze a Giustizia R. 22, ff. 18–20, 1/23/141[2]; ASVe, Giudici di Petizion, Sentenze a Giustizia, R. 39, ff. 15–16v, 11/21/1415.

26. ASVe, AC, Balla d'Oro, R. 162-1, f. 52v, 9/1/1413.

27. ASVe, Notarile Testamenti, B. 746 (Marciliano de Naresis), # 75, 11/3/1434; ASVe, Notarile Testamenti, B. 415bis (Giovanni de Buosis), #160, 7/29/1441; ASVe, Notarile Testamenti, B. 824 (Vettore Pomino), #41, 3/17/1444. I am grateful to Maarten Halff for calling the 1434 and 1444 documents to my attention and supplying me with scans of them.

28. Trevisan was a family name for both nobles and non-nobles (and could also be a geographical appellation for someone from Treviso). Angelo is termed "spectabilis et egregius vir dominus Angelus" (notable and outstanding man lord Angelo) and Nicolo is "providus et circumspectus vir dominus Nicolaus" (prudent and circumspect man lord Nicolo), all flattering terms that avoid specific designation of noble status.

29. Leonardo Mocenigo is identified as a procurator from 1425 through 1435: ASVe, Senato Misti, R. 55, f. 167v, 9/30/1425 and SM, R. 59, ff. 102–2v, 3/31/1435.

30. ASVe, AC, Strumenti per la ricerca, Matrimoni Patrizi per nome di donna, 086/ter (A-L), 121. The Querini family had eighteen members on the *Estimo*, including Ramberto with an assessment of 18,000 ducats (decile 1); it was technically one of the most prestigious "long" families, but because of its leadership of the Querini-Tiepolo conspiracy of the beginning of the fourteenth century (in which members of the Condulmer family had been participants), it was effectively barred from the dogeship.

31. ASVe, Notarile Testamenti, B. 720 (Gasparino de Mani), Quat, f. 106–7, #128, 12/30/1402. The will is crossed out in the notary's protocol with a note that it was canceled by the doge on the basis of a plea from the State Advocates. An additional note in the margin records her death in June 1413.

32. ASVe, AC, Balla d'Oro, R. 162-1, f. 108v.

33. ASVe, Notarile Testamenti, B. 1255 (Pietro Zane), R. 1, ff. 30–31, 7/27/1400.

34. ASVe, Cancelleria Inferiore, Notai, B. 226 (Angeletto da Venezia, f. Andreuccio da Bologna), fasc. 2, ff. 284v–285v, 4/1/1411. Paolo Barbo appeared in the *Estimo* with an assessment of 3,000 ducats.

35. ASVe, Notarile Testamenti, B. 719-20 (Gasparino de Mani) #31, 5/18/1418; it was finally opened more than 575 years later: "Testamento chiuso" opened in 1994 "per motivi di studio."

36. ASVe, AC, Balla d'Oro, R. 162-1, f. 22, 12/1/1434; Gaspare da Verona and Michele Canensi. *Le vite di Paolo II*, ed. Giuseppe Zippel, Rerum Italicarum Scriptores, 2nd ed., 3, part 16 (Citta di Castello, 1904) p. 74.

37. Cherubino Ghirardacci, *Della historia di Bologna, parte terza*, in *Rerum Italicarum Scriptores*, 2nd ed., vol. 33, 1, ed. A. Sorbelli (Città di Castello, 1915), 36 (passing through Bologna on December 24, 1435, on the way there and February 26, 1436, on the return voyage); *Le vite di Paolo II*, 73.

38. Stanley Chojnacki, "The Power of Love: Wives and Husbands," in *Women and Men*, 158–59.

Chapter 5

1. ASVe, Notarile Testamenti, B. 1157 (Benedetto de Croce), prot. 1, 10/10/1437: wills of Loicha and Elena Condulmer. I am grateful to Maarten Halff for supplying references to these documents and pointing out the family connection.

2. The evidence of these court cases not only illustrates the complexity of Simoneto's merchant activities over the course of his career but also testifies to the diligence of the Venetian judicial system that supported the mercantile system on which the prosperity of medieval Venice depended. The Court of Petitions was one of several courts adjudicating civil cases in medieval Venice; its jurisdiction included disputes among merchants. The extant series of registers for this period, *Sentenze a Giustizia*, includes in detail the charges made by the plaintiff and the response by the defendant, the occasional testimony of witnesses and a list of documents entered into evidence. It gives the final verdict of the three judges but does not give the basis for their decision; there are occasional additional entries documenting the settlement of these verdicts. Its extant registers include a few from the late fourteenth century and are more or less continuous for the fifteenth. As we shall see, Simoneto was a frequent plaintiff to this court after the failure of his bank; the respondents were frequently his former business partners, including several members of his own family. For further information on this court, see Giovanni Cassandro, "La Curia di Petizion," *Archivio Veneto*, ser. 5, 19 (1936), 72–144, and 20 (1937), 1–210.

3. For an introduction to Venetian banking in this period, see Mueller, *Venetian Money Market*, 1–52.

4. Mueller, *Venetian Money Market*, 99, 151–57.

5. ASVe, Giudici di Petizion, Sentenze a Giustizia, R. 4, ff. 98v–99, 8/19/1376; ASVe, Procuratori di San Marco, de Ultra, B. 106 (Federico Corner di S. Aponal), Quaterno 1, f. 8v, 5/30/1383.

6. ASVe, Giudici di Petizion, Sentenze a Giustizia, R. 5, f. 18, 12/16/1393.

7. ASVe, Giudici di Petizion, Sentenze a Giustizia R. 22, f. 63. The case is undated (between cases dated, respectively, June 1, 1412, and June 16, 1412) and has no testimony or verdict recorded. A note in the records of the Collegio set the date range for a hearing of the case for between July 4 and July 7: ASVe, Collegio Notatorio, R. 4, f. 120v, #461, 6/19/1412.

8. ASVe, Notarile Testamenti, B. 364 (Basilio Darvisio), prot., ff. 54–55v, 10/4/1400; the will is published in Reinhold Mueller, "Sull'establishment bancario veneziano: Il banchiere davanti a Dio (secoli XIV–XV)," in *Mercanti e vita economica nella Repubblica veneta (secoli XIII–XVIII)*, ed. G. Boralli (Verona, 1985), 90–94, #2. For the Benedetto bank and its successor, see Mueller, *Venetian Money Market*, 101–2, and 163–74.

9. The other executors were Andrea da Pesaro, Lorenzo Soranzo, and his son Stefano Benedetto; see the will, references above, and ASVe, Giudici di Petizion, Sentenze a Giustizia, R. 7, f. 67v, 5/25/1403.

10. ASVe, Cancelleria Inferiore, Notai, B. 34 (Pietro di Compostelli), Registro di imbreviature, f. 54, 2/8/1389. Marco is named as emancipated from his father, so was probably older than twenty at that time.

11. Mueller, *Venetian Money Market*, 163–65, citing documents in the Archivio di Stato, Prato (hereafter ASPrato), from the Papers of Francesco Datini (hereafter Datini Papers).

12. ASVe, Giudici di Petizion, Sentenze a Giustizia, R. 7, f. 67v, 5/20/1403. A case earlier that month had involved the same estate reimbursing 800 ducats to a different partnership that included Marco Condulmer; it was paid by the bank in 1401: ASVe, Giudici di Petizion, Sentenze a Giustizia 7, ff. 66v–67, 5/2/1403. In 1404, Marco appeared as one of the executors of Enrico della Piazza's estate in a dispute with the estate of Giovanni della Piazza: ASVe, Giudici di Petizion, Sentenze a Interdetti, R. 7, f. 43, 5/29/1404.

13. Mueller, *Venetian Money Market*, 166–68, citing documents in the Datini Papers.

14. ASVe, SM, R. 46, f. 162v, 11/28/1404.

15. Mueller, *Venetian Money Market*, 169–74, citing documents in the Datini Papers.

16. ASVe, Giudici di Petizion, Sentenze a Giustizia, R. 39, ff. 15–16v, 11/21/1415.

17. ASVe, Cancelleria Inferiore, Notai, B. 225 (Angeletto da Venezia, f. Andreuccio da Bologna), ff. 278v–279 (11/13/1405). Both individuals appear to have been very obscure, as I have found no other references to either.

18. ASVe, Giudici di Petizion, Sentenze a Giustizia, R. 20, ff. 4–7, 10/16/1410.

19. Giacomo Zane made out his will in 1403: ASVe, Procuratori di San Marco, de Ultra, B. 317 (Giacomo Zane q. Lorenzo di SM Mater Domini), 8/17/1403. He appears last in known documents in 1407 as the executor of the estate of Lorenzo Gradenigo: ASVe, Cancelleria Inferiore, Notai, B. 170 (Marco Rafanelli), R. 2 (no foliation in register), 9/23/1407.

20. ASVe, Collegio Notatorio, R. 3, f. 130, #480, 2/18/140[5].

21. The registers of the Forty are lacking for this period, but the provision is discussed in a lawsuit of Simonetto's of 1412: ASVe, Giudici di Petizion, Sentenze a Giustizia R. 22, ff. 18–20, 1/23/141[2].

22. ASVe, Senato Misti, R. 47, f. 14, 8/5/1405.

23. ASVe, Giudici di Petizion, Sentenze a Giustizia, R. 27, ff. 71–71v, 7/1/1407: "olim campsoris de scripta in Rialto nomine sui et sociorum banchi."

24. ASVe, Giudici di Petizion, Sentenze a Giustizia, R. 16, ff. 25–27, 2/14/140[8].

25. ASVe, Avogaria di Comun, Raspe, R. 3646, pp. 41–42, 6/1/1408.

26. ASVe, Giudici di Petizion, Sentenze a Interdetti, R. 8, ff. 52–52v, 5/28/1411 [in the ASVe computer system, this register is called Giudici del proprio, Sentenze a interdetti 8, but its cover reads "Sentenze, e interdetti Petizion"; the register seems really to be Giudici di Petizion, Sentenze a Giustizia].

27. See Chapter 6.

28. ASVe, Maggior Consiglio, Liber Ursa, f. 28v, 7/7/1418.

29. ASVe, Giudici di Petizion, Sentenze a Giustizia, R. 144, ff. 33v–42, 2/27/146[5], and ff. 63v–67v, 4/3/1465.

30. Frederic C. Lane, *Andrea Barbarigo, Merchant of Venice, 1418–1449*, Studies in Historical and Political Science, ser. 62, no. 1 (Baltimore: Johns Hopkins University Press, 1944), 17–18.

31. ASVe, Cancelleria Inferiore, Notai, B. 225 (Angeletto da Venezia, f. Andreuccio da Bologna), f. 47 (6/28/1401).

32. ASVe, Giudici di Petizion, Sentenze a Giustizia, R. 22, ff. 18–20, 1/23/141[2].

33. ASVe, Giudici di Petizion, Sentenze a Giustizia, R. 18, f. 92–93, 9/17/1410.

34. ASPrato, Datini Papers, Fondaco di Pisa, B. 550, inserto 5, codice 601773 (6/22/1396); followed up in codice 601774 (7/2/1396); codice 601775 (7/17/1396); codice 601776 (7/18/1396); codice 601777 (7/21/1396); codice 601777 (8/4/1396); and codice 601778 (8/30/1396). I am grateful to Nicolò Zennaro for these references.

35. ASVe, Cancelleria Inferiore, Notai, B. 229, 5, R. 1, Verbali del Consiglio dei mercanti Veneziani in Alessandria, f. 3, 3/20/1402. For the Council of Twelve, made up mainly of Venetian nobles, see George Christ, *Trading Conflicts: Venetian Merchants and Mamluk Officials in Late Medieval Alexandria* (Leiden: Brill, 2012), 70–71.

36. ASVe, Cancelleria Inferiore, Notai, B. 229, 5, R. 1, Verbali del Consiglio dei mercanti Veneziani in Alessandria, f. 3v, 4/10/1402.

37. ASVe, Cancelleria Inferiore, Notai, B. 229, 5, R. 1, Verbali del Consiglio dei mercanti Veneziani in Alessandria, f. 8v, 8/12/1402.

38. ASVe, Cancelleria Inferiore, Notai, B. 226 (Angeletto da Venezia, f. Andreuccio da Bologna), fasc. 1, ff. 140–140v (8/28/1403); and fasc. 1, ff. 153v–154 (9/7/1403).

39. ASVe, Giudici di Petizion, Sentenze a Giustizia, R. 12, ff. 16v–18, 1/16/140[4].

40. Three days later, the same court heard a countersuit from Marino de Michele for his contracted one-third share of the 450-ducat contract for the ship, which Simoneto was withholding because Marino had not gone to Neapolis. Finding that the voyage had been shorter than the contracted time, the court awarded Marino 90 ducats rather than the promised 150 but held Simoneto responsible for court expenses: ASVe, Giudici di Petizion, Sentenze a Giustizia, R. 11, ff. 23–23v, 1/19/140[4].

41. ASVe, Giudici di Petizion, Sentenze a Giustizia, R. 29, ff. 55–57, 5/23/1417.

42. ASVe, Giudici di Petizion, Sentenze a Giustizia, R. 11, ff. 82–82v, 6/19/1404.

43. ASVe, Giudici di Petizion, Sentenze a Giustizia, R. 22, ff. 18–20, probably 1/23/1412.

44. ASVe, Giudici di Petizion, Sentenze a Giustizia R. 20, ff. 4–7, 10/16/1410.

45. ASVe, Giudici di Petizion, Sentenze a Giustizia, R. 29, ff. 85v–88, 8/31/1417.

46. ASVe, Notarile Testamenti, B. 947 (Enrico Salomon), prot., f. 165, #223 (9/26/1421).

47. ASVe, Giudici di Petizion, Sentenze a Giustizia, R. 34, ff. 2[9]–35v. The case begins on the bottom of f. 15 but is not completed there and is recorded from the beginning on f. 29 (which is marked 28, but between folios marked 28 and 30). Both the year of the court case and of the events recounted in it are problematic. The court case is dated July 7, but no year is given. It is in a codex that begins with a case of October 1, 1423, and ends with one of June 6, 1424; it is between one of March 14, 1424, and one of April 4, 1424. The judges involved are known to have served from October 1423 to September 1424. There is no date given for the events recounted. At one point there is testimony that a certain event happened on the morning of Wednesday, April 13, but the last year before 1423 in which April 13 fell on a Wednesday was 1418; later on, it is apparent that April 15 was a Saturday, which would make 1419 the most recent year; that was soon after Gabriele Condulmer was appointed as Papal Legate to Ancona (see Chapter 6). The document is also unusual in that while the legal framework and judicial decision are presented in Latin as in other cases of this court, the testimony is recorded in vernacular; with fourteen pages of transcript, it is one of the longest case records in the Giudici di Petizion for the period. Water damage at the bottom of several pages makes some of the readings tentative.

48. Cf. Angelo Martini, *Manuale di Metrologia* (Turin, 1883), 33; Francesco Balducci Pegolotti, *La pratica della mercatura*, ed. Allen Evans (Cambridge, MA, 1936), 156.

49. Peter Partner, *The Papal State Under Martin V: The Administration and Government of the Temporal Power in the Early Fifteenth Century* (London: British School at Rome, 1958), 179–81.

50. The price set for the public purchase of oil in Venice from 1415 to 1419 varied between 39 and 42 ducats per barrel: Fabien Faugeron, *Nourrir la ville: Ravitaillement, marché et métiers dans l'alimentation à Venise dans les derniers siècles du Moyen Âge*, Bibliothèque des Écoles Françaises d'Athènes et de Rome 362 (Rome, 2014), 203–8.

51. See note 11.

Chapter 6

1. There are three general biographies of Eugene IV: Friedrich Philipp Abert, *Papst Eugen der Vierte: Ein Lebensbild aus der Kirchengeschichte des fünfzehnten Jahrhunderts* (Mainz: Kirchheim, 1884), which covers only up until his election in 1431; Joseph Gil, *Eugenius IV, Pope of Christian Union* (Westminster, 1961); and Pierluigi Sartorelli, *Eugenio IV nel vortice de eventi drammatici* (Vatican City, 1990). All rely on secondary accounts of doubtful reliability for his early life.

2. The confusion among contemporaries as to the identity and relationship between Gabriele Condulmer and Antonio Correr is reflected in the testimony of witnesses at the

Council of Pisa in 1409 about events in Siena the previous year. Gabriele is not included under the title of papal nephew by Leonardo Bruni, former secretary of Gregory, who spoke of "Gabrielem de Candelmario et Anthonium nepotem suum," or by Bartolomeo de la Capra, Bishop of Cremona, who spoke of "Anthonio episcopo Motonensi nepote dicti domini Gregorii . . . necnon Gabriele Candelmario prefati Gregorii cubiculario." However, Hermann Dwerg, the German auditor of the Palatinate, confused them in his reference to the "camerario et Gabriele nepotibus Gregorii": J. Vincke, "Acta concilii Pisani," *Römische Quartalschrift für christliche Altertumskunde und für Kirchengeschichte* 46 (1938), 251, 286–88. Some credence to the identity of Gabriele as the nephew of the pope may be found in the writings of Dietrich of Nieheim, who was in Italy at the time of the Council of Pisa and assembled a detailed compilation of documents relating to it; in chapter 24 of his treatise *De Schismate*, he characterizes Gabriele as a "consanguineum" of Antonio Correr, and in chapter 31, he specifically calls Gabriele the nephew (*nepos*) of the pope: Dietrich von Niem, *Historiarum sui Temporis Libri IIII, quorum tres priores de Schismate Universali, quartum vero Nemus unionis autor inscripsit* (Strasbourg, 1609), 185, 205.

3. *Bernardo de Rodulfis, Notaio in Venezia (1393–1399)*, ed. Giorgio Tomba, Fonti per la Storia di Venezia, sec. 3, Archivi Notarili (Venice, 1974), 65–67, #59–62.

4. Technically, the legal age for participating in a contract was twelve: *Volumen statutorum, legum ac iurium D. Venetorum* (Venice, 1564), book 2, chap. 1, 35. However, according to an act of the Great Council in 1299, a male twenty years or younger was not to be considered a man: ASVe, Maggior Consiglio, Liber Fractus, f. 94, 5/12/1299; publ. in *Il magistrato alle pompe nella Repubblica di Venezia*, ed. G. Bistort, Miscellanea di Storia Veneta, ser. 3, 5 (Venice, 1912), 323–29.

5. ASVe, Procuratori di San Marco, de Citra, B. 83 (Angelo Condulmer q. Fiornovello); copy in Procuratori di San Marco, de Ultra, B. 96 (9/9/1394).

6. Konrad Eubel, ed., *Hierarchia catholica medii aevi* (Regensberg, 1898), 1, 469.

7. ASVe, Notarile Testamenti, B. 416 (Bernardo de Rodulfis), #5, 11/20/1396.

8. ASVe, Cancelleria Inferiore, Notai, B. 169, R. 2 (Marco Rafanelli) [no foliation in codex], 6/14/1396 and 8/31/1396.

9. ASVe, Giudici di Petizion, Sentenze a Giustizia, R. 18, ff. 92–93; Reinhold Mueller, "Sull'establishment bancario veneziano: Il banchiere davanti a Dio (secoli XIV–XV)," in *Mercanti e vita economica nella Repubblica veneta (secoli XIII–XVIII)*, ed. G. Borelli (Verona, 1985), 103–4.

10. ASVe, Cancelleria Inferiore, Notai, B. 190 (Enrico Salomon), fasc. 1, f. 1v, 2/27/1[400]; Flaminio Cornaro, *Notizie storiche delle chiese e monasteri di Venezia* (Padua, 1758), 637–39. The island of San Michele would become the cemetery of Venice only in the modern era.

11. ASVe, Cancelleria Inferiore, Notai, B. 190 (Enrico Salomon), fasc. 1, f. 1v, 2/27/1[400].

12. ASVe, Cancelleria Inferiore, Notai, B. 190 (Enrico Salomon), fasc. 1, f. 2, 7/12/1400.

13. ASVe, Cancelleria Inferiore, Notai, B. 190 (Enrico Salomon), fasc. 1, f. 3, 10/20/1400.

14. ASVe, Cancelleria Inferiore, Notai, B. 190 (Enrico Salomon), fasc. 1, f. 15, 3/4/1408; Eubel, *Hierarchia*, 1, 197.

15. Donato Corner quondam Francesco appears in the 1379 *Estimo* with an assessment of 1,200 ducats, putting him in the seventh decile from the top of assessed nobles; among the thirty-one other heads of Corner households were two family members, both named Federico, one (of San Luca) with an assessment of 60,000 ducats and one (of San Aponal) of 40,000 ducats.

16. ASVe, Procuratori di San Marco, Misti, B. 182 (Guglielmo Condulmer, q. Nicolo), account book 1399–1402, f. 7.

17. ASVe, Cancelleria Inferiore, Notai, B. 190 (Enrico Salomon), fasc. 1, f. 3v, 3/25/1401.

18. ASVe, Cancelleria Inferiore, Notai, B. 190 (Enrico Salomon), fasc. 1, f. 4v, 8/12/1401.

19. Denys Hay, *The Church in Italy in the Fifteenth Century* (Cambridge, 1977), 74–75.

20. Document of the notary Enrico Salomon not in his Venetian protocol, in Archivio Segreto Vaticano, Nuntiatura Venetiorum, VI. S. Augustinus extra Vicentiam, #14, published in A. Monaci, "Una notizia inedita sulla vita di Gabriele Condulmer (Eugenio IV)," *Miscellanea di Storia e cultura ecclesiastica* 4 (1906), 425–26. The monastery has been characterized as "deserto o quasi" in this period: Giovanni Mantese, *Memorie storiche della Chiesa Vicentina*, 5 vols. (Vicenza, 1952–74), 3, 1, 313–14.

21. Ildefonso Tassi, *Ludovico Barbo (1381–1443),* Uomini e Dottrine 1 (Rome, 1952), 13, n.3.

22. Eubel, *Hierarchia,* 1, 178, 214; Dieter Girgensohn, *Venezia e il primo veneziano sulla cattedra di S. Pietro Gregorio XII (Angelo Correr), 1406–1415,* Quaderni pubblicati dal Centro tedesco di Studi Veneziani 30 (Venice, 1985), 6.

23. ASVe, Cancelleria Inferiore, Notai, B. 190 (Enrico Salomon), fasc. 1, f. 5v, 4/6/1402; Cornaro, *Notizie storiche delle chiese,* 50–58.

24. ASVe, Cancelleria Inferiore, Notai, B. 190 (Enrico Salomon), fasc. 1, f. 6v, 9/10/1402.

25. Cf. ASVe, Cancelleria Inferiore, Notai, B. 190 (Enrico Salomon), fasc. 1, f. 7, 9/28/1402.

26. ASVe, Cancelleria Inferiore, Notai, B. 190 (Enrico Salomon), fasc. 1, f. 6v, 9/10/1402.

27. Sartorelli, *Eugenio IV nel vortice,* 26, citing ASVat, Fondo Veneto, I, 4900; Giorgio Cracco, "Riforma e decadenza nel monastero di S. Agostino di Vicenza," *Rivista di Storia della Chiesa in Italia* 14 (1960), 215.

28. Jean Favier, *Les finances pontificales à l'époque du grand schisme d'Occident, 1378–1409,* Bibliothèque des Écoles Françaises d'Athènes et de Rome, fasc. 211 (Paris, 1966), 152; Cracco, "Riforma e decadenza," 217.

29. ASVe, Cancelleria Inferiore, Notai, B. 190 (Enrico Salomon), fasc. 1, f. 8, 9/20/1403.

30. ASVe, San Giorgio in Alga, B. 1, pergamene, 5/1/1203 and 8/1/1219. It was reformed in 1220 and reconsecrated in 1229: Dorigo, *Venezia romanica*, 257.

31. ASVe, San Giorgio in Alga, B. 1, pergamene, 2/3/1343.

32. ASVe, Senato Misti, R. 43, f. 176, 3/13/1397; Cesare Cenci, "Senato Veneto 'Probae' ai benefici ecclesiastici," in *Promozioni agli ordini sacri a Bologna e alle dignità ecclesiastiche nel Veneto nei secoli XIV–XV*, ed. Celestino Piana and Cesare Cenci, Specilegium Bonaventurianum 3 (Florence, 1968), 348–49, #37.

33. Tassi, *Ludovico Barbo*, 17, n.28, citing Archivio Segreto Vaticano, Nuntiatura Venetiorum, 951 (S. Georgius in Alga, 418).

34. *Bullarum, diplomatum et privilegiorum sanctorum romanorum pontificum, taurinensis editio*, 4 (1271–1431) (Turin, 1859), 645–51, #II.

35. The earliest attestation that I have found for the adoption of this color of habit is in the illustration on the first page of the 1523 manuscript of the statutes and privileges of the order: Padua, Seminario Vescovile Maggiore, Cod. 440, Statuti e privilege della Congregazione dei canonici di San Giorgio in Alga, f. 1.

36. ASVe, San Giorgio in Alga, B. 1, pergamene, 12/15/1419.

37. ASVe, Cancelleria Inferiore, Notai, B. 190 (Enrico Salomon), fasc. 1, f. 1v, 2/23/1[400]. Avonal would also act as a witness for the documents of Gabriele of 7/12/1400 and 8/20/1403.

38. Michele was probably the Michele Condulmer who in 1409, along with his father, Giovanni, received land and a house in Caranedo from Ludovico Barbo in gratitude for the support he gave to Antonio Correr on behalf of the monks of San Giorgio in Alga: Archivio di Stato di Padova, S. Giustina, Catastico VII, 14, f. 77v, cited by Silvio Tramontin, "Ludovico Barbo e la riforma di S. Giorgio in Alga," in *Riforma della Chiesa, cultura e spritualità nel quattrocento Veneto*, ed. Giovanni B. Francesco Trolese (Cesena, 1984), 105.

39. The other members documented were the priests Stefano Morosini and Francesco Barbo, the deacons Marino Querini and Lorenzo Giustinian, and the subdeacon Domenico Morosini. The Morosini house, source of a doge elected in 1382, had fifty-nine households assessed in the 1379 *Estimo*, fourteen in the top decile; it was the largest and probably most prestigious noble family of Venice. The Giustinian house was represented by thirty-one members in the *Estimo* including three in the top decile. The career of Lorenzo Giustinian would continue to intertwine with that of Gabriele; he would go on after Gabriele's death to be the first Patriarch of Venice and would be canonized in the seventeenth century. The Querini house had twenty-three households in the *Estimo*, of which two were in the top decile; because of its leadership of the 1310 conspiracy (in which two early members of the Condulmer house were also implicated), they were barred from ducal power but remained important, especially in the Aegean colonies. There were eleven Barbo households in the *Estimo*, including Pantaleone Barbo "il grande," in the top decile of nobles with an assessment of 18,450 ducats.

40. Girgensohn, *Kirche*, 153, n.63.

41. ASVe, Collegio Notatorio, R. 3, f. 140v, #514. The act is undated, between other acts dated December 11, 1405, and December 18, 1405. Barbo's name is crossed out, as is that of Domenico Duodo of the parish of San Giovanni in Bragora; the others are not.

42. It is not evident what had happened; there is no corresponding act in the registers of the Senate.

43. Girgensohn, *Venezia e il primo veneziano*, 13.

44. E. Delaruelle, E.-R. Labande, and Paul Ourliac, *L'Église au temps du Grand Schisme et de la crise conciliaire (1378–1449)*, Histoire de l'Église depuis les origines jusqu'à nos jours 14 (Paris: Bloud & Gay, 1962).

45. Noël Valois, *La France et le Grand Schisme d'Occident*, vol. 3 (Paris, 1901), 484–86.

46. Dieter Girgensohn, "Papst Gregor XII am Ende seines Lebens: Der Rücktritt, Angelo Correr als Kardinallegat in den Marken, der Streit um den Nachlass," *Mitteilungen des Instituts für Österreichische Geschichtsforschung* 124:2 (2016), 353, citing Biblioteca Apostolica Vaticana, cod. Ottob. lat. 2356, f. 235r.

47. Cenci, "Senato Veneto 'Probae' ai benefici ecclesiastici," 356, n.2.

48. Girgensohn, *Venezia e il primo veneziano*, 24–25.

49. Favier, *Les finances pontificales*, 150–51.

50. Girgensohn, *Kirche*, 186–87.

51. Girgensohn, *Venezia e il primo veneziano*, 14–15.

52. ASVe, Procuratori di San Marco, de Ultra, B. 96 (Angelo Condulmer), quat., ff. 6–9v; this is a sixteenth-century copy of a court case settled after 1431, while Gabriele was pope, seeking title to the house. This house, identified as being formerly the palazzo of the Boldin family and next to those of the Darmer and Morosini families, was left in 1394 by Gabriele's father, Angelo, to his stepmother, Franceschina; it was granted in 1439 to Nicolo Contarini, son-in-law of Simoneto, as agent for the pope's holdings in Venice: Museo Civico Correr, Biblioteca, P.D. C.2581 (#388, Galimberti, Contarini), f. 4, 7/29/1439; ff. 9–19, 4/20/1440.

53. Favier, *Les finances pontificales*, 151–52.

54. Österreichische Nationalbibliotek, Codd. 6586-6597, Antonio Morosini, *Codex*, ed. Andrea Nanetti as *Il codice Morosini: Il mondo visto da Venezia*, Quaderni della Rivista di Bizantinistica 10, 4 vols. (Spoleto: Centro Italiano di Studi sull'Alto Medioevo, 2010), 2, 629 (the chronicler mistakenly refers to Gabriele by his father's name, Angelo).

55. The best general accounts of the events leading up to and surrounding the Council of Pisa as they related to Gregory and his party are Valois, *La France et le Grand Schisme*; Peter Partner, *The Papal State Under Martin V: The Administration and Government of the Temporal Power in the Early Fifteenth Century* (London: British School at Rome, 1958); Philip J. Jones, *The Malatesta of Rimini and the Papal Court* (Cambridge, 1974); Girgensohn, *Kirche*.

56. ASVe, Senato Secreti, R. 3, f. 57, 3/2/1407; Augustin Theiner, ed., *Codex diplomaticus dominii temporalis S. Sedis*, vol. 3 (Rome, 1862), 158, #95, 2/12/1407; 159–60,

#98, 4/28/1408; Alessandro Lisini, "Papa Gregorio XII e i senesi," *La Rassegna Nazionale* 91 (1896), 111.

57. ASVe, Senato Secreti, R. 3, f. 57, 3/2/1407, publ. in Girgensohn, *Kirche*, 1, 377–78, #2.

58. ASVe, Senato Secreti, R. 3, ff. 69c–70, 7/5/1407, publ. in Girgensohn, *Kirche*, 1, 381–83, #5–6.

59. G. A. Pecci, *Storia del vescovado della città di Siena*, ed. Mario Ascheri and Mario De Gregorio (Lucca, 1748; rpt. Siena 2003), 299.

60. Eubel, *Hierarchia*, 1, 469; Sartorelli, *Eugenio IV nel vortice*, 41, citing ASVat, Reg. Lat. 131, ff. 122v–23.

61. Pecci, *Storia del vescovado*, 302–3; Alessandro Lisini, "Papa Gregorio XII e i senesi," *La Rassegna Nazionale* 18 (1896), 284.

62. Favier, *Les finances pontificales*, 433, 644.

63. Valois, *La France et le Grand Schisme*, 3, 577; Vincke, "Acta concilii Pisani," 287–88.

64. Valois, *La France et le Grand Schisme*, 3, 587.

65. P. Genequand, "Kardinäle, Schisma und Konzil: Das Kardinalskollegium im grossen abendländischen Schism (1378–1417)," in *Geschichte des Kardinalats im Mittelalter*, ed. Jürgen Dendorfer and Ralf Lützelschab, Päpste und Päpsttum 39 (Stuttgart, 2011), 495.

66. J. Miethke, ed., "Concilium Pisanum—1409," in *Conciliorum Oecumenicorum generaliumque decreta*, II/1, *The General Councils of Latin Christendom from Constantinople IV to Pavia-Siena (869–1424)* (Turnhout: Brepols, 2013), 475.

67. Genequand, "Kardinäle, Schisma und Konzil," 495. Barbarigo, who is named as one of the reformers of San Giorgio in Alga in 1404, was, like Gabriele, reputed to have been a nephew of Gregory; in this case as well, there is no contemporary documentation to support this tradition: Girgensohn, *Kirche*, 205–7.

68. Philip J. Jones, *The Malatesta of Rimini and the Papal Court* (Cambridge, 1974), 123–27.

69. Jones, *Malatesta*, 128.

70. ASVe, Senato Secreti, R. 3, ff. 129–129v, 12/9/1408, publ. Girgensohn, *Kirche*, 479–80, #56, and 483–84, #58.

71. Eubel, *Hierarchia*, 1, 214, n.10.

72. Charles-Joseph Hefele, *Histoire des Conciles d'après les documents originaux*, trans. and corr. by H. Leclercq, vol. 7, part 1 (Paris, 1916), 1–10.

73. Hefele, *Histoire des Conciles*, 7, 1, 11.

74. Hefele, *Histoire des Conciles*, 7, 1, 27.

75. Augustin Theiner, ed., *Annales ecclesiastici Cesare Baronius* [Raynaldus], vol. 27 (Bar-le-Duc, 1874), 254, c. 38.

76. Jones, *Malatesta*, 131–32.

77. Hefele, *Histoire des Conciles*, 7, 1, 45–50.

78. Genequand, "Kardinäle, Schisma und Konzil," 494; Hefele, *Histoire des Conciles*, 7, 1, 54.

79. ASVe, Senato Secreti, R. 4, f. 15, 5/18/1409, publ. Girgensohn, *Kirche,* 539, #81.

80. ASVe, Senato Secreti, R. 4, ff. 48–50, 8/18-21/1409, publ. Girgensohn, *Kirche,* 555–63, #91.

81. Delaruelle, Labande, and Ourliac, *L'Église au temps du Grand Schisme,* 158.

82. Konrad Eubel, "Das Itinerar der Päpste zur Zeit der grossen Schismas," *Historisches Jahrbuch* 16 (1895), 551–52; Jones, *Malatesta,* 134.

83. Theiner, *Annales,* 27, 319–22, #1.

84. Emil Goeller, *König Sigismunds Kirchenpolitik vom Tode Bonifaz' IX bis zur Berufung des Konstanzer Konzils* (Freiberg, 1902), 117.

85. Theiner, *Annales,* 27, 336, #4; Nanetti, *Il codice Morosini,* 1, 483, 489; Eubel, "Itinerar der Päpste," 545–64.

86. ASVe, Procuratori di San Marco, de Citra, B. 83 (Angelo Condulmer q. Fiornovello), folder 7, "Informazione e stato della commissaria de quondam Angelo Condulmer," f. 1, 3/7/1409. The deceased sisters, presumably all daughters by Franceschina as those by Pasqua did not figure in Angelo's will, were apparently Fiornovella, Elena, and Angelica, as Cataruza and Polisena are both documented as alive after this date.

87. ASVe, Giudici di Petizion, Sentenze a Giustizia, R. 18, ff. 92–93, 9/17/1410.

88. Sartorelli, *Eugenio IV nel vortice,* 51–52; Giulio Battelli, ed., *Exempla Scripturarum,* fasc. 3, *Acta Pontificum,* 2nd ed. (Vatican, 1965), 30, #28c.

89. Delaruelle, Labande, and Ourliac, *L'Église au temps du Grand Schisme,* 172.

90. Walter Brandmüller, *Das Konzil von Konstanz, 1414–1418,* 2 vols. (Paderborn, 1991, 1997), 1, 318.

91. Heinrich Finke, ed., *Acta Concilii Constanciensis,* 3 (Münster, 1926), 337–39, #152.

92. Brandmüller, *Das Konzil von Konstanz,* 1, 321.

93. Giovanni Domenico Mansi, ed., *Sacrorum conciliorum nova et amplissima collectio,* new ed., vol. 27: *1409–1418* (1903; rpt. Graz, 1961), c. 741–42.

94. Finke, ed., *Acta Consilii Constanciensis,* 2 (Münster, 1923), 256–57.

95. Nanetti, *Il codice Morosini,* 2, 629 (the chronicler mistakenly refers to Gabriele by his father's name, Angelo).

96. Mansi, *Sacrorum conciliorum,* vol. 27, c. 807.

97. Mansi, *Sacrorum conciliorum,* vol. 27, c. 811–18.

98. Finke, ed., *Acta Concilii Constanciensis,* 2 , 132–33.

99. Nanetti, *Il codice Morosini,* 2, 727–29.

100. Finke, *Acta Concilii Constanciensis,* 2, 154.

101. Mansi, *Sacrorum conciliorum,* vol. 27, c. 1169–70.

102. F.-Ch. Uginet, ed., *Le liber officialium de Martin V,* Pubblicazioni degli Archivi de Stato, Fonti e Sussidi 7 (Rome, 1975), 20. Two other members of his family do appear within the administration of the papacy: Angelo Condulmer joined the papal honor guard (*scutiferum*) in 1419 and served in the papal treasury under the vice chamberlain of the treasury, Louis Bishop of Maguelone: Uginet, *Liber officialium de Martin V,* 94;

this is probably the son of Simoneto, Gabriele's brother, even though he is identified as "nobilis"; there are no known members of the noble branch of the family with the name Angelo. Andrea Condulmer, canon of Verona, was made a papal acolyte in 1424: Uginet, *Liber officialium de Martin V*, 30; he is probably the son of Marco, brother of Gabriele's father, Angelo; cf. ASVe, Notarile Testamenti, B. 793 (Francesco Polo), quat., f. 27v, 1/11/141[2].

103. Tassi, *Ludovico Barbo*, 56.

104. Ferdinando Ughelli, *Italia sacra*, vol. 5 (Rome, 1653), c. 1285.

105. Theiner, *Codex diplomaticus*, 3, 241–42, #169. Interestingly enough, his colleague in this role was Branda Castiglione, who likewise claimed to be Cardinal Priest of San Clemente on the basis of his appointment to this same seat in 1411 by John XXIII, a papal rival to Gregory XII.

106. Theiner, *Codex diplomaticus*, 3, 268–69, #197.

107. Partner, *Papal State Under Martin V*, 109, citing *Liber constitutionum marchie anconitane* (Iesi, 1473); Antonio Leoni, *Ancona illustrata* (Ancona: Baluffi, 1832), 202.

108. Leoni, *Ancona illustrata*, 202–4.

109. *Pietra del Paragone della vera Nobilità: Discorso genealogico de Conti Ferretti* (Ancona: Serafini, 1685), 92–94.

110. *Pietra del Paragone*, 95–96.

111. *Pietra del Paragone*, 97.

112. Princeton University, Firestone Library, John Hinsdale Scheide Collection, document 7788, 9/1/1421.

113. Pietro Sella, *I sigilli dell'Archivio Vaticano*, Inventari dell'Archivio Secreto Vaticano (Vatican City, 1937), 1, 29, #145, and Table IV, 145. I am grateful to Julian Gardner for iconographic and bibliographic advice for this seal.

114. ASVe, Giudici di Petizion, Sentenze a Giustizia, R. 34, f. 2[9]–35v; see Chapter 5.

115. Francesco Scalamonti, *Vita viri clasissimi et famisissimi Kyriaci Ancontini*, ed. and trans. Charles Mitchell and Edward W. Bodnar, S.J., Transactions of the American Philosophical Society, 86, 4 (Philadelphia: American Philosophical Society, 1996), 42–47, 113–17, chaps. 47–55.

116. Partner, *Papal State Under Martin V*, 110.

117. Partner, *Papal State Under Martin V*, 142.

118. Baccio Ziliotto, "Frate Lodovico da Cividale e il suo 'Dialogus de papali potestate,'" *Memorie Storiche Forogiuliesi* 33–34 (1937–38), 151–91. There is another report of Gabriele having been instructed in Greek as a fellow student with the humanist scholar Lorenzo Valle: G. Mercati, "Intorno a Eugenio IV, Lorenzo Valla e Fra Ludovico de Strassoldo," *Rivista di Storia della Chiesa in Italia* 5 (1951), 45–52. I am grateful to Lillian Datchev for this reference.

119. Nanetti, *Il codice Morosini*, 2, 863.

120. Nanetti, *Il codice Morosini,* 2, 868; Cherubino Ghirardacci, *Historia di Bologna,* ed. Aurelio Agostino Solimane (Bologna, 1657; rpt. Bologna: Forni, 1973), vol. 2, 634–45.

121. Matteo Griffoni, *Memoriale historicum de Rebus Bononensium,* ed. Lodovico Frati and Albano Sorbelli, Rerum Italicarum Scriptores, 2nd ed., vol. 18, part 2 (Città di Castello, 1902), 106.

122. Partner, *Papal State Under Martin V,* 77–78.

123. ASVe, Cancelleria Inferiore, Notai, B. 25 (Giacomo de Brasariis), parchment dated 1/7/1424. I am grateful to Maarten Halff for supplying me with information on and a scan of this document. The act was written by a notary in Bologna in the palace of the cardinal and confirmed in Venice on May 23, 1424.

124. Partner, *Papal State Under Martin V,* 99; *Commissioni di Rinaldo degli Albizzi per il Comune di Firenze,* ed. C. Guasti, Documenti di Storia Italiana 1–3 (Florence, 1867–73), 2, 122, #569 (7/20/1424).

125. Girolamo Borselli, *Cronica Gestorum ac factorum memorabilium civitatis Bononie,* ed. Albano Sorbelli, Rerum Italicarum Scriptores, 2nd ed., vol. 23, 2 (Citta di Castello, 1912–29), 76; Ghirardacci, *Historia di Bologna,* 2, 645–46.

126. Griffoni, *Memoriale historicum,* 108.

127. Sartorelli, *Eugenio IV nel vortice,* 57; Aloysius L Taûtu, ed., *Acta Martini P.P. V,* Fontes, ser. 3, vol. 14, tomus 1 & 2 (Rome, 1980), 866, #335a. See Chapter 7 for Marco's career.

128. Sartorelli, *Eugenio IV nel vortice,* 57.

129. Ughelli, *Italia sacra,* c. 1285.

130. ASVe, Procuratori di San Marco de Citra B. 83 (Angelo Condulmer q. Fiornovello), folder 7, "Informazione e stato della comissari de quondam Angelo Condulmer," f. 1.

131. Eubel, *Hierarchia,* 1, 25–33; Genequand, "Kardinäle, Schisma und Konzil," 392–98.

132. Francesco Pizolpassi, *Summa hover cronica: 600–1440,* ed. Armando Antonelli and Riccardo Pedrini, Collana di cronache bolognesi d'epoca medioevale, moderna e contemporanea 6 (Bologna, 2001), 195–96.

133. Theiner, *Annales,* 28, 1424–1453, 88–90.

134. Walter Brandmüller, "Der Übergang vom Pontifikat Martins V zu Eugen IV," *Quellen und Forschungen aus italienischen Archiven und Bibliotheken* 47 (1967), 585–618; rpt. in his *Papst und Konzil im Grossen Schisma (1378–1431): Studien und Quellen* (Paderborn, 1990), 85–110.

135. Walter Brandmüller, "Die römischen Berichte des Pietro d'Antonio de' Micheli an das Consistoro von Siena im Frühjahr 1431," in *Papst und Konzil,* 111–54; originally published in *Bulletino Senese di Storia Patria* 74–75 (1966–68), 146–99.

136. Nanetti, *Il codice Morosini,* 3, 65, #1392.

137. ASVe, Senato Secreti, R. 11, f. 171v, 3/9/1431.

138. ASVe, Giudici di Petizion, Sentenze a Giustizia, R. 18, f. 92–93, 9/17/1410; ASVe, Giudici di Petizion, Sentenze a Giustizia, R. 22, f. 63, 6/1/1412.

139. Nanetti, *Il codice Morosini*, 3, 1482–83, 65, #1397. The ambassadors reached Rome in June and returned to Venice in July: Nanetti, *Il codice Morosini*, 3, 1504, 65, #1450, 3, 1415–16, 65, #1477.

140. ASVe, Senato Secreti, R. 11, f. 205, 6/29/1431.

141. ASVe, Senato Secreti, R. 11, f. 212, 7/28/1431; Nanetti, *Il codice Morosini*, 3, 159, 65, #1489, 7/20/1431. See Chapter 7 for the career of Antonio Condulmer.

142. ASVe, Senato Secreti, R. 12, f. 69v, 2/23/143[2].

143. Nanetti, *Il codice Morosini*, 3, 1524, 65, #1505, 8/13/1431.

144. Eubel, *Hierarchia*, 2, 7. For the actual relationship of Francesco to Gabriele and a review of Francesco's career, see Chapter 7.

145. Nanetti, *Il codice Morosini*, 3, 1526, 64, #1509. See Chapter 7 for the career of Marco Condulmer.

146. Edoardo Martinori, *Annali della Zecca di Roma*, fasc. 2 (Rome, 1918), 37–41, 2/4/1432.

147. ASVe, Senato Secreti, R. 12, f. 150, 12/18/1432.

148. ASVe, Senato Secreti, R. 12, ff. 171v–72, 4/2/1433.

149. ASVe, Senato Misti, R. 58, ff. 186v–187, 3/6/1433.

150. See, in general, Michiel Decaluwé, Thomas M. Izbicki, and Gerald Christianson, ed., *A Companion to the Council of Basel* (Leiden: Brill, 2017); and, more specifically, Joachim W. Stieber, *Pope Eugenius IV, the Council of Basel, and the Secular and Ecclesiastical Authorities in the Empire: The Conflict over Supreme Authority and Power in the Church* (Leiden: Brill, 1978).

151. ASVe, Senato Secreti, R. 12, f. 171, 3/3/1433.

152. ASVe, Senato Secreti, R. 12, ff. 171v–72, f. 178, 4/2/1433.

153. *Concilium Basiliense, Studien und Quellen zur Geschichte des Councils von Basel*, Vol. 5: *Tagerbücher und Acten*, ed. Gustav Beckmann et al. (Basel: Helbing & Lichtenhahn, 1904), 46, 73, 94.

154. Nanetti, *Il codice Morosini*, 3, 1405, 65, #1939, undated following an entry of 7/30/1433.

155. ASVe, Senato Secreti, R. 12, f. 205, 8/25/1433.

156. *Concilium Basiliense*, 5, 103.

157. Veronika Proske, *Der Romzug Kaiser Sigismunds (1431–1433): Politische Kommunikation, Herrschaftsrepräsentation und -rezeption* (Vienna, 2018).

158. ASVe, Senato Misti, R. 58, f. 214v, 6/6/1433; ASVe, Senato Secreti, R. 13, f. 195v, 7/14/1433.

159. ASVe, Senato Secreti, R. 13, f. 62, 4/11/1434.

160. ASVe, Senato Secreti, R. 13, f. 69v, 5/17/1434.

161. Pagolo di Matteo Petriboni and Matteo di Borgo Rinaldi, *Priorista (1407–1459)*, ed. Jacqueline A. Gutwirth (Rome, 2001), 249.

162. Theiner, *Codex diplomaticus*, 3, 325, #271, 6/12/1434. The Venetian Senate had urged him as early as April 1434 to leave Rome for his own safety: ASVe, Senato Secreti, R. 13, f. 62, 4/11/1434.

163. George Hofmann, ed., *Concilium Florentinum: Documenta et scriptores, epistolae pontificiae ad concilium florentinum spectantes* (Rome, 1940–46), 1, 29–30, #36–37; Maarten Halff, "The Pope's Agents in Constantinople: Eugenius IV's Legation on the Eve of the Council of Ferrara-Florence (1438–1439), *Mediterranea: International Journal on the Transfer of Knowledge* 5 (2020), 106. In general, see Sebastian Kolditz, *Johannes VIII: Palaiologos und das Konzil von Ferrara-Florenz (1438/39)* (Stuttgart, 2013).

164. *Acta Eugenii Papae IV (1431–1447)*, ed. Giorgio Fedalto, Pontificia Comissio Codici Iuris Canonici Orientalis Recognoscendo, Fontes, ser. 3, vol. 15 (Rome, 1990), 171–73, #302, 11/15/1434. It serves as the justification for the title and almost hagiographic approach of the only full-length biography of Gabriele Condulmer: Joseph Gill, *Eugenius IV, Pope of Christian Unity* (London, 1961).

165. Eugenio Cecconi, ed., *Studi storici sul concilio di Firenze* (Florence, 1869), xcvi–xcix, #32, 9/7/1434; cvi–cvii, #36, 10/20/1434.

166. Hofmann, *Concilium Florentinum*, 1, 46, #51.

167. Cecconi, *Studi storici*, clxvi–clxvii, #61, 11/ 22/1435.

168. For a detailed account of the travel arrangements for the emperor and his court to and from Italy, see Lilia Campana, "Sailing into Union, the Byzantine Naval Convoy for the Council of Ferrara-Florence (1438–1439)," *Dumbarton Oaks Papers* 73 (2019), 103–25.

169. ASVe, Senato Secreti, R. 13, f. 246–47, 6/28/1436.

170. ASVe, Senato Misti, R. 59, f. 166v, 7/17/1436.

171. ASVe, Senato Secreti, R. 14, f. 40–41, 6/9/1437; f. 44, 6/25/1437.

172. *Epistolae pontificiae ad concilium florentinum spectantes*, ed. G. Hofmann, Concilium Florentinum, 1, ser. A, 3 vols. (Rome, 1940–46), 1, 91–99, #88, 9/18/1437.

173. Georg Hofmann, ed., *Acta Camerae Apostolicae et Civitatum Venetiorum, Ferrariae, Florentiae, Ianuae de Concilio Florentino*, 3, 1 (Rome, 1950), 16–17, #20, 1/16/1438.

174. ASVe, Senato Secreti, R. 14, f. 62v, 10/4/1437.

175. ASVe, Senato Misti, R. 60, f. 46, 12/3/1437.

176. V. Laurent, ed., *Les "Mémoires" du Grand Ecclésiarque de l'Église de Constantinople Sylvestre Syropoulos sur le concile de Florence (1438–1439)*, Concilium Florentinum, ser. B, 9 (Rome, 1971), 212–224, 4, #16–25.

177. Laurent, ed., *Les "Mémoires"*, 224–27, 4, #26, 2/25/1438.

178. Laurent, ed., *Les "Mémoires"*, 226–27, 4, #18. The Council had held its seventh session in Ferrara on February 14, 1438: George Hofmann, ed., *Fragmenta protocolli, diaria privata, sermonis*, Concilium Florentinum, ser. A, vol. 3, fasc. 2 (Rome, 1951), 21–22, #7, 2/14/1438.

179. Hofmann, *Acta Camerae Apostolicae*, 48–49, #59, 12/3–13/1438.

180. *Acta Eugenii Papae IV*, 376, #785, 7/6/1439.

181. Campana, "Sailing into Union," 121–24.

182. Laurent, ed., *Les "Mémoires"*, 530–31, 11, #9.

183. Laurent, ed., *Les "Mémoires"*, 532–33, 11, #11.

184. Delaruelle, Labande, and Ourliac, *L'Église au temps du Grand Schisme*, 273-76.

185. Donald M. Nicol, *Byzantium and Venice: A Study in Diplomatic and Cultural Relations* (Cambridge: Cambridge University Press, 1988), 418-20.

186. ASVe, Senato Secreti, R. 14, f. 162, 10/23/1438.

187. ASVe, Senato Secreti, R. 14, ff. 173v-74, 12/30/1438.

188. ASVe, Senato Secreti, R. 15, ff. 55-57, 12/4/1440; ASVe, Senato Terra, R. 1, f. 25v, 5/11/1441.

189. ASVe, Senato Secreti, R. 14, f. 162, 10/23/1438.

190. ASVe, Senato Secreti, R. 14, f. 162v-163, 10/31/1438.

191. ASVe, Senato Secreti, R. 15, f. 11v, 2/13/14[40].

192. ASVe, Senato Secreti, R. 15, f. 18, 3/26/1440.

193. ASVe, Senato Secreti, R. 15, ff. 119v-20, 4/20/1442; f. 122, 5/17/1442.

194. Dennis Romano, *The Likeness of Venice; A Life of Doge Francesco Foscari, 1373-1457* (New Haven, CT: Yale University Press, 2007), 205-9.

195. ASVe, Senato Misti, R. 59, f. 167, 7/19/1436.

196. ASVe, Senato Secreti, R. 16, f. 57-58, 1/14/144[4].

197. ASVe, Senato Secreti, R. 16, f. 65, 2/13/144[4].

198. ASVe, Senato Secreti, R. 16, f. 79, 3/21/1444; ff. 95v-96, 5/25/1444

199. ASVe, Senato Secreti, R. 16, f. 103, 7/4/1444; ff. 116v-117, 8/28/144.

200. ASVe, Senato Secreti, R. 16, ff. 126v-27, 10/19/1444.

201. Kenneth Setton, *The Papacy and the Levant*, vol. 2 (Philadelphia, 1976), 89.

202. ASVe, Senato Secreti, R. 16, ff. 132-32v, 11/27/1444.

203. ASVe, Senato Secreti, R. 16, ff. 147v-47v, 2/14/144[5].

204. ASVe, Senato Secreti, R. 16, ff. 148-48v, 2/22/144[5].

205. ASVe, Senato Secreti, R. 16, ff. 158-59v, 3/18/1445.

206. ASVe, Senato Secreti, R. 16, ff. 162v-63, 4/3/1445.

207. ASVe, Senato Secreti, R. 16, ff. 179-79v, 5/11/1445.

208. ASVe, Senato Secreti, R. 16, ff. 180v-181, 5/14/1445.

209. ASVe, Senato Secreti, R. 16, ff. 211-11v, 8/11/1445.

210. Nicolai Iorga, *Notes et extraits pour server à l'histoire des croisades au XVe siècle*, vol. 3 (Paris, 1902), 206, n.1.

211. Georg M. Thomas and Riccardo Predelli, eds., *Diplomatarium veneto-levantinum*, Monumenti Storici, ser. 1, 9, vol. 2 (Venice, 1899), 366-68, #198, 2/25/144[6].

212. ASVe, Senato Secreti, R. 17, f. 68, 10/25/1446.

213. Herman Diener and Brigide Schwarz, "Das Itinerar Papst Eugens IV (1431-1447)," *Quellen und Forschungen aus italienanischen Archiven und Bibliotheken* 82 (2002), 228-29.

214. ASVe, Senato Secreti, R. 17, ff. 112v-13, 3/3/1447.

215. ASVe, Senato Secreti, R. 17, ff. 117v-19, 3/20/1447.

216. Romano, *Patricians and Popolani*, 42-43.

217. Vespasiano da Bisticci, *Vite di uomini illustra del secolo XV,* ed. Angelo Mai and Adolfo Bartoli (Florence, 1859), 6-7.

218. It may also be relevant that the early fifteenth century marked a period of greatly increased prosecution of sodomy in Venice, with public capital punishment: Stanley Chojnacki, "Gender and the Early Renaissance State," in his *Women and Men*, 35; Guido Ruggiero, *The Boundaries of Eros: Sex Crime and Sexuality in Renaissance Venice* (Oxford: Oxford University Press, 1985), 74–75.

219. For a study of this pattern in Florence, see Michael Rocke, *Forbidden Friendships: Homosexuality and Male Culture in Renaissance Florence* (Oxford, 1996); for the Venetian case, see Ruggiero, *The Boundaries of Eros*, 121–24.

220. Pio Paschini, "Da medico a Patriarca d'Aquileia, Camerlengo e Cardinale di S. Romana Chiesa," *Memorie Storiche Forogiuliesi* 23 (1927), 4.

221. Paschini, "Da medico a Patriarca," 5.

222. Paschini, "Da medico a Patriarca," 8–11.

223. Paschini, "Da medico a Patriarca," 15–29. Noël Valois, in a detailed and well-documented but patently pro-Basel and antipapal study, considers Alvise Trevisan unsuitable for the Curia and role of papal adviser "si l'on considère les moeurs douteuses et l'humeur impitoyable de l'ancien petit médecin passé grand condottiere," (if one considers the dubious morals and ruthless character of this former humble doctor become a great condottiere): Valois, *La crise religieuse du XVe siècle, Le pape e le concile (1418–1450)*, 2 vols. (Paris, 1909), 2, 273.

224. ASVe, Bolle ed Atti della Curia Romana, B. 6 (1417–1446), #65, 2/1/1435. The only mention I have found of it is in an unpublished Tesi di Laurea, which cites it as evidence that Gabriele's branch of the family was not ennobled by his elevation to the papacy: Maria Teresa Todesco, *Aggregati ed esclusi: Le cooptazioni al maggior consiglio al tempo della Guerra di Chioggia*, PhD diss., Tesi di Laurea, Università degli Studi di Venezia, Facoltà di Lettere e Filosofia, Dipartimento di Studi Storici, 1986–87, 172. I am grateful to Reinhold Mueller for loaning me his copy of this thesis, which he directed.

225. The closest parallel I am aware of is the case of Gotardo, the spiritual son, "fio danema," of the noble Venetian merchant Nicolo da cha da Pesaro, whom he had taken in as a young man and to whom in 1396 he left the Pesaro family's Ca' Grande in Cannaregio, but who was eventually hounded out of the palace by Nicolo's other heirs: documents in ASVe, Procuratori di San Marco, Misti, B. 150 (Nicolo da cha da Pesaro).

226. Giuseppe Del Torre, *Patrizi e cardinali: Venezia e le istituzioni ecclesiastiche nella prima età moderna* (Milan: FrancoAngeli, 2010), 52.

227. Luca Boschetto, *Società e cultura a Firenze al tempo del Concilio: Eugenio IV tra curiali, mercanti e umanisti (1434–1443)* (Rome: Edizioni di Storia e Letteratura, 2012), 283.

228. ASVe, Bolle ed Atti della Curia Romana, B. 6 (1417–1446), #71–72, 7/6/1440.

229. ASVe, Collegio Notatorio, R. 7, f. 71, 9/28/1443.

230. Carol Richardson, *Reclaiming Rome: Cardinals in the Fifteenth Century* (Leiden, 2009), 347–49.

231. Elizabeth McCahill, *Reviving the Eternal City: Rome and the Papal Court, 1420–1447* (Cambridge, MA: Harvard University Press, 2013), 168–69.

232. ASVe, Giudici di Petizion, Sentenze a Giustizia, R. 107, ff. 194–96, 7/28/1449.

Chapter 7

1. ASVe, Avogaria di Comun, Raspe, R. 3643, part 1, f. 110v, 10/30/1368.

2. ASVe, Cancelleria Inferiore, Notai, B. 114 (Marino, pr. di San Tomà, plebano Ss. Gervasio e Trovaso, cancelliere ducale), R. 5, f. 63, 12/7/1380.

3. Chinazzo, *Cronica de la guerra*, 19–20.

4. ASVe, Segretario alle Voci, R. 3, f. 22, 11/6/1384; R. 3, f. 26v, 12/22/1387; ASVe, Senato Secreti, R. E, f. 44, 11/28/1388; ASVe, Collegio Notatorio, R. 2, f. 120, #341, 8/23/1388.

5. ASVe, Notarile Testamenti, B. 615 (Conte di Bertoldo), #115, 4/11/1380.

6. ASVe, Procuratori di San Marco, de Ultra, B. 96 (Pietro Condulmer, S. Tomà), quaterno.

7. ASVe, Scuole Piccole e Suffragi, B. 406 (S. Cristofalo alla Madonna dell' Orto), Mariegola.

8. ASVe, Notarile Testamenti, B. 830 (Nicolò Benedetto), #171, 4/7/1370.

9. ASVe, Segretario alle Voci, R. 3, f. 1 8, 9/21/1384; ASVe, Senato Misti, R. 39, f. 137, 8/28/1385; ASVe, Segretario alle Voci, R. 3, f. 24, 12/10/1385; R. 3, f. 20v, 4/29/1386; R.3, f. 24v, 11/27/1387.

10. ASVe, Scuola Grande di S. Giovanni Evangelista, R. 4, f. 10.

11. ASVe, Collegio Notatorio, R. 2, f. 117v, #331, 7/5/1388.

12. ASVe, Giudici di Petizion, Sentenze a Giustizia, R. 5, f. 55, 4/29/1394.

13. ASVe, Cancellaria Inferiore, Notai, B. 223 (Angeletto da Venezia f. Andreuccio da Bologna), 2/1/139[9]; and B. 224, f. 291, f. 291v (2/1/139[9]). I am grateful to Nicola Carotenuto for supplying me with this reference. This dowry receipt carried the unusual provision that if Ursia predeceased Paolo, only 300 of the 500 ducats would go to her estate, with him keeping the balance; if he died first, she would get it all back.

14. ASVe, Avogaria di Comun, Balla d'Oro, R. 162-1, f. 117, 12/2/1427. For Bernardo's other son, Antonio, see below.

15. ASVe, Procuratori di San Marco, Misti, B. 182 (Guglielmo Condulmer, q. Nicolo), parchment dated 12/6/1456; most of the account book kept by the Procurators in settling the account is in such poor condition as to be illegible.

16. ASVe, Cancelleria Inferiore, Miscellanea notai diversi, B.134 bis, document of 8/3/1429. I am grateful to Hannah Barker for this reference. Marco Barbaro, Arbori de' patritii venetii, ASVe, Miscellanea Codici, Ser. I: Storia veneta, R. 18, 413.

17. ASVe, Procuratori di San Marco, de Citra, B. 83 (Angelo Condulmer q. Fiornovello), folder 7, "Informazione e stato della comissari de quondam Angelo Condulmer," f. 1, 2/22/143[1].

18. ASVe, Cancelleria Inferiore, Notai, B. 25 (Giacomo de Brasariis), parchment dated 1/7/1424. I am grateful to Maarten Halff for supplying me with information on

and a scan of this document. The act was written by a notary in Bologna in the palace of the cardinal and confirmed in Venice on May 23, 1424.

19. ASVe, Procuratori di San Marco, de Ultra, B. 96 (Angelo Condulmer q. Fiornovello), quaterno, f. 5v.

20. ASVe, Avogaria di Comun, Matrimoni patrizi per nome di donna, 086/ter (A-L), 121.

21. ASVe, Procuratori di San Marco, de Ultra, B. 96 (Angelo Condulmer q. Fiornovello), quaterno [16th century?], ff. 6–18v; Museo Civico Correr, Biblioteca, P.D. C. 2581 (#388, Galimberti, Contarini), f. 4, 7/27/1439; ff. 9–10, 4/20/1440.

22. ASVe, Giudici di Petizion, Sentenze a Giustizia, R. 107, f. 194–96, 7/28/1449.

23. ASVe, Giudice del Procurator, Sentenze a Legge, R. 4, ff. 63v–66, 6/9/1455. The case is canceled in the register with a reference to a ruling in June 1457 by Doge Francesco Foscari. I am grateful to Reinhold Mueller for this reference.

24. ASVe, Avogaria di Comun, Matrimoni patrizi per nome di donna, indice 86/ter I, p. 121. I am grateful to Maarten Halff for this reference.

25. ASVe, Notarile Testamenti, B. 1157 (Benedetto de Croce), prot. 1, ff. 73v–74, 10/10/1437. I am grateful to Maarten Halff for this reference.

26. ASVe, Matrimoni patrizi per nome di donna, indice 89/ter I, p. 385.

27. ASVe, Notarile Testamenti, B. 1155 (Benedetto de Croce), #233, 2/10/143[5].

28. ASVe, Giudice di Petizion, Sentenze a Giustizia, R. 144, ff. 33v–42, 2/27/146[5].

29. Partner, *Papal State Under Martin V*, 194.

30. He is specified as brother to Marina Condulmer, daughter of Marco, in her will of 1415: ASVe, Notarile Testamenti, B. 915/1 (Bartolomeo Bon), #22, 3/13/1415.

31. He is identified as *protonotarius* of the Apostolic See in the will of his sister Clara, for which he served as executor and received half of the estate: ASVe, Notarile Testamenti, B. 947 (Enrico Salomon,) prot., f. 113, #147, 12/10/1429. He appears with another sister Franceschina as "Apostolicae Sedis Protonotarius" and "quondam Marci Condolmario" in their purchase of land of their late mother: ASVe, Cancelleria Inferiore, Notai, B. 190 (Enrico Salomon), fasc. 8, f. 2v, 8/8/1430.

32. *Repertorium Germanicum. Regesten aus den Päpstlichen Archiven zur Geschichte des Deutschen Reichs. Pontifikat Eugens IV (1431–1447)*, ed. Robert Arnold (Berlin, 1897); *vicecamerarius*: 1, 143, #867, 4/20/1431; *protonotarius*: 1, 169, #1022, 5/12/1431; *camerarius*: 1, 437, #2729, 2/ 21/1432.

33. ASVe, Senato Misti, R. 58, f. 80, 8/23/1431.

34. Theiner, *Annales*, t. 28, 110; Eubel, *Hierarchia*, 2, 7.

35. Valois, *La crise religieuse*, 1, 337, n.1.

36. Nanetti, *Il codice Morosini*, 3, 1526, 64, #1509; 3, 1515, 65, #1480.

37. G. Hofmann, ed., *Epistolae pontificiae ad concilium florentinum spectantes*, Concilium Florentinum, vol. 1, ser. A, 3 vols. (Rome, 1940–46), 1, 21–24, #29–30, 11/12/1431.

38. Eubel, *Hierarchia*, 2, 199; J. Haller, ed., *Concilium Basiliense, Studien und Quellen zur Geschichte des Concils von Basel*, 1 (Basel, 1896), 435–39, #67, November 1936. The florin was equivalent in value to the ducat.

39. Haller, *Concilium Basiliense*, 1, 311–12, #26, 5/12/1433; Theiner, *Annales*, t. 28, 1424–1453, 190.

40. Valois, *La crise religieuse*, 1, 359; F. Palacky, *Monumenta conciliorum generalium*, 4 vols. (Vienna, 1857–86), 2, 718; Luca Boschetto, *Società e cultura a Firenze al tempo del Concilio: Eugenio IV tra curiali, mercanti e umanisti (1434–1443)* (Rome: Edizioni di Storia e Letteratura, 2012), 14–18, 56.

41. Concetta Bianca, "I cardinali al Concilio di Firenze," in *Firenze e il Concilio del 1439*, ed. Paolo Viti, 2 vols. (Florence: Olschki, 1994), 147–73.

42. ASVe, Senato Secreti, R. 13, 142–42v, 3/2/1435; Theiner, ed. *Codex Diplomaticus*, vol. 3, 326–29, #275, 7/16/1435; Theiner, *Annales*, vol. 28, 188; ASVe, Senato Secreti, R. 14, ff. 40–41, 6/9/1437.

43. Eubel, *Hierarchia*, 2, 86, 106.

44. G. Hofmann, ed, *Fragmenta protocolli, diaria privata, sermonis*, Concilium Florentinum, vol. 3, fasc. 2, ser. A (Rome, 1951), 38, #d.

45. G. Hofmann, ed., *Acta Camerae Apostolicae et Civitatum Venetiarum, Ferrariae, Florentinae, Ianuae de Concilio Florentino*, Concilium Florentinum, vol. 3, fasc. 1, ser. A (Rome, 1950), 31, #34, 3/8/1438; 35–36, #39, 5/4/1438.

46. Hofmann, *Acta Camerae Apostolicae*, 45–46, #54, 10/28/1438, and *passim*, 89, #108, 12/21/1439.

47. Adolf Gottlob, *Aus der Camera Apostolica des 15. Jahrhunderts* (Innsbruck, 1889), 268.

48. N. Iorga, ed., "Excerpt from Jehan de Wavrin, *Anciennes chroniques d'Angleterre*," in *The Crusade of Varna*, ed. Colin Imber (Aldershot, 2006), 107–66.

49. Wavrin, *Anciennes chroniques*, 127.

50. Wavrin, *Anciennes chroniques*, 142.

51. Eubel, *Hierarchia*, 2, 28, #90.

52. Eubel, *Hierarchia*, 2, 29, #100, 101.

53. Eubel, *Hierarchia*, 2, 29, #122.

54. Eubel, *Hierarchia*, 2, 31, #157; A. Olivieri, "Condulmer, Francesco," in *Dizionario biografico degli italiani*, vol. 27 (Rome, 1982), 761–65.

55. Ernst Gerland, *Neue Quellen zur Geschichte des lateinischen Erzbistums Patras* (Leipzig, 1903), 199–201, #13, 10/23/1420; Aloysius L Taûtu, ed., *Acta Martini P.P. V*, Fontes, ser.3, vol. 14 (Rome, 1980), 2, 866, #335a, 7/27/1426.

56. Nanetti, *Il codice Morosini*, 3, 1526, 64, #1509. Marco does not appear among the names of the offspring of Simoneto: Procuratori di San Marco de Ultra, B. 96 (Angelo Condulmer), quat. [16th century?], f. 5v. As he was considered a possible university student in 1426, this is not likely to have been the same Marco Condulmer who had been a monk at San Giorgio in Alga in 1404 or the Marco who was a banking partner of Simoneto in 1400.

57. Valois, *La crise religieuse*, 1, 167, n.3.

58. Georgios Phrantzes, *Cronaca*, ed. and trans. Riccardo Maisano (Rome, 1990), 44–45.

59. Nanetti, *Il codice Morosini*, 3, 1526, 64, #1509; Robert Arnold, ed., *Repertorium Germanicum: Regesten aus den päpstlichen Archiven zur Geschichte des deutschen Reichs—Pontifikat Eugens IV (1431–1447)* (Berlin, 1897), bd. 1, 384, #2386.

60. Valois, *La crise religieuse*, 1, 166; Eubel, *Hierarchia*, 2, 100.

61. Valois, *La crise religieuse*, 1, 168–74.

62. Valois, *La crise religieuse*, 2, 262–69; Eubel, *Hierarchia*, 2, 245.

63. Cherubino Ghirardacci, *Della historia di Bologna, parte terza, in RIS*, 2nd ed. 33, 1, ed. A. Sorbelli, (Città di Castello, 1915), 33–39.

64. ASVe, Senato Secreti, R. 13, ff. 139–39v, 2/4/143[5]; ASVe, Senato Secreti, R. 14, f. 50, 8/2/1437.

65. Hofmann, *Epistolae*, 1, 76–77, #76, 7/6/1437; 1, 80, #80, 7/10/1437; 1, 82–83, #83, 7/15/1437.

66. *Acta Eugenii Papae IV (1431–1447)*, ed. Giorgio Fedalto, Pontificia Comissio Codici Iuris Canonici Orientalis Recognoscendo, Fontes, ser. 3, vol. 15 (Rome, 1990), 289–93, #564–67, 7/15/1437.

67. Georgios Phrantzes, *Cronica*, ed. and trans Riccardo Maisano (Rome, 1990), 79.

68. Laurent, ed., *Les "Mémoires,"* 198–99, 4, 2; 208–9, 4, 11.

69. Hofmann, *Concilium Florentinum*, vol. 3, fasc. 2, ser. A, *Fragmenta protocolli, diaria privata, sermonis* (Rome, 1951), 21–22, #7, 2/14/1438.

70. Eubel, *Hierarchia*, 2, 160; Hofmann, *Epistolae*, 2, 33–34, #139, 5/20/1438.

71. Hofmann, *Epistolae*, 2, 68–79, #176, 7/6/1439.

72. ASVe, Senato Secreti, R. 16, f. 13v, 5/25/1443.

73. Fedalto, *Acta*, 555, #1124, 12/16/1444.

74. Fedalto, *Acta*, 556–58, #1227, 1/1/1445; 561, #1234, 1/9/1445.

75. A. Olivieri, "Condulmer, Marco," in *Dizionario biografico degli italiani*, 27 (Rome, 1982), 765–66.

76. See Chapter 2.

77. ASVe, Avogaria di Comun, Balla d'Oro, R. 162-1, f. 52v, 9/1/1413.

78. ASVe, Senato Misti, R. 56, f. 179, 7/13/1428.

79. Nanetti, *Il codice Morosini*, 2, 882, #64, 908, 1/12/142[1]; 2, 1097, #65, 377, March 1426; ASVe, Senato Misti, R. 56, f. 76v, 2/8/142[7]; ASVe, Collegio Notatorio, R. 6, f. 31, 4/14/1427; 3, 1293, #65, 887, 7/22/1428; 3, 1426, #65, 1256, 7/11/1430; 2, 918, #65, 1000, July 1422; 3, 1415, #65, 1235, April 1430.

80. ASVe, Senato Misti, R. 55, f. 106, 4/2/1425; Senato Secreti, R. 9, ff. 5–8v, 4/2/1425.

81. ASVe, Senato Secreti, R. 11, f. 212, 7/28/1431; Nanetti, *Il codice Morosini*, 3, 1519, #1489; 7/20/1431. The Morosini chronicle adds that they brought 8,000 ducats from the papacy with them to pay for the expenses.

82. Nicolae Iorga, *Notes et extraits pour servir à l'histoire des croisades au XVe siècle*, 6 vols. (Paris 1899), 2, 2, 7/10/1431.

83. ASVe, Senato Secreti, R. 12, f. 69b, 2/ 23/143[2]; Nanetti, *Il codice Morosini*, 3, 1643, #65, 1789. For details on this voyage, see Halff, "Pope's Agents," 113.

84. ASVe, Senato Misti, R. 58, f. 168, 1/8/143[3].

85. ASVe, Senato Misti, R. 59, ff. 29–32, 2/20/143[4]; Doris Stöckly, *Le système de l'incanto des galées du marché à Venise (fin XIIIe–milieu XVe siècle)* (Leiden: Brill, 1955), 158.

86. Iorga, *Notes et extraits*, 2, 7–9; Hofmann, *Concilium Florentinum*, vol. 3, fasc. 1, ser. A, *Acta Camerae Apostolicae et Civitatum Venetiarum, Ferrariae, Florentinae, Ianuae de Concilio Florentino* (Rome, 1950), 35–36, #39–40.

87. Laurent, ed., *Les "Mémoires,"* 176–79, 3, 15.

88. ASVe, Cancelleria Inferiore, Notai, Miscellanea notai diversi, B. 11, # 157, [unidentified notary], f. 41v, 5/4/1438. I am grateful to Maarten Halff for providing me with this reference.

89. *The Book of Michael of Rhodes: A Fifteenth-Century Maritime Manuscript*, vol. 2, *Transcription and Translation*, ed. Alan M. Stahl (Cambridge, MA: MIT Press, 2009), 280–81.

90. ASVe, Spirito Santo, Pergamene, B. 4.

91. ASVe, Senato Mar, R. 1, f. 226b, 3/23/1444, where he is listed first and characterized as "maior."

92. ASVe, Senato Secreti, R. 16, f. 180v–81, 5/14/1445.

93. ASVe, Avogaria di Comun, Prove di età per patroni di galere, reg. 178-2, fol. 71v, 9/31/1450; f. 98v, 9/6/1453. I am grateful to Maarten Halff for these references.

94. See Chapter 4.

95. Giuseppe Zippel, ed., *Le vite di Paolo II di Gaspare da Verona e Michele Canensi*, Rerum Italicarum Scriptores, ed. L. A Muratori, 2nd ed., 3, part 16 (Citta di Castello, 1904), 74.

96. Ian Robertson, *Tyranny Under the Mantle of St. Peter: Pope Paul II and Bologna* (Turnhout: Brepols, 2002), 18–20.

97. Eubel, *Hierarchia*, 2, 8, and 2, 126.

98. ASVe, Senato Terra, R. 1, f. 47, 11/5/1441; ASVe, Senato Terra, R. 1, f. 153v, 3/15/1445.

99. Eubel, *Hierarchia*, 2, 28, #89; 2, 29, #100.

100. Eubel, *Hierarchia*, 2, 267, and n.1.

101. A. Baiocchi, "Condulmer, Antonio," in *Dizionario biografico degli italiani*, vol. 27 (Rome, 1982), 758–61.

102. Brown, *Private Lives in Renaissance Venice*, 173–86.

103. J. Temple Leader, *Libro dei nobili veneti* (Florence, 1884), 27–28.

104. ASVe, Miscellanea codici, Storia veneta, B. 18 (Genealogie Barbaro), 2, 414, 417.

105. Paolo Pazzi, *Lo stradario di Venezia* (Venice, 2001), 2, 653.

BIBLIOGRAPHY

Archival and Manuscript Documents

Padua. Seminario Vescovile Maggiore

Cod. 440, Statuti e privilege della Congregazione dei canonici di San Giorgio in Alga.

Prato. Archivio di Stato. Papers of Francesco Datini

Fondaco di Pisa. B. 550, inserto 5.

Princeton. Firestone Library

John Hinsdale Scheide Collection. Document 7788.

Venice, Archivio di Stato

Atti diplomatici. Miscellanea. R. 127.
Avogaria di Comun. Balla d'Oro. R. 162.
Avogaria di Comun. Matrimoni Patrizi per nome di donna. R. 086/ter.
Avogaria di Comun. Prove di età per patroni di galere. R. 178-2.
Avogaria di Comun, Raspe. R. 3642, 3463, 3646.
Bolle ed Atti della Curia Romana, B. 6.
Cancelleria Inferiore. Notai. B. 16 (Suriano Belli).
Cancelleria Inferiore. Notai. B. 18 (Andrea Bianco).
Cancelleria Inferiore. Notai. B. 19 (Benedetto Bianco).
Cancelleria Inferiore. Notai. B. 25 (Giacomo de Brasariis).
Cancelleria Inferiore. Notai. B. 34 (Pietro di Compostelli).
Cancelleria Inferiore. Notai. B. 73 (Ermolao, pievano of San Marco).
Cancelleria Inferiore. Notai. B. 136 (Nicolo, prete in S. Cancian).
Cancelleria Inferiore. Notai. B. 114 (Marino, prete di San Tomà, plebano Ss. Gervasio e Trovaso, Cancelliere ducale).
Cancelleria Inferiore. Notai. B. 136 (Ognibene, pievano di S. Giovanni di Rialto, arciprete di Castello).
Cancelleria Inferiore. Notai. B. 146 (Bernardo Panza, detto di Ghibellino).
Cancelleria Inferiore. Notai. B. 164 (Francesco Recovrati).
Cancelleria Inferiore. Notai. B. 169–70 (Marco Rafanelli).
Cancelleria Inferiore. Notai. B. 190 (Enrico Salomon).
Cancelleria Inferiore. Notai. B. 199 (Marco de Tocci).

Cancelleria Inferiore. Notai. B. 225–26. (Angeletto da Venezia, f. Andreuccio da Bologna).

Cancelleria Inferiore. Notai. B. 229, 5, R. 1, Verbali del Consiglio dei mercanti Veneziani in Alessandria.

Cancelleria Inferiore. Notai. Miscellanea notai diversi. B. 6.

Cancellaria Inferiore. Notai. Miscellanea notai diversi. B. 134 bis.

Cassierie della Bolla Ducale. Grazie, R. 3, 5, 7, 8, 9, 11, 12.

Collegio Notatorio. R. 2, 3, 4, 5, 6, 7.

Giudici del Procurator. Sentenze a Legge. R. 1, 2, 4.

Giudici di Petizion. Sentenze a Giustizia. R. 2, 4, 5, 7, 11, 12, 16, 18, 20, 22, 27, 29, 32, 34, 39, 107, 144.

Giudici di Petizion. Sentenze a Interdetti. R. 7, 8.

Libri Commemoriali. R. 1, 2, 5, 6, 7.

Maggior Consiglio. Liber Ursa, Liber Fractus.

Miscellanea atti non appartenenti a nesssun archivio. B. 28.

Miscellanea Codici, Ser. I: Storia veneta. R. 18 (Marco Barbaro, Arbori de' patritii venetii).

Notarile Testamenti. B. 55a (Amizo, plebano di S. Moise).

Notarile Testamenti. B. 364 (Basilio Darvisio).

Notarile Testamenti. B. 415bis (Giovanni de Buosis).

Notarile Testamenti. B. 416 (Bernardo di Rodulfi).

Notarile Testamenti. B. 435a (Nicolo Ferranti).

Notarile Testamenti. B. 466 (Giovanni Gazo).

Notarile Testamenti. B. 557 (Leone da Rovelone).

Notarile Testamenti. B. 571 (Giorgio di Ghibellino).

Notarile Testamenti. B. 615 (Conte di Bertoldo).

Notarile Testamenti. B. 719–20 (Gasparino de Mani).

Notarile Testamenti. B. 746 (Marciliano de Naresis).

Notarile Testamenti. B. 753 (Nicolo Leonardi).

Notarile Testamenti. B. 763c (Nicolo Rosso, S. Simeone Apostolo).

Notarile Testamenti. B. 793 (Francesco Polo).

Notarile Testamenti. B. 824 (Vettore Pomino).

Notarile Testamenti. B. 830 (Nicolo Benedetto).

Notarile Testamenti, B. 915/1 (Bartolomeo Bon).

Notarile Testamenti. B. 947 (Enrico Salomon).

Notarile Testamenti. B. 1157 (Benedetto de Croce).

Notarile Testamenti. B. 1255 (Pietro Zane).

Procuratori di San Marco, de Citra. B. 27 (Doge Antonio Venier).

Procuratori di San Marco, de Citra. B. 83 (Angelo Condulmer q. Fiornovello).

Procuratori di San Marco, de Ultra. B. 96 (Agnese Condulmer, rel. Giacomello. S. Luca).

Procuratori di San Marco, de Ultra, B. 96 (Angelo Condulmer).

Procuratori di San Marco, de Ultra. B. 96 (Giacomo Condulmer).

Procuratori di San Marco, de Ultra. B. 96 (Nicoletta Condulmer ved. Giacomo dal conf. S. Lucia).

Procuratori di San Marco, de Ultra, B. 96 (Pietro Condulmer di S. Tomà).

Procuratori di San Marco, de Ultra, B. 96 (Tutella e commissaria di Zanino Condulmer).

Procuratori di San Marco, de Ultra. B. 96 (Tutella figli minori di Alvise Condulmer).

Procuratori di San Marco, de Ultra. B. 97 (Nicolo Condulmer di S. Cassiano).

Procuratori di San Marco, de Ultra. B. 106 (Federico Corner di S. Aponal).

Procuratori di San Marco, de Ultra. B. 262 (Nicolo Condulmer and Paolo Signolo).

Procuratori di San Marco, de Ultra. B. 317 (Giacomo Zane q. Lorenzo di SM Mater Domini).

Procuratori di San Marco. Misti. Commissarie. B. 51 (Andriolo Betin q. Marco, Santa Maria Formosa).

Procuratori di San Marco. Misti. Commissarie. B. 103 (Gasparino Morosini), testamento 1401.

Procuratori di San Marco. Misti. Commissarie. B. 127a (Pietro Stornello q. Marco).

Procuratori di San Marco. Misti. Commissarie. B.150 (Nicolo da cha da Pesaro).

Procuratori di San Marco. Misti. Commissarie. B. 182 (Guglielmo Condulmer, q. Nicolo).

Procuratori di San Marco. Misti. Miscellanea Pergamena. B. 34.

San Giorgio in Alga. B. 1.

Santa Maria della Misericordia o della Valverde. R. 1 [Mariegola].

Scuola Grande di S. Giovanni Evangelista. R. 4.

Scuole Piccole e Suffrage. B. 406. S. Cristofalo alla Madonna del Orto. Mariegola.

Scuole Piccole e Suffrage. B. 410. SS. Maria e Cristoforo dei mercanti, scuola alla Madonna dell'Orto, 1215–1806. Pergamene 1350–1399.

Segretario alle Voci. R. 3, 4.

Senato. Mar. R. 1.

Senato. Misti. R. 30, 36, 39, 44, 41, 46, 47, 51, 55, 56, 58, 59.

Senato. Secreti. R. E, 3, 4, 9, 11, 12, 13, 14, 15, 16, 17.

Senato. Terra. R. 1.

Spirito Santo. Pergamene, B. 4.

Venice, Biblioteca Nazionale Marciana,

Dolfin, Giorgio. *Chronica.* MSS Ital, Cl. VII, 794 (8503).

Venice. Biblioteca del Museo Civico Correr,

P.D. C. 2581 (#388, Galimberti, Contarini).

Published Documents

Acta Camerae Apostolicae et Civitatum Venetiorum, Ferrariae, Florentiae, Ianuae de Concilio Florentino. Ed. Georg Hofmann. Concilium Florentinum documenta et scriptores. Ser. A, vol. 3, fasc. 1. Rome, 1950.

Acta Eugenii Papae IV (1431–1447). Ed. Giorgio Fedalto. Pontificia Comissio Codici
    Iuris Canonici Orientalis Recognoscendo, Fontes, ser. 3, vol. 15. Rome, 1990.

Balducci Pegolotti, Francesco. *La pratica della mercatura.* Ed. Allen Evans. Cambridge,
    MA, 1936.

Battelli, Giulio, ed. *Exempla Scripturarum.* Fasc. 3: *Acta Pontificum.* 2nd ed. Vatican,
    1965.

Bernardo de Rodulfis: Notaio in Venezia (1392–1399). Ed. Giorgio Tamba. Fonti per la
    Storia di Venezia, sec. 3. Venice, 1974.

Bilanci Generali della Repubblica di Venezia. R. Accadema Nazionale dei Lincei. Docu-
    menti Finanziari, I, 1. Venice, 1912.

Borselli, Girolamo. *Cronica Gestorum ac factorum memorabilium civitatis Bononie.* Ed.
    Albano Sorbelli. Rerum Italicarum Scriptores, 2nd ed. Vol. 23, 2. Citta di Castello,
    1912–29.

*Bullarum, diplomatum et privilegiorum sanctorum romanorum pontificum, Taurinensis
    edition.* Vol. 4 (1271–1431). Turin, 1859.

Caroldo, Giovanni Giacomo. *Cronaca.* Ed. Şerban V. Marin. *Istorii Veneţiene,* vol. 2.
    Bucharest, 2009.

Cecconi, Eugenio, ed. *Studi storici sul concilio di Firenze.* Florence, 1869.

Cessi, Roberto, ed. *Deliberazioni del Maggior Consiglio di Venezia.* Accademia Nazionale
    dei Lincei, 3 vols. Bologna, 1950, 1931, 1934.

Chinazzo, Daniele di. *Cronica de la Guerra de Veneciani a Zenovesi.* Ed. V. Lazzarini.
    Monumenti Storici, n.s. 11. Venice, 1958.

Commissioni di Rinaldo degli Albizzi per il Comune di Firenze. Ed. Cesare Guasti. Docu-
    menti di Storia Italiana 1–3. Florence, 1867–73.

Concilium Basiliense, Studien und Quellen zur Geschichte des Councils von Basel. Vol. 1.
    Ed. Johannes Haller. Basel, 1904.

Concilium Basiliense, Studien und Quellen zur Geschichte des Councils von Basel. Vol. 5:
    Tagerbücher und Acten. Ed. Gustav Beckmann et al. Basel, 1904.

*Concilium Florentinum: Documenta et scriptores, epistolae pontificiae ad concilium flo-
    rentinum spectantes.* Ed. George Hofmann. 11 vols. Rome, 1940–76.

Dietrich von Niem. *Historiarum sui Temporis Libri IIII, quorum tres priores de Schismate
    Universali, quartum vero Nemus unionis autor inscripsit.* Strasbourg, 1609.

Diplomatarium veneto-levantinum. Ed. Georg M. Thomas and Riccardo Predelli. Mon-
    umenti Storici, ser. 1, 9. 2 vols. Venice, 1880–1901.

Dolfin, Giorgio. *Chronicha dela nobil città de Venetia.* Ed. Angela Carraciolo Aricò. Ven-
    ice, 2009.

Epistolae pontificiae ad concilium florentinum spectantes. Ed. G. Hofmann. Concilium
    Florentinum. Vol. 1, ser. A, 3 vols. Rome, 1940–46.

Finke, Heinrich, ed. *Acta Consilii Constanciensis.* 4 vols. Münster, 1896–1928.

Gaspare da Verona and Michele Canensi. *Le vite di Paolo II.* Ed. Giuseppe Zippel. Rerum
    Italicarum Scriptores. 2nd ed., 3, part 16. Citta di Castello, 1904.

Gerland, Ernst, ed. *Neue Quellen zur Geschichte des Lateinischen Erzbistums Patras.* Leipzig, 1903.

Ghirardacci, Cherubino. *Historia di Bologna.* Ed. A. A. Solimane. Bologna, 1657; rpt. 1973.

———. *Della historia di Bologna, parte terza.* Ed. A. Sorbelli. Rerum Italicarum Scriptores, 2nd ed., vol. 33. Città di Castello, 1915.

Griffoni, Matteo. *Memoriale Historicum de Rebus Bononensium.* Ed. Lodovico Frati and Albano Sorbelli. Rerum Italicarum Scriptores, 2nd ed., vol. 18, part 2. Città di Castello, 1902.

Hofmann, George, ed. *Fragmenta protocolli, diaria privata, sermonis.* Concilium Florentinum. Ser. A, vol. 3, fasc. 2. Rome, 1951.

Iorga, Nicolai, ed. "Excerpt from Jehan de Wavrin, *Anciennes chroniques d'Angleterre.*" In *The Crusade of Varna.* Ed. Colin Imber. Aldershot, 2006.

———. *Notes et extraits pour servir à l'histoire des croisades au XVe siècle.* 6 vols. Paris, 1899–1916.

Luzzatto, Gino, ed. *I prestiti della Repubblica di Venezia.* R. Accademia dei Lincei, Document Finanziari. 3rd ser., vol. 1, part 1. Padua, 1929.

Mansi, Giovanni Domenico, ed. *Sacrorum conciliorum nova et amplissima collectio.* 2nd ed. Vol. 27: *1409–1418.* 1903; rpt. Graz, 1961.

Martinori, Edoardo. *Annali della Zecca di Roma.* Rome, 1918.

Michael of Rhodes. *The Book of Michael of Rhodes: A Fifteenth-Century Maritime Manuscript.* Vol. 2: *Transcription and Translation.* Ed. Alan M. Stahl. Cambridge, MA, 2009.

Miethke, Jürgen, ed. "Concilium Pisanum–1409." In *Conciliorum Oecumenicorum generaliumque decreta,* II/1, 471–516. *The General Councils of Latin Christendom from Constantinople IV to Pavia-Siena (869–1424).* Turnhout, 2013.

Monacis, Lorenzo de. *De gestis, moribus et nobilitate civitatis Venetiarum.* Ed. Flaminio Corner, as *Chronicon de rebus gestis.* Venice, 1758.

Morosini, Antonio. *Codex.* Österreichische Nationalbibliotek, Codd. 6586-6597. Ed. M. P. Ghezzo, J. R. Melville-Jones, and A. Rizzi, as *The Morosini Codex.* 4 vols. Padua, 2000–2010.

———. *Codex.* Ed. Andrea Nanetti, as *Il Codice Morosini: Il mondo visto da Venezia.* Quaderni della Rivista di Bizantinistica 10. 4 vols. Spoleto: Centro Italiano di Studi sull'Alto Medioevo, 2010.

Morozzo della Rocca, Raimondo, ed. *Lettere di Mercanti a Pignol Zucchello (1336–1350).* Fonti per la Storia di Venezia. Sec. 4, Archivi Privati. Venice, 1957.

Palacky, Frantisek, ed. *Monumenta conciliorum generalium.* 4 vols. Vienna, 1857–1886.

Petriboni, Pagolo di Matteo, and Matteo di Borgo Rinaldi. *Priorista (1407–1459).* Ed. Jacqueline A. Gutwirth. Rome, 2001.

Phrantzes, Georgios. *Cronaca.* Ed. and trans. Riccardo Maisano. Rome, 1990.

Pizolpassi, Francesco. *Summa hover cronia: 600–1440.* Ed. Armando Antonelli and Riccardo Pedrini. Collana di cronache bolognesi d'epoca medioevale, moderna e contemporanea 6. Bologna, 2001.

Predelli, Riccardo, ed. *I libri commemoriali della repubblica di Venezia: Registri.* Monumenti Storici, ser. 1, vol. 1, 3. Venice, 1876.

Repertorium Germanicum: Regesten aus den päpstlichen Archiven zur Geschichte des deutschen Reichs—Pontifikat Eugens IV (1431–1447). Ed. Robert Arnold. Berlin, 1897.

Sansovino, Francesco. *Venetia citta nobilissima e singolare.* Venice, 1581; rpt. Bergamo, 2002.

Sanudo, Marin. *De origine, situ et magistratibus urbis Venetiae ovvero la città di Venetia (1493–1530).* Ed. Angela Caracciolo Aricò. Collana di testi inediti e rari 1. Cisalpino, 1980.

———. *Vite dei duchi di Venezia.* Ed. Lodovico Antonio Muratori. Rerum Italicarum Scriptores, vol. 22. Milan, 1733.

———. *Vite dei dogi. Ed.* Giovanni Monticolo. Rerum Italicarum Scriptores, 2nd ed., vol. 22, part 4. Città di Castello, 1900.

Syropoulos, Sylvester. *Les "Mémoires" du Grand Ecclésiarque de l'Église de Constantinople Sylvestre Syropoulos sur le Concile de Florence (1438–1439).* Ed. Vitalien Laurent. Concilium Florentinum, ser. B, 9. Rome, 1971.

Taûtu, Aloysius L., ed. *Acta Martini P.P. V.* Fontes, ser. 3, vol. 14, 1 & 2. Rome, 1980.

Theiner, Augustin, ed. *Annales ecclesiastici Cesare Baronius* [Raynaldus]. 37 vols. Bar-le-Duc, 1864–83.

———. *Codex diplomaticus dominii temporalis S. Sedis.* 3 vols. Rome, 1861–62.

Uginet, François-Charles, ed. *Le liber officialium de Martin V.* Pubblicazioni degli Archivi de Stato–Fonti e Sussidi 7. Rome, 1975.

Vespasiano da Bisticci. *Vite di uomini illustra del secolo XV.* Ed. Angelo Mai and Adolfor Bartoli. Florence, 1859.

Vincke, Johannes, ed. "Acta concilii Pisani." *Römische Quartalschrift für christliche Altertumskunde und für Kirchengeschichte* 46 (1938).

Le vite di Paolo II di Gaspare da Verona e Michele Canensi. Ed. Giuseppe Zippel. *Raccolta degli Storici Italiani,* 2ⁿᵈ ed., 3, part 16. Citta di Castello, 1904.

Zago, Ferruccio, ed. *Consiglio dei dieci: Deliberazioni miste—Registri I–II (1310–1325).* Fonti per la Storia de Venezia, sec. 1. Venice, 1962.

Secondary Works

Abert, Friedrich Philipp. *Papst Eugen der Vierte: Ein Lebensbild aus der Kirchengeschichte des fünfzehnten Jahrhunderts.* Mainz, 1884.

Baiocchi, A. "Condulmer, Antonio." In *Dizionario biografico degli italiani.* Vol. 27, 758–61. Rome, 1982.

Barker, Hannah. *That Most Precious Merchandise: The Mediterranean Trade in Black Sea Slaves.* Philadelphia, 2019.

Belich, James. *The World the Plague Made: The Black Death and the Rise of Europe.* Princeton, NJ, 2022.

Bianca, Concetta. "I cardinali al Concilio di Firenze." In *Firenze e il Concilio del 1439.* Ed. Paolo Viti. 2 vols. Florence, 1994.

Bloch, March. *La société féodale*. Paris, 1939–40.

Boerio, Giuseppe. *Dizionario del dialetto veneziano*. Venice, 1856.

Boschetto, Luca. *Società e cultura a Firenze al tempo del Concilio: Eugenio IV tra curiali, mercanti e umanisti (1434–1443)*. Rome, 2012.

Boyd, Catherine E. *Tithes and Parishes in Medieval Italy: The Historical Roots of a Modern Problem*. Ithaca, NY, 1952.

Brandmüller, Walter. *Das Konzil von Konstanz, 1414–1418*. 2 vols. Paderborn, 1991, 1997.

———. "Die römischen Berichte des Pietro d'Antonio de' Micheli an das Concistoro von Siena im Frühjahr 1431." *Bulletino Senese di Storia Patria* 73–75 (1966–68); rpt. in Brandmüller, *Papst und Konzil im Grossen Schisma (1378–1431): Studien und Quellen*, 111–154. Paderborn, 1990.

———. "Der Übergang vom Pontifikat Martins V zu Eugen IV." *Quellen und Forschungen aus Italienischen Archiven und Bibliotheken* 47 (1967): 585–618; rpt. in *Papst und Konzil im Grossen Schisma (1378–1431): Studien und Quellen*, 85–110. Paderborn, 1990.

Brunetti, Mario. "Venezia durante la peste del 1348." *Ateneo Veneto* 32:1 (1909): 289–311.

Brown, Patricia Fortini. *Narrative Painting in the Age of Carpaccio*. New Haven, CT, 1988.

———. *Private Lives in Renaissance Venice*. New Haven, CT, 2004.

Campana, Lilia. "Sailing into Union, the Byzantine Naval Convoy for the Council of Ferrara-Florence (1438–1439)." *Dumbarton Oaks Papers* 73 (2019): 103–25.

Carocci, Sandro. "Social Mobility and the Middle Ages." *Continuity and Change* 26:2 (2011): 367–404.

Cassandro, Giovanni. "La Curia di Petizion." *Archivio Veneto*, ser. 5, 19 (1936): 72–144; 20 (1937): 1–210.

———. *Le rappresaglie e il fallimento a Venezia nei secoli XIII–XVI*. Turin, 1938.

Cecchetti, Bartolomeo. *La vita dei veneziani nel 1300*. Part 2, *La città, la laguna*. 1885; rpt. Bologna, 1980.

———. *La vita dei veneziani nel 1300*. Part 3, *Le veste*. 1886; rpt. Bologna, 1980.

Cenci, Cesare, ed. "Senato Veneto 'Probae' ai benefici ecclesiastici." In *Promozioni agli ordini sacri a Bologna e alle dignità ecclesiastiche nel Veneto nei secoli XIV–XV*. Ed. Celestino Piana and Cesare Cenci, 313–54. Specilegium Bonaventurianum 3. Florence, 1968.

Cessi, Roberto. "La finanza veneziana al tempo della Guerra di Chioggia." In *Politica ed economia di Venezia nel Trecento, 179–248*. Rome, 1952.

———. *Storia della repubblica di Venezia*. 2nd ed. 1968; rpt. Florence, 1981.

Chojnacki, Stanley. "La formazione della nobilità dopo la serrata." In *Storia di Venezia: Dalle origini alla caduta della Serenissima*. Vol. 3: *La formazione dello stato patrizio*. Ed. Girolamo Arnaldi et al., 641–725. Rome, 1997.

———. "From Trousseau to Groomgift." In *Women and Men in Renaissance Venice*, 76–94. Baltimore, 2000.

———. "Getting Back the Dowry." In *Women and Men in Renaissance Venice*, 95–111. Baltimore, 2000.

———. "Kinship Ties and Young Patricians." In *Women and Men in Renaissance Venice*, 206–26. Baltimore, 2000.

———. "Measuring Adulthood: Adolescence and Gender." In *Women and Men in Renaissance Venice*, 185–205. Baltimore, 2000.

———. "The Power of Love: Wives and Husbands." In *Women and Men in Renaissance Venice*, 153–68. Baltimore, 2000.

Christ, George. *Trading Conflicts: Venetian Merchants and Mamluk Officials in Late Medieval Alexandria*. Leiden, 2012.

Cracco, Giorgio. *"Un altro mondo," Venezia nel medioevo dal secolo XI al secolo XIV*. Turin, 1986.

———. "Riforma e decadenza nel monastero di S. Agostino di Vicenza." *Rivista di Storia della Chiesa in Italia* 14 (1960): 203–34.

———. *Società e stato nel medioevo veneziano (secoli XII–XIV)*. Florence, 1967.

Crouzet-Pavan, Elisabeth. *"Sopra le acque salse": Espaces, pouvoir et société à Venise à la fin du Moyen Âge*. Istituto Storico Italiano per il Medio Evo, Nuovi Studi Storici 14. Rome, 1992.

———. *Venice Triumphant: The Horizons of a Myth*. Trans. Lydia G. Cochrane. Baltimore, 1999.

Decaluwé, Michiel, Thomas M. Izbicki, and Gerald Christianson, eds. *A Companion to the Council of Basel*. Leiden, 2017.

Del Torre, Giuseppe. *Patrizi e cardinali: Venezia e le istituzioni ecclesiastiche nella prima età moderna*. Milan, 2010.

Delaruelle, Etienne, Edmond René Labande, and Paul Ourliac. *L'Église au temps du Grand Schisme et de la crise conciliaire (1378–1449)*. Histoire de l'Église depuis les origines jusqu'à nos jours 14. Paris, 1962.

Diener, Herman, and Brigide Schwarz. "Das Itinerar Papst Eugens IV (1431–1447)." *Quellen und Forschungen aus italienanischen Archiven und Bibliotheken* 82 (2002): 193–230.

Dohrn-van Rossum, Gerhard. *History of the Hour: Clocks and Modern Temporal Orders*. Trans. Thomas Dunlap, Chicago, 1996.

Dorigo, Wladimiro. *Venezia romanica: La formazione della città medioevale fino all'età gotica*. Istituto Veneto di Scienze, Lettere ed Arti, Monumenta Veneta 3. 2 vols. Venice, 2003.

Eubel, Konrad, ed. *Hierarchia catholica medii aevi*. 2 vols. Regensberg, 1898.

———. "Das Itinerar der Päpste zur Zeit der grossen Schismas." *Historisches Jahrbuch* 16 (1895): 545–64.

Faugeron, Fabien. "L'art du compromis politique: Venise au lendemain de la conjuration Tiepolo-Querini (1310)." *Journal des Savants* (2004): 357–421.

———. *Nourrir la ville: Ravitaillement, marché et métiers dans l'alimentation à Venise dans les derniers siècles du Moyen Âge*. Bibliothèque des Écoles Françaises d'Athènes et de Rome 362. Rome, 2014.

Favier, Jean. *Les finances pontificales à l'époque du grand schisme d'Occident, 1378–1409.* Bibliothèque des Écoles Françaises d'Athènes et de Rome, fasc. 211. Paris, 1966.

Genequand, Philippe. "Kardinäle, Schisma und Konzil: Das Kardinalskollegium im grossen abendländischen Schism (1378–1417)." In *Geschichte des Kardinalats im Mittelalter.* Ed. Jürgen Dendorfer and Ralf Lützelschab, 303–98. Päpste und Päpsttum 39 (Stuttgart, 2011).

Gill, Joseph. *Eugenius IV, Pope of Christian Union.* Westminster, 1961.

Girgensohn, Dieter. *Kirche, Politik und adelige Regierung in der Republik Venedig zu Beginn des 15. Jahrhunderts.* Veröffentlichungen des Max-Planck-Instituts für Geschichte 118. 2 vols. Göttingen, 1996.

———. "Papst Gregor XII. am Ende seines Lebens: Der Rücktritt, Angelo Correr als Kardinallegat in den Marken, der Streit um den Nachlass." *Mitteilungen des Instituts für Österreichische Geschichtsforschung* 124:2 (2016): 350–90.

———. *Venezia e il primo veneziano sulla cattedra di S. Pietro Gregorio XII (Angelo Correr), 1406–1415.* Quaderni pubblicati dal Centro tedesco di Studi Veneziani 30. Venice, 1985.

Goeller, Emil. *König Sigismunds Kirchenpolitik vom Tode Bonifaz' IX bis zur Berufung des Konstanzer Konzils.* Freiberg, 1902.

Gottlob, Adolf. *Aus der Camera Apostolica des 15. Jahrhunderts.* Innsbruck, 1889.

Goy, Richard J. *Venetian Vernacular Architecture: Traditional Housing in the Venetian Lagoon.* Cambridge, 1989.

Gullino, Giuseppe. "Garzoni, Francesco." *Dizionario biografico degli italiani.* Vol. 52, 430–32. Rome, 1999.

———. "Garzoni, Marino." *Dizionario biografico degli italiani.* Vol. 52, 444. Rome, 1999.

Halff, Maarten. "The Pope's Agents in Constantinople: Eugenius IV's Legation on the Eve of the Council of Ferrara-Florence (1438–1439). *Mediterranea: International Journal on the Transfer of Knowledge* 5 (2020): 91–151.

Hay, Denys. *The Church in Italy in the Fifteenth Century.* Cambridge, 1977.

Hefele, Charles-Joseph. *Histoire des Conciles d'après les documents originaux.* Trans. and corr. Henri Leclercq. 11 vols. Paris, 1907–52.

Herlihy, David. "Three Patterns of Social Mobility in Medieval Society." *Journal of Interdisciplinary History* 3 (1973): 623–47.

Humfrey, Peter. "Competitive Devotions: The Venetian Scuole Piccole as Donors of Altarpieces in the Years Around 1500." *Art Bulletin* 70:3 (September 1988): 401–23.

Jones, Philip J. *The Italian City-State: From Commune to Signoria.* Oxford, 1997.

———. *The Malatesta of Rimini and the Papal Court.* Cambridge, 1974.

Kim, David Young. "Gentile in Red." *I Tatti Studies in the Italian Renaissance* 18:1 (2015): 157–92.

Kojic, Desanka Kovačević. "Serbian Silver at the Venetian Mint in the First Half of the Fifteenth Century." *Balcanica* 50 (2019): 58–71.

Kolditz, Sebastian. *Johannes VIII: Palaiologos und das Konzil von Ferrara-Florenz (1438/39)*. Stuttgart, 2013.

Kretschmeyr, Heinrich. *Geschichte von Venedig*. 3 vols. 1905–33; rpt. Aalen, 1964.

Lane, Frederic C. *Andrea Barbarigo, Merchant of Venice, 1418–1449*. Johns Hopkins University Studies in Historical and Political Science, ser. 62, no. 1. Baltimore, 1944.

———. "The Enlargement of the Great Council in Venice." In *Florilegium Historiale, Essays Presented to Wallace K. Ferguson*. Ed. J. G. Rowe and W. H. Stockdale, 237–74. Toronto, 1971; rpt. in Lane, *Studies in Venetian and Social History*. Ed. Benjamin G. Kohl and Reinhold C. Mueller. London, 1987.

———. "The Funded Debt of the Venetian Republic, 1262–1482." In *Venice and History: The Collected Papers of Frederic C. Lane*, 87–98. Baltimore, 1966.

Lane, Frederic C., and Reinhold C. Mueller. *Money and Banking in Medieval and Early Renaissance Venice*. Vol. 1: *Coins and Moneys of Account*. Baltimore, 1985.

Lazzarini, Vittorio. "Aneddoti della congiura Quirini-Tiepolo." *Nuovo Archivio Veneto* 10 (1895): 81–96.

Leoni, Antonio. *Ancona illustrata*. Ancona, 1832.

Lisini, Alessandro. "Papa Gregorio XII e i senesi." *La Rassegna Nazionale* 91 (1896): 280–321.

Mantese, Giovanni. *Memorie storiche della Chiesa Vicentina*. 5 vols. Vicenza, 1952–74.

Maranini, Giuseppe. *La costituzione di Venezia*. Vol. 2: *Dopo la serrata del Maggior Consiglio*. 1931; rpt. Florence, 1974.

Martini, Angelo. *Manuale di Metrologia*. Turin, 1883.

McCahill, Elizabeth. *Reviving the Eternal City: Rome and the Papal Court, 1420–1447*. Cambridge, MA, 2013.

Mercati, G. "Intorno a Eugenio IV, Lorenzo Valla e Fra Ludovico de Strassoldo." *Rivista di Storia della Chiesa in Italia* 5 (1951): 45–52.

Monaci, Alfredo. "Una notizia inedita sulla vita di Gabriele Condulmer (Eugenio IV)." *Miscellanea di Storia e Cultura Ecclesiastica* 4 (1906): 425–26.

Monnas, Lisa. "Some Medieval Colour Terms for Textiles." *Medieval Clothing and Textiles* 10 (2014): 25–58.

Moretti, Lino, Antonio Niero, and Paola Rossi. *La chiesa del Tintoretto: Madonna dell'Orto*. Venice, 1994.

Mueller, Reinhold C. "Aspetti sociali ed economici della peste a Venezia nel medioevo." In *Venezia e la peste, 1348–1797*. Venice, 1979.

———. "Effetti della Guerra di Chioggia (1378–1381) sulla vita economica e sociale di Venezia." *Ateneo Veneto* 19 (1981): 27–41.

———. "Sull'establishment bancario veneziano: Il banchiere davanti a Dio (secoli XIV–XV)." In *Mercanti e vita economica nella Repubblica veneta (secoli XIII–XVIII)*. Ed. G. Borelli, 45–103. Verona, 1985.

———. *The Venetian Money Market: Banks, Panics, and the Public Debt, 1200–1500*. Money and Banking in Medieval and Renaissance Venice 2. Baltimore, 1997.

Nicol, Donald M. *Byzantium and Venice: A Study in Diplomatic and Cultural Relations.* Cambridge, 1988.

O'Connell, Monique. *Men of Empire: Power and Negotiation in Venice's Maritime State.* Baltimore, 2009.

Olivieri, A. "Condulmer, Francesco." In *Dizionario biografico degli italiani.* Vol. 27, 761–65. Rome, 1982.

———. "Condulmer, Marco." In *Dizionario biografico degli italiani.* Vol. 27, 765–66. Rome, 1982.

Partner, Peter. *The Papal State Under Martin V: The Administration and Government of the Temporal Power in the Early Fifteenth Century.* London, 1958.

Paschini, Pio. "Da medico a Patriarca d'Aquileia, Camerlengo e Cardinale di S. Romana Chiesa." *Memorie Storiche Forogiuliesi* 23 (1927): 1–56.

Pazzi, Piero. *Lo Stradario di Venezia.* 3rd ed. Venice, 2001.

Pecci, Giovanni Antonio. *Storia del vescovado della città di Siena.* 1748; rpt. Siena, 2003.

Petralia, Giuseppe. "Problemi della mobilità sociale dei mercanti (secoli XII–XIV, Italia e Mediterraneo europeo)." In *La mobilità sociale nel medioevo.* Ed. Sandro Carocci, 247–71. Rome, 2010.

Pietra del Paragone della vera Nobilità: Discorso genealogico de Conti Ferretti. Ancona, 1685.

Pozza, Marco. "*Marco Polo Milion*: An Unknown Source Concerning Marco Polo." *Mediaeval Studies* 68 (2006): 285–301.

Proske, Veronika. *Der Romzug Kaiser Sigismunds (1431–1433): Politische Kommunikation, Herrschaftsrepräsentation und -rezeption.* Vienna, 2019.

Queller, Donald E. *The Venetian Patriciate: Reality Versus Myth.* Urbana, IL, 1986.

Raines, Dorit. *L'invention du mythe aristocratique: L'image de soi du patriciat vénitien au temps de a Sérénissime.* Istituto Veneto di Scienze, Lettere ed Arti, Memorie, Classe di Scienze Morali, Lettere ed Arti 113. Venice, 2006.

Ravid, Benjamin. "The Legal Status of the Jews in Venice to 1509." *Proceedings of the American Academy for Jewish Research* 54 (1987): 169–202.

Richardson, Carol. *Reclaiming Rome: Cardinals in the Fifteenth Century.* Leiden, 2009.

Robertson, Ian. *Tyranny Under the Mantle of St. Peter: Pope Paul II and Bologna.* Turnhout, 2002.

Rocke, Michael. *Forbidden Friendships: Homosexuality and Male Culture in Renaissance Florence.* Oxford, 1996.

Romano, Dennis. *The Likeness of Venice; A Life of Doge Francesco Foscari, 1373–1457.* New Haven, CT, 2007.

———. *Patricians and Popolani: The Social Foundations of the Venetian Renaissance State.* Baltimore, 1987.

Ruggiero, Guido. *The Boundaries of Eros: Sex Crime and Sexuality in Renaissance Venice.* Oxford, 1985.

Sartorelli, Pierluigi. *Eugenio IV nel vortice di eventi drammatici.* Vatican City, 1990.

Scalamonti, Francesco. *Vita viri clasissimi et famisissimi Kyriaci Ancontin.* Ed. and trans.
Charles Mitchell and Edward W. Bodnar, S.J. Transactions of the American Philosophical Society, 86, 4. Philadelphia, 1996.

Sella, Pietro. *I sigilli dell'Archivio Vaticano.* Inventari dell'Archivio Secreto Vaticano. Vatican City, 1937.

Semi, Franca. *Gli ospizi di Venezia.* Venice, 1984.

Setton, Kenneth. *The Papacy and the Levant.* 4 vols. Philadelphia, 1976–84.

Stahl, Alan M. "Ingots and the Venetian Mint in the Later Middle Ages: The Accounts
of Guglielmo Condulmer." In *Money and Its Use in Medieval Europe Three Decades
On: Essays in Honour of Professor Peter Spufford.* Ed. Martin Allen and Nicholas Mayhew, 75–84. Royal Numismatic Society Special Publications 52. London,
2017.

———. "The Mint of Venice in the Face of the Great Bullion Famine." in *Le crisi finanziarie: Gestione, implicazioni sociali e conseguenze nell'età preindustriale.* Ed. Giampiero
Nigro, 223–37. Istituto Francesco Datini, Settimane di Studi 47. Florence, 2016.

———. "Venice in the Transformation of Northern Bullion to Mediterranean Money."
In *Bullion Trade in Medieval and Early Modern Europe: 3rd Prague Conference in
Economic History.* Ed. Roman Zaoral and Claudio Marsilio. Prague, forthcoming
2024.

———. "Vielmo Condulmer, a Moneychanger as Would-Be Noble in Medieval Venice."
In *Cultures of Exchange.* Ed. Susanna Barsella and Germano Maifreda. Toronto,
forthcoming 2024.

———. "Where the Silk Road Met the Wool Trade: Venetian and Muslim Merchants in
Tana in the Late Middle Ages." In *Crusading and Trading Between West and East:
Studies in Honour of David Jacoby.* Ed. Sophia Menache et al., 351–64. Crusades-
Subsidia 12. London, 2018.

———. *Zecca: The Mint of Venice in the Middle Ages.* Baltimore, 2000.

Stahl, Alan M., and Louis Waldman. "The Earliest Known Medalists: The Sesto Brothers
of Venice." *American Journal of Numismatics,* ser. 2, 5:6 (1993–94): 167–88.

Stieber, Joachim W. *Pope Eugenius IV, the Council of Basel and the Secular and Ecclesiastical Authorities in the Empire: The Conflict over Supreme Authority and Power in
the Church.* Leiden, 1978.

Stöckly, Doris. *Le système de l'incanto des galées du marché à Venise (fin XIIIᵉ‑milieu XVᵉ
siècle).* Leiden, 1955.

Tassi, Ildefonso. *Ludovico Barbo (1381–1443).* Uomini e Dottrine 1. Rome, 1952.

Temple Leader, John. *Libro dei nobili veneti.* Florence, 1884.

Todesco, Maria Teresa. *Aggregati ed esclusi: Le cooptazioni al maggior consiglio al tempo
della Guerra di Chioggia.* PhD dissertation. Tesi di Laurea, Università degli Studi di
Venezia, Facoltà di Lettere e Filosofia, Dipartimento di Studi Storici, 1986–87.

Tognetti, Sergio. "Businessmen and Social Mobility in Late Medieval Italy." In *Social
Mobility in Medieval Italy (1100–1500).* Ed. Sandro Carocci and Isabella Lazzarini,
199–215. Rome, 2018.

Tramontin, Silvio. "Ludovico Barbo e la riforma di S. Giorgio in Alga." In *Riforma della chiesa, cultura e spritualità nel quattrocento Veneto*. Ed. Giovanni B. Francesco Trolese, 91–107. Cesena, 1984.

Ughelli, Ferdinando. *Italia sacra*. 9 vols. Rome, 1643–62.

Valois, Noël. *La crise religieuse du XVe siècle, le pape e le concile (1418–1450)*. 2 vols. Paris, 1909.

———. *La France et le Grand Schisme d'Occident*. 4 vols. Paris, 1896–1902.

Varlik, Nükhet. *Plague and Empire in the Early Modern Mediterranean World: The Ottoman Experience, 1347–1600*. Cambridge, 2015.

Vio, Gastone. *Le Scuole Piccole nella Venezia dei Dogi: Note d'archivio per la storia delle confraternite veneziane*. Costabissara, Italy, 2004.

Waley, Daniel, and Trevor Dean. *The Italian City-Republics*. 4th ed. London, 2013.

White, Lynn, Jr. *Medieval Technology and Social Change*. Oxford, 1962.

Wolters, Wolfgang. *La scultura veneziana gotica (1300–1460)*. Venice, 1976.

Zanetti, Vincenzo. *La chiesa della Madonna dell'Orto in Venezia*. Venice, 1870.

———. *Guida di Murano*. Venice, 1866.

Ziliotto, Baccio. "Frate Lodovico da Cividale e il suo 'Dialogus de papali potestate.'" *Memorie Storiche Forogiuliesi* 33–34 (1937–38): 151–91.

INDEX

Printed in the USA
CPSIA information can be obtained
at www.ICGtesting.com
JSHW021454140624
64817JS00001B/2